POSTWAR GERMAN LITERATURE

POSTWAR GERMAN LITERATURE

A Critical Introduction

PETER DEMETZ

Schocken Books • New York

TO HANA, *the family novelist*

Contents

Preface

MORE THAN one hundred and sixty years ago, when Madame de Staël was formulating her thoughts on Germany, she emphatically suggested that the productivity of the German mind (in some contrast to the marked centralism of French literature) constituted a *douce et paisible anarchie*, a sweet and peaceful anarchy. Madame de Staël had her own romantic ax to grind, but she had also recognized an essential element in German intellectual life, and I suspect that much of what she said then is still well worth considering today; the sweet anarchy of German literary life may be less peaceful than before, but the youthful force and rich vitality of recent German writing continue to imply a contradictory, "federal" principle of intellectual activity rather than the hegemony of one metropolis or institution able to dictate styles, opinions, and ideas. Younger and older writers in the German-speaking countries all share a fundamental concern with the Nazi past, but their intimate and everyday experience in Switzerland, Austria, the German Democratic Republic, and the Federal Republic of Germany differs widely, and their attitudes differ accordingly. I certainly do not want to substitute an idea of *four* national literatures for the *one* that long blurred our vision in the past, but I believe I cannot ignore the importance of the four political "stages" on which literary life has been developing for nearly twenty-five years.

I do not wish to conceal my almost instinctive assumption that the richness and vitality of any literature reside in the individual works of art or the individual creative minds rather than in "patterns" and "trends" hatched in the brains of professors, but since I am a professor myself, I have tried to organize my discussion of German writing since World War II in a convenient manner that takes note of sociological developments or general trends in literary forms and yet stresses the contribution of the productive individual, no matter where he was born or now resides.

In my four introductory chapters I discuss social and intellectual transformations that have occurred since 1945 in Switzerland, Austria, the German Democratic Republic, and the Federal Republic of Germany; and after paying my tribute to these changes in the *Zeitgeist* I turn to three brief intermezzi concerned with the literary forms of poetry, drama, and fiction. My discussion centers on twenty-two critical portraits of important writers, grouped more or less according to the forms in which they feel most at home. This arrangement is a compromise that will satisfy neither the purists on the New Left nor the extreme formalists (with whom I usually sympathize); and if I impose a few methodological idiosyncrasies upon my readers, they are those of an avid reader who has lived under both Nazi and Stalinist regimes and has come to realize that literature suffocates whenever topical concerns take exclusive precedence over questions of craft and quality. Within the space of an introduction intended for the general reader rather than for my fellow specialists, I have tried to be as inclusive as possible, and to combine essential information with interpretations of important texts and value judgments which may or may not challenge the reader to further explorations on his own. I do not think it necessary to wait fifty years before judging a poem, a play, or a novel produced in our own time.

Throughout my discussion I have used my own translations for the infrequent quotations from the German, not because I fail to appreciate the published translations, but because the critic engaged in close combat with individual authors cannot resist the temptation to rely on his own rendering rather than accept help from the outside. In a few instances, including two or three lines from Wilhelm Lehmann (translator: Gertrude C. Schwebell), Nelly Sachs (Michael Roloff), and Rolf Hochhuth (Robert David McDonald), I used the extant translations; and I would like to add that I am among those who deeply appreciate what the Winstons, Michael Hamburger, Christopher Middleton, and many others have done for students and readers of German literature.

In preparing my manuscript I enjoyed the encouragement and the tolerant help of many students, colleagues, and friends. I should like to express my particular gratitude to Mrs. Margaret Broekhuysen and Miss Krishna Winston, who had a difficult time checking on my outlandish grammar and the factual details, and to Mr. Donald Fuller, who, with the eagle eye of the professional writer, quickly spotted inconsistencies of presentation and argument. If, with their generous help, I should be able to convince one of my readers to add a single book or poem to his future reading, I would feel amply rewarded in my attempt to mediate between countries, languages, and sensibilities.

Ezra Stiles College/Yale University   PETER DEMETZ
October 1969

A Note on Technicalities

ALL TITLES are given in the original German, followed by the date of publication and an English rendering of the original title; dates after the English title (if given) refer to published translations.

> E.g., *Die Dämonen*, 1956 / *The Demons*, 1961

IF THE ENGLISH TITLE of a published translation differs considerably from the sense of the original German title, I interpolate a more literal translation of the German in square brackets.

> E.g., *Märkische Argonautenfahrt*, 1950 / [Argonauts of the Mark Brandenburg] *The Quest*, 1960

IN MY DISCUSSIONS of the drama, the date in square brackets following the original German title indicates the first performance, while the date occasionally following the English title indicates the publication of a book translation.

> E.g., *Die Ermittlung* [1965] / *The Investigation*, 1966

COMPLETE German and English titles with dates of publication or performance are given only when books or plays are mentioned for the first time; they are simplified in the subsequent discussion.

POSTWAR GERMAN LITERATURE

1. Switzerland

A Stubborn Confederation: 1933–1949

IN THE EARLY 'thirties, Switzerland suffered as severely from the economic crisis as other countries of Central Europe (by 1935, there were nearly eighty-five thousand unemployed), but the stubborn Confederation was far less prone to totalitarian temptations than its neighbors; Switzerland was partly infected by fascism but was not maimed by the disease. By 1933, a number of right-wing organizations, in the German- as well as the French-speaking regions, voiced distaste for the inherited multi-party system, demanded an interventionist economy, and, aping the organizational forms of the German Nazis or Italian Fascists, followed their "leaders" rather than their elected representatives. There was much talk of a "spring of the front movements" (*Frontenfrühling*), and yet the combined groups were unable to rally enough popular support to dominate the political scene. Two years after Hitler had come to power in Germany, the right-wing "fronts" put their demands for a total if not totalitarian transformation of the inherited liberal constitution to a practical test by plebiscite, and were promptly defeated, 511,578 to 196,135 (1935). Hitler's march to Vienna and Prague reduced rather than increased the fervor of the Swiss nationalists (who did not dream of an *Anschluss*), and when war came, mobilization orders were executed promptly and with precision. Henri Guisan of the Vaud was elected general (the Swiss do not have a general in peacetime); and on July 25, 1940, the staff officers of the army, regardless of social origin, language, or religion, renewed (in the famous *Rütli* glen, where their forefathers had gathered in 1291 to defend their ancient privileges against the outsiders) an enthusiastic pledge to resist potential invaders. The Germans seemed to have scheduled their *Aktion Schweiz* for late March of 1943, but orders were never given to the SS commandos to execute the existing plans that included a swift occupation of the Basel Rhine bridges. General Guisan's later secret negotiations with SS General Schellenberg (who found neutral Switzerland a convenient place for contacts with the Allies) do not necessarily fit a textbook image of the stalwart Swiss military man; but Guisan would hardly have been successful if his discussions with Schellenberg had not been conducted against the backdrop of mined bridges, a system of tank traps, and the possibility of protracted and costly warfare against Swiss partisans in forlorn Alpine valleys. The Swiss demonstrated little tolerance toward saboteurs; in mid-war, the death penalty was introduced for certain crimes against the state, and fourteen Swiss citizens were, after due trial, shot for actively abetting the National Socialist enemy. The Swiss Confederation (74% of its inhabitants speaking a German dialect) was defended against Hitler's armies by means of cunning and military resolution; it is another question entirely whether the Swiss really did what was humanly possible for the refugees of many nations who desperately wanted to cross the borders into Switzerland.

Helvetian democracy, the product of long experience in local self-administration, has strongly masculine, puritan, and practical strains; we still feel that it was originally practiced by peasants, shepherds, and hardworking artisans who wanted to protect their own way of life against the Austrian and German dynasties. Many techniques of direct democracy (akin to New England town meetings) have been preserved through the centuries, but, with a few exceptions, women are still excluded from the electorate; and it is true that Swiss political traditions (like those of the United States) are hardly saturated with aesthetic interests. For a long time, patriotic historians declared that Swiss literature was basically one of educative involvement and dedicated service to the community. Only more recently have critics come to admit that the strong current of didactic, political, and "realistic" writing was again and again countered by the protests, dreams, anxieties, and neuroses of those more aesthetically inclined writers who considered civic togetherness to be, if not a curse, at least a terrible burden, and who tried to escape into a creative solitude where they might go undisturbed by communal do-gooders; some of the greatest found their solitude in the insane asylum. There were, to be sure, Johann Heinrich Pestalozzi (1746–1827), Jeremias Gotthelf (1797–1854), and Gottfried Keller (1819–1890), who taught, preached, and served; but there were also Conrad Ferdinand Meyer (1825–1898), who dreamed, behind drawn blinds, of fiery supermen; melancholy Heinrich Leuthold (1827–1879), who wrote strangely moving verse of classicist perfection; paranoiac Robert Walser (1878–1956), immensely admired by Kafka; and the talented novelist Jakob Schaffner (1875–1944), who in his longing to escape from life in a petty community took refuge in a mystique of the German *Reich* and turned into a minor Nazi propagandist. The dense pressures of the community are to Swiss writers a matter of both pride and pain; geographical limitations combine with the traditional Swiss preference for practical action over audacious inquiry, and the almost instinctive will to serve the neighbor clashes with a recurrent need for open spaces, unfettered contemplation, fulfillment of the individual imagination, and political irresponsibility. The alternative to the image of the narrow Swiss petit bourgeois community, be it Gottfried Keller's Seldwyla, Max Frisch's Andorra, or Friedrich Dürrenmatt's Güllen, is the perennial dream of the unbourgeois wild blue yonder.

But Swiss writers of the German language labor under an additional burden not shared by most of their German and Austrian colleagues. Swiss writers live and work close to linguistic schizophrenia. As children, lovers, fathers, and neighbors they speak, each according to his specific place of habitation, a highly differentiated Alemannic dialect; but as writers who want to communicate beyond the confines of their intimate community they have to use *Schriftdeutsch* (as High German is called in Switzerland). While they are literally at home in their dialect, they have to learn the written language in school; literary High German is as foreign to them as was Latin to Burgundian monks. The trouble is that there does not exist a uniform dialect (as the term *Schwyzerdütsch* wrongly suggests), but rather an almost infinite variety of local variations; the citizen of Zurich may easily understand the phonetic intricacies of *Basel-Dütsch*, yet he will have considerable difficulty understanding his compatriot from the isolated valleys of the Bernese *Oberland*. Far from being a monolithic affair, Swiss literature in German really consists of interlocking and shifting levels, each of which has its own problems of genre and generations: first, close to the homely roots of daily life, a flourishing literature in the local dialects (e.g., Rudolf von Tavel, Bern; Meinrad Lienert, Schwyz; Albert Bächtold, Schaffhausen); a goodly number of highly urbane literary works in *Schriftdeutsch* which, unfortunately, have remained an entirely Swiss German concern (including the masterly prose of Meinrad Inglin [b. 1893] and the sophisticated verse of Albin Zollinger [1895–1941], Switzerland's Stephen Spender); and finally, the *Schriftdeutsch* writings of a select group of authors who have successfully broken the barriers of provincial isolation and speak to readers on both sides of the Atlantic. Frisch and Dürrenmatt are not a Swiss miracle but richly talented members of a complex community of creative writers who display many gifts.

As in Germany and Austria, the first years after the war were a curious time of possibilities in abeyance; Switzerland quickly reasserted its international commercial interests, but the deeper transformations of the *Eidgenossenschaft*, caused by the war and the metamorphosis of Europe, were not yet visible in sharp outline. I suspect that recent Swiss intellectual developments tend to follow the rhythm of systole (inhaling) and diastole (exhaling) pointed out, in a different context, by the scientist Goethe: in time of grave danger to their inherited institutions the Swiss, intellectuals included, instinctively reaffirm "the idea hovering in the mountains" (Gottfried Keller) or, in less metaphorical terms, the political options that unite the four linguistic groups; as soon as pressures subside, forces of cohesion weaken, disturbing questions reappear, and a younger generation longs to throw open all the windows of the stuffy house. Max Frisch's *Tagebuch 1946–49 / Diary* emerges from the immediate postwar years as an outstanding record of a troubled sensibility which, leaving the isolation of a country surrounded by enemies, resolutely confronts new issues and allegiances; and discussion of the traditional problem of the Swiss writer and his community is combined with a new search for a commitment that would be binding far beyond Switzerland. Almost on the first page of his *Diary* Frisch (b. 1911) identifies Switzerland with "Andorra," a curious little country of "distrustful and ambitious people," and again confirms the native Swiss desire for "the great and flat horizons . . . the desire for the waters" which would link the Swiss "to all shores of the world." But something has changed: after a short trip to devastated Germany, with its ruins, refugees, and black marketeers, Frisch returns to tidy Switzerland and suddenly feels that in his literary efforts he has proceeded on obsolete assumptions: "We write sonnets" which assume certainty of "where man ends, where Heaven begins, how God and devil rhyme. . . . What is a world? An inclusive consciousness? But whose?" It is remarkable to see that young Frisch (in sharp contrast to the generation of the 'sixties) fully reaffirms his belief in the Swiss political tradition; it is better, he suggests, to have a "rough" democracy than to indulge in the cultural aestheticism of the "butchers." Culture, to the Swiss, implies the civilized political achievements of the entire community, not the aesthetic masterpiece of a unique individual; and if the artists find the atmosphere of their Swiss homeland rather "dry," Frisch holds that they fare better living in that dry air than being caught up in a purely aesthetic "culture" indifferent to the most cruel inhumanity. These are sentiments of a passing moment, however; within a few years Max Frisch's Stiller (a romantic artist in search of his true self) will grant his "dry" homeland far less credit, and the former defender of a rough-hewn liberalism will bitterly attack an ossified establishment of bureaucrats, "squares," and bourgeois enemies of true sensitivity. Evidently, Frisch's *Diary, 1946–1949*, still belongs to the systolic aftermath of the war, while his later novel about Stiller (1954) articulates the diastolic era of wintry discontent.

The Swiss Establishment and Anatol Ludwig Stiller: 1950–1960

SWITZERLAND IS basically a poor country, but the Swiss, driven by a Calvinist devotion to hard work (fully shared by the Catholics), have accepted the challenges of dearth; the traditional watch industry demonstrates the Swiss response to a shortage of natural resources. In the last year of the war, Switzerland had to be fed by the Allies, but since the late 'forties, Switzerland has generously if not uniformly contributed to European recovery; the export volume increased by 50% (1950-1959), real hourly wages rose meteorically, and the national income doubled within fifteen years (1948-1963). Yet there were early trouble spots which indicated problematical industrial and sociological changes: the metal, chemical, and electronics industries expanded rapidly while traditional textile production was losing many of its international customers; a high trade deficit had to be balanced by income from banking, insurance, and tourism, chronically lagging in some regions (Vaud); and the high rate of production was only sustained by Italian and Spanish workers, whose arrival *en masse* was to create inevitable problems affecting the fundaments of Swiss political tradition.

Rapid economic expansion was accompanied by political stabilization of a particular kind. The Swiss federative system has long cultivated a compromise which assures the effective coexistence of all twenty-five cantons (including half-cantons). During the war, the political parties became convinced that it was both useful and possible to underplay ideological conflicts, concentrate on pragmatic issues, and cultivate compromise not as an art but as an institution. In the past, there had always existed some kind of "cantonal" apportionment to make sure that a representative of powerful Zurich or of Canton Vaud was seated in the Federal Council and that at least two seats were reserved for delegates of the French- and Italian-speaking regions; during the 'fifties, the idea of proportioning power in the Federal Council according to political allegiances began gaining ground. After the elections of 1959, a new form of a *Bundesratsproporz* was elaborated by which representation was divided, the seven seats to be distributed among the Liberals (2), Conservative-Christians (2), Social Democrats (2), and the Peasants, Artisans, and Citizens Party (1). In marked contrast to the Austrian *Proporz* of the 'fifties, however, the Swiss did not develop an inflexible system of black and red featherbedding at every level down to the village post office, but rather a working hypothesis constantly checked in the cantons and the communities, where local political constellations continued to prevail: in Zurich, the Social Democrats have long been the determining power group (1963: ten seats in the National Council); in Bern, the Social Democrats (12) compete with the Peasants, Artisans, and Citizens Party (11); Conservatives are strong in Lucerne (5), Fribourg (3), and St. Gallen (6). Critics are right in insisting that the proportional formula works, but only at a high price: effective opposition practically vanishes, and extremist groups, including the Jura Separatists, resort to bombing railway lines and courthouses rather than to parliamentary discussion. But in a society of agreeable politicians and expert administrators, creative minds also turn into "separatists," for they suspect that they serve the establishment only as exquisite adornments rather than as critics formulating essential challenges; they dislike the idea of being the frosting on the consumer's cake. I do not want to reduce Max Frisch's novel *Stiller*, 1954 / *I'm Not Stiller*, 1958, which made the young playwright known far beyond the Swiss frontiers, to a mere social allegory of intellectual unrest in the self-satisfied 'fifties; the "civic" strand constitutes a fundamental element in its rich texture. *Stiller* combines the story of an artist in search of his true self with a Strindbergian (and indeed autobiographical) portrait of a tortured marriage destroyed from within because man and wife make absolute demands upon each other. The sculptor, Anatol Ludwig Stiller, a reluctant citizen of Zurich, has escaped from his frustrations into the wide-open cities of America and the deserts of Mexico, but after a suicide attempt fails, he decides to go home as a different, "newborn" man. At the Swiss border he is arrested because of his fake U.S. passport, and while the Swiss authorities are trying to establish his true identity, he is asked by the State Prosecutor, who happens to be married to Stiller's former mistress, to write a frank report on his recent restless life. Stiller's aversion to his old self implies a strong dislike for the good, average Swiss citizen, whose life is regulated, confined, and ruled by the local bureaucracies; he refuses "to play the role which they would like so much." Arguing his case with the defense attorney, a Swiss citizen of the most correct kind, Stiller has

ample opportunity to rail against the Swiss "lack of temperament" and "desire to make no mistake"; his compatriots, he feels,
are unfortunately quite satisfied "with dry laurel behind their
mirrors," because they have ceased to ask the kinds of questions
that demand unexpected, harsh, disturbing answers. Feeling
acutely the frustrations of entire generations of Swiss artists from
C. F. Meyer to Albin Zollinger, Stiller does not want to share
in that "cheap disregard of greatness (the whole, the perfect, the
radical)" which inevitably results in spiritual sterility. It is not
political compromise which he dislikes; he cannot bear the
thought that his fellow citizens never suffer when they have to
make compromises in matters of the intellect; and although
Stiller remains in Switzerland, he characterizes his existence as
that of "German Jews in New York"; he and his ailing wife,
Julika, are, as he ironically suggests to the State Prosecutor, "a
Swiss couple of inner émigrés." I suspect that Stiller's, and perhaps Frisch's, relationship to his Swiss compatriots resembles
Byron's trouble with women: he can live neither with nor without
them; and he is left a hesitant prisoner of an inescapable dialectic
of acceptance and rejection, escape and return.

The Swiss 'Sixties: David's Dream

FAR-REACHING CHANGES in the accustomed way of life were well
under way in the 'fifties but became more visible in the early
'sixties, when the country was harshly confronted with the consequences of an industrial expansion based mainly on imported
foreign labor. Industrialization means urbanization, and in Switzerland, too, the population movement away from the agricultural
and Alpine regions into the exploding cities rapidly changed the
country; within ten years (1950–1960) the number of people
active in agriculture decreased by nearly sixty thousand. There
are now five metropolitan agglomerations (Basel, Bern, Zurich,
Lausanne, and Geneva) which dominate the social structure and,
by an irrevocable mechanism, create entire "rings" of commuter
bedroom communities where the new middle classes are concentrated: the population of Zurich increased by 22.5% within
ten years (1950–1960) and that of Dietikon (where the commuters

dwell) by 109.2%. Swiss sociologists are beginning to fear that an urban "gold coast" is developing in contrast to the depleted hinterlands, and just when they are trying to decentralize new industries (and the accompanying infrastructure), people continue moving away from the Swiss heartlands. Cantons like Glarus, Appenzell, or the Valais are barely holding their own or are even decreasing in population; mountain villages are deserted and, as in southern France, old farmhouses are being rapidly bought up by fashionable urban weekenders who want to have a chic place for the next party. Demographically, the traditional image of Switzerland as the country of the radiant mountain farmer blowing his long horn or yodeling across the valleys has become almost a Potemkinian stage set of rather dubious reality.

But sociological transformations are intensified by the massive involvement of foreign labor in Swiss economic affairs; expanding industries and progressing urbanization are based on a rapid population increase which to a significant degree consists of laborers excluded from the political life of the country: Italians and Spaniards may work but not vote. One year after the war, Switzerland employed about fifty thousand foreigners; by 1961, there were half a million working in factories, agriculture, and services; and in the late 'sixties the number increased to nearly 800,000, or almost 15% of the entire population. In some of the key industries (including machines and construction) nearly one-third of the entire labor force comes from abroad. Swiss planners had not had much experience with massive movements of workers, yet the alternatives which they faced were equally difficult: if "aliens" are "rotated" (as they were for some time by the authorities) the guest worker is degraded to a migrant, and the product of his work will lack quality; if permission to settle is granted liberally, living conditions will rapidly deteriorate when families join their heads in cities that lack proper accommodations, and rising rents and real estate prices will further dislocate the economy. Yet the basic problem is one of political participation—the Italians and Spaniards cannot even vote on matters of local importance (including bus fares or the salaries of civil servants) traditionally decided by a referendum of the entire population. They have their transistor radios and special movies at which they congregate on Sundays, but they remain as underprivileged as Mexican migrant workers in the American Southwest.

The youngest writers have a difficult time coping with both their craft and the radical, yet long invisible, transformation of Swiss life; in a society more fluid than ever before they cannot simply turn back to the admirable masters of the past—the new universe does not resemble that of Gottfried Keller or even, perhaps, of Thomas Mann. Switzerland may be neutral in international affairs, but it intimately shares in general European vicissitudes; the new commuter may be as Swiss as an old Glarus shepherd, but his daily experience seems far less direct, substantial, and colorful. In such a different world, Frisch's Stiller seems a character with obsolete, romantic inclinations: his personal concern with "eros" and "art" belongs to a distant age, of which little survives in the minds of the young. I am tempted to read Otto F. Walter's (b. 1928) novel *Herr Tourel*, 1962, as a formidable counterstatement to Frisch's story of the exceptionally sensitive and endangered artist. Herr Tourel, a Swiss underground man from the borders of the Jura, writes his hectic personal confession in a lonely hut on the border of the Aare River, but as he describes his unexceptional life (that of a local photographer with occasional artistic leanings), his obsessions increasingly poison his remembering mind. Pursued by childhood memories and the false talk of his fellow citizens (or so he says), Tourel wants to clear his life of all shadows. "I shall wash myself clean, I shall, I shall," he says, and yet his mind sinks into final darkness and confusion. Human life as such, not only the aristocratic existence of the alienated artist has become questionable; and while Otto F. Walter does not want to define the totality of the social situation, he amply succeeds in darkly illuminating the destructive anxieties potentially present in the mind of every man. Walter's *Herr Tourel* is an exercise in Swiss Gothic that haunts the imagination with its ghostly precision.

Hugo Loetscher (b. 1929), another gifted writer of the youngest generation, has not yet made up his mind whether to cope with the new issues in a more traditional mode close to realism, or to employ the ironic parable, derived ultimately from Kafka. I prefer his earlier novel *Die Kranzflechterin*, 1964 / *The Wreath Maker* to his parable of *Noah*, 1967, because the earlier story displays a bitter energy of language which I miss in the amusing if casual reworking of the Biblical story. In his tale of the German peasant girl, Anna, who comes to Switzerland to make a living, Loetscher—often against his epic intent—encompasses an entire epoch of teeming Zurich life: Anna fails with a little grocery store but discovers that funeral wreaths are always needed. She rears a daughter born out of wedlock, sleeps with the young men who rent her extra room, watches the growing city from the roof of the apartment block, visits her former country (which has turned into a ghost land under the Nazis), and dies surrounded by wreaths of her own making. Clearly, she is a distant cousin of Brecht's Mother Courage, who thrives where other people die and challenges death by her lean and vital tenacity of purpose. There is high comedy in Loetscher's novel (Anna does make a good living from death); and an inimitable combination of terse irony with exuberant, almost "Flemish," genre scenes from the life of humble folk demonstrates rare sophistication of craft.

Walter Matthias Diggelmann (b. 1927), Switzerland's angriest young man, prefers message to craftsmanship, and his novel *Die Hinterlassenschaft*, 1965 / *The Inheritance* unsparingly attacks the Swiss establishment by challenging the legend "of courageous and Christian Switzerland." The Swiss, Diggelmann says, were guilty of abetting mass murder when they turned away many refugees during World War II; and the same people who were then active in the fascist "fronts" and supported a strict immigration policy are now actively promoting a crude anti-Communism aimed at suffocating all public criticism of social affairs. Diggelmann openly refuses to share the "symbolic" leanings of the older generation (including Max Frisch); he does not want to construct a parable of antisemitism, as Frisch did in *Andorra*, but prefers to call a spade a spade. In practice, Diggelmann returns to the collage technique of Dos Passos and Alfred Döblin. His story of young David, who, himself of partly Jewish origin, wants to find out who became responsible for the death of his parents by refusing to admit them to Switzerland, is combined with newspaper clippings from the Swiss right-wing press of 1933, memoranda concerning Swiss refugee policy, and the official report on the refugee question submitted to the government and the Swiss people by the renowned Basel lawyer Dr. Carl Ludwig. I wonder whether Diggelmann's carefully compiled documentation impresses the responding reader as intensely as the moral energy of his hero, who takes sides with all the Swiss underprivileged, including the foreign workers, and dies in a tavern brawl prearranged by some conservatives. The story certainly suffers from Diggelmann's attempt to deal with two or more issues at once, and the second part, which deals with the organization of a conservative "pogrom" against a Marxist intellectual living in a small Swiss town, lacks the highly concentrated effect of the first. But David has a dream about the Christian Swiss which has more than local relevance: "And there came hundreds of thousands [of refugees to Switzerland], most of them with only what they were able to carry on their shoulders, and every Swiss citizen who had more than one shirt, gave them one, and whoever had two pairs of shoes, gave them one." Hidden in David's dream is an accusation about what *should* have happened but did not; and few people, inside or outside Switzerland, can answer it with easy conscience.

2. Austria

Austria without Schmaltz: 1945–1948

THE FIRST Austrian Republic (1918–1938) was troubled by destructive self-doubt, which continually strengthened its powerful enemies. After the breakup of the Monarchy, the parliament proclaimed that *Deutsch-Österreich* was part of the Socialist German Republic then emerging from the debris of the Wilhelmine Empire; and in the first years after World War I the plebiscites held in most provinces confirmed that many Austrians did not believe their country had a viable future as an independent state. In the Geneva protocols (1922) the Allies combined their political insistence on Austrian independence with financial guarantees which stabilized the currency but did not solve the structural deficiencies of a dislocated economy. Of a population of approximately 6.7 million, one-half million were chronically unemployed; they contributed markedly to the political unrest which resulted in a brutal civil war (1934), an authoritarian reorganization of the state under Dollfuss and Schuschnigg (1934–1938) and, finally, Hitler's triumphant drive to Vienna.

But Hitler's henchmen taught many of those who had enthusiastically welcomed the *Führer* to share the feelings of those other seventy thousand uncompromising Austrians rounded up and imprisoned as potential enemies by advance units of the Gestapo in the spring of 1938. After the new rulers had wiped out Austrian selfhood, including the name of the country, hopes faded rapidly. Little was done to save the Austrian Jews from coming disasters, but in the early 'forties the tide of opposition at last began to turn with some force; and when Dr. Carl Goerdeler, the leader of the German conservative resistance, came to Vienna to discuss a "greater Germany" without Hitler, he was astonished to discover that prominent Austrians no longer anticipated such a political possibility. The officers' revolt of July 20, 1944, failed in Vienna as it did elsewhere; although the *Wehrmacht* for a few hours held high party functionaries, the defeat of the Berlin Group quickly reversed the situation. Local resistance groups, however, had long been working on creating a compact organization ("05") which could establish close contact with allied strategic services; Austrian battalions were incorporated into Tito's army, and highly placed *Wehrmacht* officers of Austrian origin successfully transferred their compatriots to command posts on Austrian soil. When the allied armies approached, the resistance often helped by disposing of the Nazi rulers in fierce street skirmishes (Innsbruck) or by applying quiet pressure (Graz); in Vienna, a number of *Wehrmacht* units engaged, under Russian fire, in protracted street battles with the SS in order to take points of political and administrative importance; and where the SS temporarily prevailed, *Wehrmacht* officers of Austrian sympathies were shot a few hours before the Soviet army penetrated the city.

Within days a provisional government was formed by representatives of the Catholic conservatives, the Social Democrats, and the Communist rank and file, all of whom had come to tolerate each other in Hitler's prisons and concentration camps and, in marked contrast to their predecessors of 1918, had little doubt that it was their fundamental task to create a free and independent Austria; even the Communist functionaries flown in by the Soviets did their best to stress their Austrian heritage. The first national elections were held in November, 1945, throughout occupied Austria. Reestablishing traditional prewar balances, they gave strong mandates to the Catholic and conservative Austrian People's Party, which prudently underplayed its personal links to the authoritarian phase of the First Republic, and to the Austrian Socialist Party, preserving the aspirations of the well-organized old Social Democracy; the Communists' hopes were shattered when they received a bare 5.42% of the vote (an outcome not lost on Ulbricht's collaborators in East Germany).

The reconsolidation of intellectual life (apart from the rapid blossoming of the theater) was a slow and meandering process; I suspect that the deepest wounds and the most incisive shocks were not to be felt until twenty, if not thirty, years later. In some contrast to West Germany, where the return of the exiles caused protracted discussions or, as in East Germany, constituted an entirely new beginning of literary life, the Austrian situation lacked melodramatic conflicts or uniform answers. Many distinguished writers, including Richard Beer-Hofmann (1866–1945), Robert Musil (1880–1942), and Franz Werfel (1890–1945), had died in exile; others, like Hermann Broch (1886-1951), Elias Canetti (b. 1905), Ernst Waldinger (b. 1896), Johannes Urzidil (b. 1896), or, among the youngest, Erich Fried (b. 1921), stayed on in the United States or England; among those who soon returned were Franz Theodor Csokor (1885–1968), the grand old man of Austrian letters, and the critic Hans Weigel (b. 1908), who actively encouraged the young. The transitional years between the end of the war and the beginning of economic stabilization were faithfully reflected in *Plan* (1945–1948), a short-lived but many-splendored literary periodical edited by Otto Basil (b. 1901), a poet and critic of wide intellectual interests. While the Nazis had favored robust poetry and the old-fashioned peasant novel (popular among middle- and lowbrow Austrian readers long before the Nazis), the editor of *Plan* was eager to explore the forbidden past of Expressionism, as well as French Surrealism, which had never attracted much interest among German writers and yet suddenly triumphed among the youngest group of Viennese painters. Paul Celan (b. 1920), Christine Busta (b. 1915), Friedericke Mayröcker (b. 1924), Milo Dor (b. 1923), and Reinhard Federmann (b. 1923) published their early verse and prose in Otto Basil's periodical; Heimito von Doderer (1896–1966), under the name René von Stangeler (who appears as a central character in his major novels), analyzed the distinguished work of his friend, the artist and writer Albert Paris Gütersloh (b. 1887); and a lone new playwright, Fritz Hochwälder (b. 1911), here published (1946) the first scenes of *Das heilige Experiment* / [The Holy Experiment] *The Strong Are Lonely*, 1954, which made him internationally known within a few years. It was characteristic of the Austrian situation that old and the new were able to coexist without discrimination: Felix Braun (b. 1885), Rudolf Felmayer (b. 1897), and Paula von Preradović (1887–1951) continued writing their distinctive poetry in the classical tradition and were joined by the young, among them Ilse Aichinger (b. 1921), who in her astonishing first novel *Die grössere Hoffnung*, 1948 / [The Greater Hope] *Herod's Children*, 1963, explored the hopes and fears of children considered "racially impure" by the dictators. Life was still too difficult to allow separating the generations, at least for the time being.

The Burdens of Prosperity:
Austria in the 'Fifties

AUSTRIANS ARE FOND OF SPEAKING about their own *Wirtschaftswunder*, which within a decade transformed their hungry country into a modern consumer society, but I am tempted to speak of a simultaneous political feat which enabled them to organize a more or less functioning democracy under the very nose of the Soviet occupation power; Austria's neighbor Czechoslovakia was far less fortunate. Economic stabilization began when the government, against Soviet exhortations, agreed to accept Marshall Plan aid, and American money was poured into the (speedily nationalized) basic industries to increase production levels; the combination of new American gifts and wartime German investments in the steel industry proved extremely effective in reforming the Austrian economic structure. In 1947, industrial production was still far below the prewar level (1937 = 100), but in 1950 it reached 145 and had more than tripled by 1963 (338).

Yet the painful beginnings of economic reorganization caused problems which the Communists tried to exploit in their final bid for power. Marshall Plan funds were not invested in developing the trades; agricultural production remained inefficient; uncontrolled inflationary tendencies emerged; and peasants in many regions withheld their products from the markets until price ceilings should be raised. The Communists, relying on heavily infiltrated security forces in the Soviet zone, on the workers' "commandos" which they had established in the Soviet-controlled industries, as well as on the legitimate grievances of the workers, attempted to organize a wave of strikes in late September and early October, 1950, to seize control of the powerful trade unions and topple the coalition government; in many places groups of Communist strikers blocked railways and telegraph communications to and from Vienna, in order to isolate the government from the rest of the country. Their attempt failed for a number of reasons: the Soviets did not intervene directly (except in Wiener-Neustadt); Oscar Helmer, the resilient Socialist Minister of the Interior, shrewdly neutralized the Communist police forces by deploying the newly trained *gendarmerie*, equipped by the United States, outside the Soviet zone; and Socialist and Catholic workers did not obey the Communist call for a general strike. By October 6, 1950, it was clear that the strike had failed. The Communists withdrew to their 5% limbo and were further weakened by the consequences of the Hungarian revolution and the exuberance of the consumer society.

But the Soviet Union was concerned with long-range strategic planning rather than with ideology. Shortly after Stalin's death (1953), the Soviets opted for a neutralized Austria rather than for the risks of establishing another People's Democracy geographically confined to their own zone of occupation. On April 15, 1955, an Austrian delegation came to Moscow to discuss the future of the country; and a few days after a successful conference of the ambassadors of the occupying powers, an Austrian State Treaty was signed in Vienna on May 15, 1955, to end the occupation and to guarantee an "independent and free" Austria. In late October, 1955, the last soldiers of the occupying armies left the country and the parliament solemnly declared Austria a permanently neutral state.

Independence and neutrality strengthened the Austrians' natural feeling of pride, but unfortunately they also resulted in the ossification of the "red" and "black" coalition system which had been extremely effective for a decade. The intimate collaboration of the two great traditional parties (which a generation previously had fought a gory civil war) had been useful under the occupation, but the august principle of "togetherness" rapidly deteriorated into the dubious practices of a proportional system (*Proporz*) which developed more vices than virtues. Basically, the proportional system consisted of prearranged bargains between the two parties that determined their policies and divided up the spoils. These secret (later, semisecret) and unconstitutional agreements contributed to political stability but blunted intellectual activities in many ways: in an impotent parliament, dialectics and the incisive language of inquisitive criticism were replaced by recurrent clichés; the dullness of the newspapers was only occasionally relieved by the witty theater reviews that have long provided an outlet for much of Austrian intellect; and the mass media, ineffective economically and overstaffed with political functionaries, repulsed rather than attracted new writers, who more and more tended to sell their manuscripts to the more courageous West German broadcasting stations, and consequently to West German publishers as well.

Prosperity, independence, neutrality, and the *Proporz* system coincided, in the 'fifties at least, with a great deal of intellectual ossification or creeping provincialism; one of the worried critics rightly suggested that Austria was being "balkanized." Nazi criminals were not tried; intellectual discussion remained less than intense; sociological inquiry languished; and for a decade the festive clichés and a frozen "Chamber of Commerce" image of Austria (White Stallions, Grinzing, and all) obfuscated the

incisive changes that had taken place in the Austrian political
and sociological structure. Austrian literary life had traditionally
been determined by the productive tension between Vienna, the
center of restless inquiry, criticism, and experiment, and the
calmer provinces, in which more conservative writers and audiences preferred the inherited, the sound, and the "sane." In the
old Monarchy as well as in the First Republic, Viennese Jews
provided an essential element of relentless intellectual search and
uncompromising exploration in literature, philosophy, and many
sciences, but after they had been killed or driven from the country, a tremendous gap opened up, one which self-satisfied
speeches about Austrian traditions cannot fill; Vienna, the young
Austrian critic Paul Kruntorad suggests, has turned into a prov-
ince of its own past. There are additional sociological reasons
why Vienna continues to suffer losses of strength while the
Austrian provinces increasingly gain in importance. The Austrian
population and economy is shifting from Vienna and the east
to the west of the country. Two regions of different sociological
texture are emerging; the Enns River today separates a "poorer"
east from the "richer" west. In 1934, 3.7 of 6.7 million inhabitants
lived in the eastern provinces, but in 1961, only 3.2 of 7 million
remained. Sociologists provide telling statistical evidence: from
1934 to 1961 Vienna lost 16% of its inhabitants, while the western
provinces gained from 33% (Tyrol) to 46% (Vorarlberg). It is hard
to assess the final consequences of these continuing shifts:
Carnap, Freud, Musil, and Broch thrived in metropolitan Vienna;
but I wonder whether their successors, or potential disciples, will
find the extremely pleasant provincial climate an adequate substitute for a lively capital.

Austria in the 'fifties was dominated by traditional literary
issues that did not reflect current sociological change; and in
Georg Saiko's novel *Auf dem Floss*, 1954 (revised version) / *On
the Raft*, the most noble elements of the past are blended with
unusual finesse, distinction, and depth. Unconcerned with recent
social transformation, Saiko (1892–1962) returns once more to
a world of melancholy princes, wellborn girls educated in fashionable Catholic schools, pensive aristocrats and, within the
horizon of the old estates, a feudal landscape of villages,

shepherds, and passionate gypsies. But Saiko skillfully distances even the most melodramatic events (including murder by poison and drowning): conversations unfold, as it were, behind a silver veil, elegant tea tables are set in the park, an aging countess has to compete with her sixteen-year-old daughter for the attentions of older cavaliers, and the dry clicking of the croquet balls echoes on the still summer air. Deriving inspiration from Freud and from Turgenev, Georg Saiko concerns himself not with the events but with the hidden motives behind them: he wants to know how deeper impulses break through rational conventions and, as one of the great Viennese writers of Musil's, Broch's, and Doderer's generation, he suggests with considerable artistry a vision of humanity drifting "on a raft" of social rules, on the dark waters of prerational and unconscious desires.

Gerhard Fritsch's first novel *Moos auf den Steinen,* 1955 / *Moss on the Stones* is an extraordinary attempt by a young writer to cope with the burdens of the Austrian past and those of the traditional novel as well. His simple love story, or legend, certainly invites an almost allegorical interpretation: Baroness Jutta, who lives in the dark Castle Schwarzwasser ("Dark Waters"), for a fateful moment is torn between an intellectual "operator," who wants to organize fashionable symposia in the neglected park, and a shy poet, who offers Jutta his love in order to rescue her from her oppressive memories of injury and rape (shades of May, 1945). She refuses the organization man, but the poet dies in an accident, and Jutta, an incarnation of Austria itself, has to find her way on her own. Leaving her future life in abeyance, Gerhard Fritsch (1924–1968) resolutely breaks with the traditional rules of the novel, merely sketching in a fragmentary final chapter in which he suggests that historical experience must provide the further plot.

Austrian traditionalism of the more provincial kind managed by sly indifference to counteract the imaginative efforts of a loose grouping of younger intellectuals and artists whose search for new art forms went hand in hand with a bohemianism that wavered curiously between reminiscences of the *fin de siècle* and anticipations of future "happenings." In 1953, young Gerhard Rühm (b. 1930) and H. C. Artmann (b. 1921), who had just returned to Vienna from Switzerland, defined their "Eight-Point Proclamation of the Poetic Act" and in late July of the same year organized a *Soirée aux amants funèbres*, a mock funeral procession through the center of Vienna, interrupted by ceremonial recitations of Baudelaire and Nerval at the busiest intersections. But the "Vienna group," as it was later called, was never unified by principle or practice; Rühm early tended toward "constructivist" and "concrete" poetry and later allied himself with Eugen Gomringer, while H. C. Artmann, possibly after reading Federico García Lorca, used Viennese dialect in his own phonetic transcription to create a macabre and funny poetry rich in texture—he wrote his verse, first gathered in *Med ana schwoazzn Dintn*, 1958 / *Witt Black Inkk*, in rebellion against the middle-class establishment and quickly found himself with a middle-class best seller on his hands. During the late 'fifties, the underground groups slowly emerged from their cellars and cafés to organize jam sessions, revolutions, and children's operas, but once again West German publishers and radio stations exerted a stronger pull than native institutions, and many of the most talented men, including Rühm and Artmann, left Vienna for Munich or Berlin. Among the camp followers of the Vienna group, the poet Ernst Jandl (b. 1925) today continues to impress by his wit, ingenuity, and verve.

The Restive 'Sixties: In Search of a Past

IN THE 'sixties, the proportional system of divided spoils increasingly failed to respond to the economic and political needs of a country transformed, within less than twenty years, from a belated baroque affair into a modern society; and with the popular referendum demanding incisive changes in the State Broadcasting Organization and the subsequent crisis concerning Otto von Habsburg's passport, the exhausted coalition system cracked wide open. In the national elections of March, 1966, the People's Party, which had steered a more pragmatic course of action, was considerably more successful than its Socialist coalition partner (85 seats vs. 74) and, after brief and halfhearted negotiations on continuing the old system, Chancellor Josef Klaus formed a *Volkspartei* cabinet to run the country, while the Socialists (hardly prepared at that moment for such a productive task) again assumed the function of the opposition. At the time when the Grand Coalition was formed in the Federal Republic of Germany, Austria returned to a more legitimate relationship of government and opposition in order to face a decreasing growth rate of the gross national product (1955–1960: 5.2; 1960–1965: 4.1), a sagging economy burdened with an inefficient nationalized industry, and the many unsolved problems of the preceding decades, including a costly system of subsidized theaters lacking in intellectual vitality and primitive housing for most of the citizens (1961: 52% of all apartments had outside toilets and 36% lacked inside water faucets).

Austria's *Kultur* has still to be civilized, but the process is irrevocably under way. Political-minded writers, journalists, and sociologists, including Günther Nenning, Karl Bednarik, Alexander Vodopivec, and Otto Schulmeister, the editor-in-chief of *Die Presse* (Austria's only cosmopolitan daily), explore the situation in pragmatic terms; and in an internationally known "television interview" the indefatigable Carl Merz and Hellmuth Qualtinger have characterized and condemned the "ugly Austrian" *Der Herr Karl*, 1962, who, by betraying every one of his friends and girls, has survived all the different regimes and continues to vegetate in perspiring self-satisfaction, stealing booze and spying on young Sunday lovers in the Danube marshes.

Perhaps more ferment of talent is developing than the managers of the tourist trade would care to admit; many younger novelists demonstrate a highly committed view of their world, resolutely search the more recent Austrian past for the deeper causes of failures and crimes, and show an intense awareness of modern prose experimentation. Hans Lebert's *Die Wolfshaut*, 1960 / *The Wolf's Skin* unmasks a sleepy Austrian village in which almost everybody wants to hide what has happened during the war; forgetful people eat, drink, and make love; and unpunished evil lurks around the damp houses like a hungry wolf in the snow. Lebert (b. 1919) does not grind an ideological ax; he relies instead on a web of moral and symbolic implications. Lebert coolly analyzes the obsessions of a man who has participated in the mass executions in Poland, works with ironic reversals, and successfully creates mounting tension in a dense world of flesh, fog, and mud.

Thomas Bernhard (an intense talent [b. 1913] of far more than local relevance) stares fixedly at sickness, infertility, and death. In *Frost*, 1963, a young intern observes a painter who has morbidly withdrawn to a forlorn mountain village, and quickly discovers that he will have to report on ontological issues rather than on medical problems (as his superior assumes). The painter drags him through darkness and snow, explicates his philosophy of decay, and confronts him with the stench of the Old People's Asylum, the gore of the *abattoir*, ghostly accidents and funerals, and terribly vivid memories of the mutilated war dead rotting in the forests. The young man tries in vain to return to his reading of Henry James, but the painter (who prefers Pascal) relentlessly trudges with him through a putrescent landscape and speaks of the coming of the great frost that will silence all life: "The stars will flash like nails closing the lids of heaven." Thomas Bernhard's attitude implies a stark protest against literary tradition as well: in the dark and the cold of ugly villages pretenses are shattered, Austria appears as "Europe's brothel, with a good transatlantic reputation," and the inherited romantic images of the strong peasants and sweet landscapes are mercilessly destroyed.

Herbert Eisenreich (b. 1925), a highly gifted writer and critic, began publishing in the mid-'fifties, but his substantial promise has yet to be realized in a full performance. In his best short stories he likes to deal with ironic twists in the lives of his modest Austrian contemporaries: a loquacious commercial traveler complains about his wife's many friends, only to conceal the fact that he is having a pleasant affair with a willing girl; in the conversation of some small-town dignitaries a lie is told that implies the "naked truth." In his *récit, Der Urgrossvater*, 1964 / *The Great-Grandfather*, a young man suddenly feels fascinated by the portrait of an ancestor about whom dark rumors are told, and sets out to discover whether his great-grandfather was of Jewish origin or really an aristocrat as people imply. For his quest he retains the services of some shabby detective agencies, finds himself involved with two sisters who ask him to pay for an (entirely unnecessary) abortion, and finally tries to open a grave to come closer to the truth. He is arrested; later, following his instincts, he travels to a small Austrian town where he finds his son and, at the end of his quest, shows that he accepts being a husband and a father when he philosophically watches his son kissing a girl. As literary critic, Eisenreich has published first-rate essays on Doderer and Adalbert Stifter, and (challenged by the fashionable modernism of his contemporaries) proudly defends an old-fashioned realism, praises the ironic art of Thackeray, and tries to define the legitimate function of the Austrian writer today. It is good to see intellectuals continue Hugo von Hofmannsthal's and Robert Musil's search for the specific meaning of being Austrian; and although I do not see much sense in speaking of an "Austrian man" or in saying, as does Professor Gerhart Baumann, that Austrian literature fuses "the Ancient and the Christian, the Romance and the Germanic, past and future," I find much illumination in Herbert Eisenreich's insistence that being Austrian means to be deeply distrustful of what people generally call right and correct. Perhaps we are not far from the renewed discovery that, in Austria's best days, a strong "culinary" strain of festive theater, six kinds of goulash, Johann Strauss waltzes, and half-articulate feelings were decisively counterbalanced by the "analytical" strain of an intellectual tradition which is incarnated in the rationalist discipline of the later eighteenth century, in psychoanalytical research, in Viennese neopositivism, and in a lynx-eyed rather than maudlin literature.

3. The German Democratic Republic

The "Antifascist Democratic Order" And the Kulturbund: 1945–1949

THE SPRING OF 1945 was a time of great expectations for many German intellectuals, exiles, liberated prisoners, and returning soldiers; and the Communist functionaries in the Soviet zone of occupation tried to avoid endangering these hopes. The Ulbricht Group (among them the critic Fritz Erpenbeck, who later viciously attacked Brecht) were flown by Soviet plane into Brandenburg on April 30, 1945, to begin organizing efficient district administrations in smoldering Berlin and later in the entire zone under the Soviet military administration. Banks and heavy industry were nationalized, the large estates were redistributed, the school system was reorganized, but Communist administrators, hard pressed by ruthless Soviet *démontage,* employed the political soft sell; the practices of a Popular Front, still largely untried on German soil, were considered highly appropriate.

It is impossible to overlook the fact that most members of the nascent literary establishment had once been founding members of the *Bund proletarisch-revolutionärer Schriftsteller Deutschlands* (Association of German Proletarian and Revolutionary Writers), established on October 19, 1928, to support Communist policies in connection with the Soviet First Five-Year Plan, and exactly patterned in its organization and aims after the Russian Association of Proletarian Writers (RAPP), which dominated the Soviet literary scene in the late 'twenties and early 'thirties. There were indeed a few proletarians like Willi Bredel (b. 1901) or Hans Marchwitza (b. 1890), but others, like Johannes R. Becher (1891–1958) or the highly talented Anna Seghers (b. 1900), came from middle-class families and had their difficulties sacrificing sophisticated literary experimentation to *agitprop* short stories and partisan reportage. These writers were unified, however, by their historical fate as refugees, soldiers, or commissars in the Spanish Civil War, and, in their later exile in the Soviet Union or Mexico, as faithful apologists for Stalin's Socialist Realism, which most of them accepted as a matter of organizational discipline; when Anna Seghers boldly protested, she was silenced by Georg Lukács, who in the late 'thirties defended the administrative point of view. They were all experienced functionaries, resilient, infinitely patient, and, alone among the many German exiles, willing to identify themselves completely with the policies of an occupying army; in exile they had raised their voices against the inhumanities of fascism, but when they returned home and rapidly rose to power, their sensibilities ossified in the sudden confrontation with a coarse reality which bore little resemblance to their dreams.

As early as July 3, 1945, the *Kulturbund zur demokratischen Erneuerung Deutschlands* (Cultural Union for the Democratic Reconstruction of Germany) was established in the Soviet zone in order "to unite all constructive forces in the cultural field." Gerhart Hauptmann (1862–1946) had kind words for the undertaking; and in Thuringia, Ricarda Huch (1864–1947), a venerable humanist in the German idealist tradition, accepted the honorary chairmanship of the local branch of this new organization, whose functionaries solemnly proclaimed that they would "not impose an ideology like the Nazis, but would awaken and further the spirit of true humanity." The tolerant latitude of tastes was publicly supported in the pages of *Aufbau / Construction*, the official periodical of the Cultural Union, and one of the early important literary magazines of liberated Germany. Along with contributions by famous Marxist critics such as the Hungarian Lukács, there appeared essays by Heinrich and Thomas Mann, Hermann Broch, Paul Valéry, and Virginia Woolf; the art of James Joyce, long proscribed in the Soviet Union, was interpreted to his new German readers; and occasionally, to satisfy the insatiable German intellectuals, questions were discussed that were officially ignored in the Soviet Union, e.g., the theatrical innovations of Alexander Tairov. It was a difficult time, marked by suspense, hunger, and groping hopes, all reflected perhaps less in the new poems and novels that slowly began to appear than in a spate of memorable films, produced by Wolfgang Staudte, Erich Engel, and Kurt Maetzig, who were eager to continue the cinematographic achievements of the late 'twenties.

The Hegemony of Socialist Realism: 1949–1956

TACTICAL TOLERANCE, practiced to attract the widest possible support for the administration, did not last more than a few uneasy years. As Soviet policy turned bitterly anti-Western, vestiges of "decadent bourgeois" culture in the Soviet Union and elsewhere came under attack. Early in 1950 the precepts of Socialist Realism were discussed with increasing vehemence in the newspapers of the German Democratic Republic (established on October 7, 1949), and the Stalinist norms for aesthetic value (commitment to the party, typicality, and optimism) emerged from the prescribed discussion in the mass organizations. In the spring of 1951, the Central Committee of the German Socialist Unity Party (SED) adopted the anticipated resolution, "Against Formalism in Art and Literature: For a Progressive German Culture" (March 15–17), and seventeen years after it had been imposed on Soviet writers, Socialist Realism was declared to be the sole doctrine binding on all East German artists and intellectuals, who were thenceforth to be controlled by the newly created State Commission for Affairs of Art. Carl Hofer, highly honored a few years previously as one of the great masters of German expressionist painting, was now suddenly denounced for working against "the vital interests of the German people"; Otto Dix, whose avant-garde painting had been condemned by the Nazis, was proclaimed a "mere technician caught in the morass of decadent form," and Bertolt Brecht found himself accused of being a "formalist." This was not a matter to be taken lightly, for the new State Commission stated clearly that "formalism encouraged cosmopolitan ideas and thus implied direct support for the aggressive policy of American imperialism."

But constant threats and close supervision did not contribute to producing good literature, and while the doctrine triumphed, the practical results were rather meager. The older generation, including Arnold Zweig and Anna Seghers, chose to look backward and continued to write social novels in which the conflicts of World War I or the Weimar Republic were scrupulously analyzed; and Eduard Claudius (b. 1911), who had written a first-rate book about his experiences in the Spanish Civil War (*Grüne Oliven und nackte Berge,* 1945 / *Green Olives and Bare Mountains*), was far less convincing when he touched on human relationships in the new socialist society in *Menschen an unserer Seite,* 1951 / *Side by Side with Others.* There was more hope for poetry: while Stephan Hermlin (b. 1915), a highly talented disciple of the modern French, stooped for some years to writing bald political verse, younger poets began groping to transcend the idiom of classicism and Rilke. Franz Fühmann (b. 1922), who had written his first remarkable poems as a German soldier on the Finnish front, published his long poem *Die Fahrt nach Stalingrad / The Journey to Stalingrad* in 1953, which analyzed his conversion from an enthusiastic member of the Hitler Youth to Communism and demonstrated his great gifts in bold and burning metaphors.

A Fragile "Thaw" and the Aftermath: 1956–

WRITERS AND WORKERS were becoming increasingly estranged in their economic and political interests, and there was no immediate connection between the workers' uprising of June 17, 1953 (originally a local protest against increased work quotas), and the explosive unrest among the intellectuals after Stalin's death. Signs of the post-Stalin "thaw" appeared very slowly; by early 1955, however, East German intellectuals were astir, and philosophers as well as writers were beginning to formulate new ideas and demands within a Marxist context. The philosopher Ernst Bloch, who had reversed his earlier emigration by returning from Cambridge, Massachusetts, to East Germany in 1948, and his many talented pupils at the University of Leipzig formed one of the cores of resistance against orthodoxy. Bloch's Marxist, if highly poetic, anthropology impressed younger readers both by its wide range and by a prophetic language of expressionist power and extraordinary intensity. Three lectures delivered by Bloch in East Berlin expressed restlessness in half-veiled terms; and in the *Deutsche Zeitschrift für Philosophie (German Journal of Philosophy)*, edited by the erratic Walter Harich, the younger generation tried to combine Marxism, existentialist ideas, and the heritage of philosophical phenomenology in a new image of man that would correspond to their intimate experiences.

It was the fourth Writers' Congress in East Berlin, held from January 9 to 14, 1956, which briefly united some pre-Stalinist functionaries with the younger intellectuals of the post-Stalinist generation against the oppressive restrictions of official doctrine. The Congress was not, as has been suggested, a demonstration against Communism by friends of representative democracy; the most vigorous voices of protest were those of aging pre-Stalinist party members who well remembered the Bolshevik avant-garde and its pioneering achievements. The first to express his disgust with the dominant inflexibility in cultural matters was Willi Bredel, who had been a party man all his adult life; he was followed by Anna Seghers and even by Georg Lukács, the grand old man of Marxist criticism. Submitting to pressure, the administration announced a temporary retreat; and while insisting that "Socialist Realism offered the widest freedom for artistic achievements and provided creative opportunities for all talents, personalities, and individual modes of style," the functionaries suggested that the time for dogmatic rules had passed and that writers "should not be afraid to take up artistic experimentation again." The triumphant writers, in East Berlin and in the provinces, at once proceeded to broaden their demands: they declared that contacts with Western, above all American, literature ought to be intensified and the publishing houses of the Republic made independent of the state. But it was a late and fleeting spring, followed by recurrent, and almost fatal, wintry blasts. The Hungarian Revolution and the Soviet intervention put a swift end to the fragile "thaw" in East Germany. The screws were tightened again; and the harshest measures were directed against the philosophers, whom the regime considered particularly dangerous. The state police broke into the editorial offices of the *German Journal of Philosophy*, impounded its manuscripts, and arrested several of its contributors; the youthful editor-in-chief was sentenced to ten years in prison and has only recently been released. After the disciples, it was the turn of the teachers: Ernst Bloch was forced to give up teaching, his philosophical efforts were condemned by obedient colleagues, and his assistants dispersed.

During the days of the brutal campaign against the intellectuals, some of the most talented men of the older and younger generations made their way to the West; for the first time the stream of ordinary citizens escaping from East to West was joined by intellectuals of the Left who were being persecuted by a government which they had helped to sustain. The administration swiftly mobilized its conservative functionaries, who at ritual conferences reaffirmed their willingness to fight against "ideological coexistence" and for the development of realist art; and conservative and obedient authors were pitted against the restless intellectuals. After the Middle German Publishing House in Halle, acting on behalf of the administration, had called a writers' conference in Bitterfeld, the showcase of industrial development, an official "Bitterfeld Movement" was launched (April 24, 1959) to pamper talented and loyal industrial workers who might want to become writers; as in the Soviet Union in the late 'twenties, it was hoped that the workingman, untouched by any closer knowledge of Joyce, Apollinaire, or Kafka, would be a natural ally in the fight for a conservative, traditional, and provincial view of the arts. Alfred Kurella (b. 1895), who well remembers the *Proletkult* of the 'twenties, and the poet Kuba (b. 1914), a zealous servant of the Central Committee of the SED, were particularly active organizing peasant theaters, mass festivals, and writing courses for the workers who were to be trained to compete with the unreliable intellectuals: the government slogan was "Start Writing, Buddy!" (*Greif zur Feder, Kumpel!*). On April 24 and 25, 1964, a second Bitterfeld Conference was held in order to evaluate the results, and the presence of Walter Ulbricht himself plainly demonstrated the government's unremitting determination to insist on a socialist and popular art (*sozialistische Volkskunst*) which the rebellious writers consider obsolete and naïve.

Tensions of the 'Sixties: The Protest against the Establishment

THE OFFICIAL PHRASES of the GDR functionaries (and those of their counterparts in the Federal Republic) obscure the complicated and often meandering course of real experience. For the ordinary citizen of the GDR, daily life has changed considerably in the past decade; it is not a question of unqualified progress or of total frustration but one of the coexistence of rapid developments and increased conflict. Perhaps it is not unfair to say that the Ulbricht government has pinned its hope on a liberalized, more efficient economy increasingly oriented toward satisfying the rising demands of the individual consumer, rather than on consistently liberalized creative thought.

Industrial normalization began in the mid-'fifties, when the Soviets, reversing their policy, ceased dismantling factories and offered small credits, and an economy bled white by *démontage* and dogmatically imposed production schedules tottered toward its own remarkable *Wirtschaftswunder*, increasing industrial production from 1955 to 1963 by 75%. The odds were overwhelming: a country notoriously poor in raw materials; a working force overage and depleted by the unceasing stream of refugees (1949–1961: approximately two and one-half million); a per capita debt far higher than in the Federal Republic. Yet advances were visible within a few years: work became more rewarding, earning power increased, hard goods appeared in the nationalized shops, ration cards were discontinued thirteen years after the war (1958), and for the first time non-Communist citizens felt growing pride in what had been achieved. From 1957 to 1959, the yearly number of refugees decreased from 260,000 to 143,000.

These developments were unexpectedly interrupted by the crisis of 1958–1961 which finally resulted in the building of the wall sealing off the territory of the GDR from the open gates of West Berlin. Ernst Richert has shown that this crisis actually consisted of a series of interrelated economic events and political countermeasures: in 1958 the Socialist Unity Party suddenly decided to overtake the production level of the "capitalist" neighbor within a few years and decreed that the race with the Federal Republic was to have top priority; and after a catastrophically dry summer in 1959 which endangered agricultural productivity in all of central and eastern Europe, Ulbricht ordered a sudden and merciless drive for the total collectivization of all farmland. The collectivization drive and the accompanying police terror immediately increased the number of refugees (440,000 within sixteen months) and threatened to disrupt industrial production. Ulbricht gave the order to build the wall (August 13, 1963), the state was transformed into a geographical prison, and the population was forced into further psychological accommodation with the regime. But the stream of highly skilled refugees was stopped, and the gradual normalization of industrial production played into the hands of a powerful force of young managers, who wanted the economy efficient, "profitable," and rationalized. Early advocates of the profit motive were still considered dangerous "revisionists," but within ten months after the publication of Liberman's famous article on the functioning of the profit motive in the Communist economy (*Pravda*, 1962), the SED announced the New Economic Policy, and Erich Apel

(1917–1965) became the new head of the State Planning Commission and elaborated an inclusive plan of economic transformation which fired the imagination of the managerial élite as well as the hopes of the ordinary citizen. Apel was the architect, and the martyr, of economic change: he shot himself on December 3, 1965, in his office when the Republic was forced by the Soviet Union to sign a new trade agreement which endangered his plans; but in spite of his death and Ulbricht's efforts to reduce the intensity of the reform, Apel's friends and allies in almost all branches of industry (and recently even in agriculture) are still carrying on his work. "Libermanism" has been pushed further in the GDR than in any other country of the Soviet bloc, and the new generation of industrial managers despises political phrases and resists the central planners. Rational "management" rather than the anachronistic five-year plan set up by political functionaries seems to be the order of the day.

But the administration is not equally willing to tolerate liberalization in the arts and, furthering the Bitterfeld Movement, officially insists on a conservative, i.e., a socialist and realistic, literature. These wishes are answered by a number of middle-aged writers (like Erwin Strittmatter [b. 1912] or Erik Neutsch) who dare to criticize the errors of the Stalinist past in popular human-interest stories but who, when it comes to political and literary nuances, more often than not fully support the demands of the party and an old-fashioned realism conveying unvarnished messages. Christa Wolf (b. 1929) was officially praised for her love story *Der geteilte Himmel*, 1963 / *Divided Heaven*, the heroine of which decides to return from West Berlin to the spartan challenges of the Republic, but her autobiographical narrative *Nachdenken über Christa T.*, 1968 / *Thoughts about Christa T.* was condemned by the authorities because it reasserted the privileges of the individual in a lifeless, functionary-ridden society.

It is evident that the young GDR generation which has grown up in a closed Marxist universe has intimate friends among the dissatisfied intellectuals in Poland and Czechoslovakia and derives many of its ideas from the essays of nonconformist Communists like Ernst Fischer (Vienna), Leszek Kolakowski (Warsaw), or Roger Garaudy (Paris) who, returning to young Marx and late Engels, articulate the fundamental thought of the Communist Reformation. At the seminal Kafka Conference at Liblice near Prague (May, 1963), organized by Eduard Göldstücker (sentenced in the Stalinist show trials in the early 'fifties and later released to become professor of German literature at Prague's Charles University), the GDR representatives defended obsolete views. They interpreted Kafka as a historical phenomenon while other intellectuals from many countries almost unanimously agreed that Kafka was an eminently relevant author, because he revealed the alienation ever present in capitalist as well as socialist states.

The mounting intellectual unrest of the 'sixties finds its clearest expression in the essays of the philosophically inclined physicist Robert Havemann (b. 1910), and in the antiestablishment ballads of Wolf Biermann (b. 1936), a legitimate ally of Joan Baez. Havemann, who was a Communist before Hitler came to power (he was condemned to death by the Nazis and survived in a laboratory which the army established in his prison), unsparingly ridiculed ideological rigidity at a scientific conference in Leipzig (1962) and consequently attracted the academic élite to his course on the philosophy of science at the University of Berlin (1963–1964). Basically concerned with scientific aspects of philosophical problems, his wide-ranging lectures that touched on Heisenberg, marriage, and art boldly attacked a dogmatism which blocked scientific progress and objective thought; and while defending cybernetics and pragmatic sociology, Havemann did not hesitate to say that those philosophers who were fighting dogmatism would be doing their share toward changing the political situation. After his lectures were published in West Germany and he came out in support of a parliamentary opposition in the GDR (as well as a legal Communist party in the Federal Republic), Havemann lost his academic post, just as Ernst Bloch had almost ten years previously. But the administration did not find enough support among his colleagues to have him voted out of the Academy of Sciences; his membership had to be canceled by decree, and the government was immediately attacked by the powerful Italian Communist party, which was intolerant of any such blatant relapses into Stalinism.

Wolf Biermann irritates the "office elephants," as he calls the functionaries, in a different way: his record is impeccable, and he composes his provocative songs in the "progressive" tradition of Villon, Heine, and Brecht. Biermann belongs to a generation not anticipated by Marxist planning: vital, irreverent, disrespectful, guitar-strumming, and absolutely impatient with its elders, who after all their battles have consented to obediently mull over clichés of future happiness while tolerating present injustice: "Those who once boldly faced the machine guns / are now afraid of my guitar." In his sequence of poems dedicated to the older comrades, Biermann touches on the core of the matter: half-saddened, half-angry, he observes the "tired eyes" and "old hands" of the comrades who have fought faraway battles, but still he insists on his dissatisfaction with the new order. The old comrades are amazed and hurt when they hear him speak, and they complain bitterly about his lack of gratitude—yet the cause would be best served if they simply abdicated. "Provide a good end to your work," Biermann demands of them, "and leave to us the new beginnings." The Central Council of the ruling party, convened in the fall of 1965, angrily condemned Wolf Biermann and his alleged allies (including Robert Havemann and the writer Stephan Heym) and made them responsible for the rapidly emerging beatnik groups in the cities of the Republic. Ulbricht himself, usually not interested in literary matters, solemnly contrasted Peter Weiss and Rolf Hochhuth, who had pronounced "the great truth of the age," with the irresponsible writers who wallowed in "nihilism, half-baked anarchism, pornography, and other modes of the American way of life." There is little chance that the recurrent exhortations of the Communist fathers will convince their sons that they must change their way or respect, as Ulbricht demanded, the "national interest." They respect the national interest in their own way, and time is not on Ulbricht's side.

4. The Federal Republic of Germany

"Zero Point" and Beyond: 1945–1948

THE ALLIES were united when battling the German armies, but less unanimous when dealing with the defeated *Reich*. After Hitler's suicide in his dreary bunker, the unconditional surrender of the *Wehrmacht*, and the summary arrest of Admiral Dönitz's interim government, the Allied Control Council declared on June 5, 1945, that the commanders-in-chief were to assume the supreme power in Germany and that all territories west of the Oder-Neisse line were to be divided into four zones of military occupation, the city of Berlin to be occupied by all four powers. At the Potsdam Conference (July 17 to August 2, 1945) the Allies once more affirmed their intention to treat defeated Germany as a single economic unit, but their mutual distrust, steadily on the increase since Hiroshima, worked at cross-purposes with their theoretical proclamations; the first days of peace turned out to be the first days of the Cold War, and the haphazardly sketched military demarcation lines were soon hardening into political boundaries. The Western allies were far more hesitant to revive German political groups than the Soviets: in the Soviet zone, blueprints prepared long before were immediately put into effect, while in the American zone, grassroots political groups were not permitted to form until late summer, and in the French zone, not until a year after the fighting had ended. Catholic and Protestant groups, the nucleus of the future Christian Democrats (CDU/CSU), convened in Cologne and Berlin to consider new social policies, including the nationalization of the basic industries (an idea quickly dropped after the currency reform); and the delegates from the rapidly reemerging local organizations of the Social Democrats (SPD) first met near Hanover on October 5, 1945, without being able, at least for the time being, to resolve the tensions between the local representatives and the members of the Central Committee returning from their London exile. We have become used to calling the summer of 1945 and the subsequent months the "zero point" in German history, but the popular metaphor hides rather than reveals the consequences of total defeat: the resilience, the corruption, the sincere concern with new values, the tawdry opportunism and the ceaseless shifting of entire populations of prisoners, slave laborers, and refugees. Ruined railway stations suddenly became new centers of life, densely peopled with families on the move, homeless peasants, black marketeers, and disheveled women who spent their days near the tracks showing snapshots of their missing sons and husbands to the returning soldiers. In the eating places, even the spoons, once almost worthless, had to be chained to the tables.

Within a few weeks after the unconditional surrender, the central issue of the intellectuals' responsibility for the abominations of the Hitler regime was discussed in the South German newspapers, recently licensed by the American military government. In a message from Santa Monica that appeared on May 18, 1945, in the *Bayrische Landeszeitung*, Thomas Mann suggested that "it was not a small number of criminals" who were responsible for what had happened, but "hundreds of thousands of the so-called German élite" who, submitting to demented ideas, had perpetrated crimes "in sick lust"; and he implored his German readers to return to a spiritual tradition and, instead of admiring power, to contribute to "the development of the free spirit." These remarks on the crimes of the élite challenged many writers who had stayed in Germany and continued working; defending their past decisions, they formulated their apologetical concept of an "inner emigration" no less creative than that of the lonely men in exile. The first response to Mann's message was moderate, if not particularly moving; the conservative writer Walter von Molo asked Thomas Mann (on August 13, in the *Münchner Zeitung*) to return to Germany and console the wounded sensibilities of his fellow countrymen. Taking up Mann's medical metaphor, Molo suggested that he return as a "good physician" who knew that the German people's disease was not incurable. The response of Frank Thiess (whose novels had been tolerated by Goebbels but censored by the central party offices) was far more aggressive and self-righteous, both in argument and in tone. Thiess explicitly declared (on August 18, also in the *Münchner Zeitung*) that the "inner emigration" (including, among others,

Erich Kästner and Werner Bergengruen) had built an "inscape" untouched by Hitler, adding that he had gathered far more intense experience by staying in Germany than he would have by watching the German tragedy from the "dress circle and first-row seats abroad." It was more difficult, he claimed, to preserve one's personality in Hitler's *Reich* than to broadcast messages from outside. Thomas Mann's answer to both correspondents, published on October 12, 1945, in the *Augsburger Anzeiger*, combined patient confessions of the most personal nature with a good deal of irate bitterness. He quietly explained that those who had stayed in Germany could never have experienced the "coronary spasms" of the uprooted exile, and he left little doubt as to what he thought of those who had gone on publishing in Hitler's Germany: "It might be superstitious, but in my eyes books that could be printed from 1933 to 1945 in Germany are less than worthless, and they are not good to handle. An odor of blood and shame sticks to them. They should all be destroyed (*eingestampft*)." I respect Thomas Mann's anger, but I would exclude many books from his denunciation, among them the novels of Elisabeth Langgässer, who managed to publish for a few years under Nazi rule, those by Jochen Klepper, who killed himself and his family before they could be deported (1942), the essays of Friedrich Reck-Malleczewen, who died in the Dachau concentration camp (February, 1945), as well as the many publications of the Jewish Cultural Union (*Jüdischer Kulturbund*), which paradoxically remained alive until the beginning of the war.

There was not much awareness among the exiles or the "inner emigration" that a third literary force was rapidly consolidating and was to dictate the central interests of new German writing for some time to come. Close to four hundred thousand German prisoners of war were scattered in 425 camps (including branch camps) throughout the United States, and State Department planners began to seek out and transfer POW's with antifascist records to a few camps on the Atlantic seaboard, where they were to attend courses in the social sciences as training for becoming the future administrators of a liberated Germany. Among the antifascist prisoners gathered at Fort Kearney and Fort Getty were

Alfred Andersch (b. 1914), Walter Mannzen (b. 1905), Walter Kolbenhoff (b. 1908), and Hans Werner Richter (b. 1908), and from their group emerged *Der Ruf / The Call*, the most intelligent and liberal German camp newspaper in America (1945–1946). After Andersch was released and sent home, he convinced the military government that publication should continue in Germany, and together with Hans Werner Richter he edited a German *Ruf* (August, 1946 to April, 1947), which boldly articulated the views of the younger generation. Discussion of topical issues, including collective guilt and American distrust of German political spontaneity, was acute and intelligent, and after sixteen issues the U.S. Military Government intervened to put an end to the editorial activities of these antifascists trained on the shores of Narragansett Bay; some people believe the ban was issued at the prompting of the Soviet authorities, provoked by Hans Werner Richter's open letter to the French Stalinist Marcel Cachin (February 15, 1947). It was Richter who hoped to continue the efforts of *Der Ruf* in a new satirical periodical, but the military government refused a license, and the frustrated editor arranged for an improvised meeting of friends and potential contributors in September, 1947, at the house of Ilse Schneider-Lengyel at Bannwaldsee in the Allgäu region. Manuscripts were read and discussed (the first reader being Wolfdietrich Schnurre), and the meeting has gone down in literary history as the birth of Group 47. While *Der Ruf* had been a predominantly political publication, the continuing meetings of Group 47 were gatherings of imaginative writers, removed from and yet concerned with concrete politics.

But most contributors to the German *Ruf* and many of those who first attended the Group 47 meetings shared certain political inclinations and an intense concern with the German language, grievously deformed by the National Socialists. In politics they were definitely left of center, in an instinctive rather than theoretical way, and occasionally interested in existentialist ideas, reimported to Germany from France; in literary matters they were deeply suspicious of complex grammar, flights of poetry, and Hölderlin. In a symptomatic article (November 15, 1946) in *Der Ruf*, Gustav René Hocke, the future historian of European mannerism, discussed the tradition of elaborate writing which he dubbed "calligraphy," and while attesting to its potential political function in the past, resolutely rejected it for a literature of the future that was to stay close to the basic "contents" of life. Analogous ideas preoccupied those who attended the Group 47 gatherings, at least for two or three years: the German language had been defiled by war and dictatorship, and the only hope was in a salutary reduction of vocabulary to "about three hundred words," corresponding to a spartan existence free of inherited luxuries. Rilkean and Nazi turns of phrase were hard to avoid, but young writers liked the idea of "clearing the thickets" (*Kahlschlag*), suggested by Wolfgang Weyrauch in 1949, and embraced the most fundamental verbal materials, paratactical syntax, factual reportage, and the sober short story. In Philip Rahv's terms, these younger writers were all for the "redskins" (Hemingway) and against the "palefaces" (Henry James) and expressed radical doubts about the traditional German inwardness, the poetry of the "flower-pickers," and politically irrelevant surrealism. Literature was to be as simple as smoking a cigarette in a world without light or warmth.

Good intentions were more numerous than new manuscripts, and what publications there were (1945: 2409 titles, including the sciences) followed literary tradition instead of breaking new ground; the surrender of the German armies was not a signal for a glorious revolution in literature like the volcanic eruption of the Spartacus period (1918/19). The first poetry anthology, *De Profundis* (1946), was rather conservative in tone and modes; it contained the belated classicism of the "inner emigration" and the inevitable folksong stanzas on cities in ruins, but only a few of the poems, including those by Günter Eich, Rudolf Hagelstange, and Elisabeth Langgässer, suggested potential changes of poetic idiom. Gunter Groll, the editor of the anthology, contributed verse in the surrealist mode, long proscribed in the Nazi state, and sensing the dearth of experimental courage among his other contributors, invented at least three avant-garde authors, complete with astonishing (antifascist) biographies, and wrote their poetry himself.

Carl Zuckmayer's *Des Teufels General* [1946] / *The Devil's General,* combining striking portraits in the naturalist tradition of Nazi functionaries and *Wehrmacht* officers with an expressionistic third act, was the greatest popular theatrical success of these years. With an uncanny ear for idiom, Zuckmayer sketches a precise picture of Berlin society during the war and asks pertinent questions about guilt and responsibility. But his vitalist leanings interfere with exact analysis; his characters are far more clearly profiled than his thoughts. His General Harras detests the Nazis, but he serves the regime because he does not want to give up flying. Before crashing and dying in a defective plane (sabotaged by his closest collaborator in order to hasten the German defeat), Harras expresses his hope that the future of Germany will be in the hands of his two (prototypal) friends—the saboteur who actively resisted inhumanity, and a young officer, once an enthusiastic member of the Hitler Youth, who has come to realize the brutality of the regime. Young audiences in the Western zones eagerly discussed the political implications of the play, while many of their elders took pleasure in seeing the splendor of the old uniforms resurrected—on stage, at least.

The metaphysical restlessness of the transitional moment emerges most intensely from Elisabeth Langgässer's *Märkische Argonautenfahrt*, 1950 / [Argonauts of the Mark Brandenburg] *The Quest*, 1960. In a novel full of shifting time sequences and interpolated meditations, seven persons, all deeply scarred by traumatic experiences, set out on a hot August day in 1945 from Berlin, still rank with rotting corpses and black flies, to rediscover the lost meaning of their lives at Anastasiendorf, a Benedictine monastery in a remote corner of the Mark. Almost instinctively, they join in the quest for personal salvation—a baptized Jewish couple, too eager to begin again as if little had happened; a young architect burdened with guilt; his sister, who is obsessed by sexual memories of her missing husband; a returning soldier; a bored actor; and a girl who has been imprisoned for her part in the resistance. But Elisabeth Langgässer (who has learned a good deal from Virginia Woolf) does not offer explicit solutions: the ineffable is merely touched upon in a concluding story about hungry children and black marketeers hiding out in the Berlin sewers, and the fate of the seven seekers is left in suggestive abeyance. I think it was symptomatic that the difficult works of Elisabeth Langgässer, who was persecuted by the National Socialists, attracted wider attention only for a brief moment. Her fellow Catholics she offended by using sultry images of vegetative sex, and her leftist readers anxious for earthbound relevance, by revealing the white heat of her mystical passions. Today she is read only by the happy few.

The "Economic Miracle" and the Intellectuals: 1949–1963

AFTER THE London Conference of Foreign Ministers had failed and French worries that a reorganized Germany might be all too cohesive were partly assuaged by a gathering of the Six Powers, the Western Allies resolved to push ahead with the formation of a German state. Economic and political measures followed hard upon each other: new incentives to industrial production were created by the currency reform of June 20, 1948 (which also resulted in the Berlin blockade), and on May 8, 1949, the Parliamentary Council, consisting of delegates from the West German diets, agreed on the text of the "Basic Law" defining the rights of citizens, the federative structure of the West German territory, and the prerogatives of the future president, sharply curtailed because of political experiences in the last years of the Weimar Republic. General elections were held on August 14, 1949 (CDU/CSU: 31%, SPD: 29.2%), and the new government of the Federal Republic which took office in September, 1949, was made up of representatives of the Christian Democrats, the Free Democrats, and the ultraconservative German Party. Again, as in the early years of the Weimar Republic, the Social Democrats were pushed into the opposition, and in the continuing power struggle, Kurt Schumacher, a tense and rather inflexible Prussian socialist, lost out to the Rhenish Catholic Konrad Adenauer, who shrewdly exploited to his and his party's advantage the changes in the international situation since the Korean War, the Germans' desire for material prosperity, the Allies' demands for a German contribution to NATO, and (last but not least) reawakening feelings of national pride. Throughout the 'fifties, the Christian Democrats were widely supported by the electorate and had by 1957 won an absolute majority in parliament (CDU/CSU: 50.2%, SPD: 31.8%), compelling the Social Democrats to revise their strategies. In the Godesberg Program (1958), many Marxist ideas, of little appeal to the new consumer, were dropped. In his sturdy and autocratic manner, Adenauer fulfilled the wishes of many Germans, concerned after the defeat only with rebuilding their lives in peace and prosperity; but he achieved his indubitable if ambivalent success only by ignoring essential problems that were to plague his own government and successors in the 'sixties. In 1955 he achieved complete national sovereignty for the rearming Federal Republic but was unable (or unwilling) to develop flexible policies toward the Soviet Union and its restive allies. He resolutely rebuilt constitutional political life, yet for years he tolerated former Nazi functionaries and prominent fellow travelers in high administrative offices and, while eager to solve the problems of businessmen, civil servants, and the heavily subsidized farmers, did not encourage creative initiatives for correcting obsolete educational policies and spurring lagging scientific research.

In the 'fifties the Federal Republic made an unprecedented economic recovery which affected the life of every citizen. Within eleven years (1950–1961) industrial production increased by 164%, and the Federal Republic joined the United States and the Soviet Union as one of the world's leading industrial powers. During this time, nominal weekly wages roughly tripled, as did the average monthly salary (1950: 240 DM; 1962: nearly 600 DM); and within some ten years twenty million Germans moved into new apartments. The "economic miracle," which did not solve the problems of the aged, of the coal miners, and of people in other pockets of poverty, grew out of the interaction of many elements and forces. After the rubble had been cleared, it turned out that German industry had suffered far less destruction than previously assumed (on an average about 15%); air raids and *démontage* freed industry of obsolete machinery and forced producers to develop new technological procedures; about 10% of all Marshall Plan aid was assigned to the Federal Republic; and the many millions of refugees constituted a highly trained and mobile labor and consumer force, as eager as other Germans to work hard for a secure place in the sun. Throughout the rehabilitation period capital investment was, as Michael Balfour suggests, rather high, and the Germans (despite appearances) consumed only 59% of the gross national product, as compared with 65% in Great Britain. It remains a question whether the "economic miracle" was accompanied by an inclusive spiritual transformation, or whether the new accumulation of goods introduced a wholly restorative period. The often repeated slogan of "restoration" surely deserves closer scrutiny: if social critics of the 'fifties were suggesting that "restoration" implied the total absence of any of the nationalization expected after the war (but quickly rejected by many after the currency reform), they had touched on a legitimate issue, but they were certainly wrong when they saw a wholesale return to older structures of society. German society of pre-Hitler days could not be brought back to life; pragmatically inclined sociologists boldly point out today that the plebeian National Socialists destroyed the older élite of the Junkers and aristocrats, greatly reduced inherited loyalties to region, religion, and profession by ruthless administrative intervention and, contrary to their own intent, opened the way for a mobile society that had room for conflicting groups and clashing interests.

The Group 47 did not attract many older authors and returning exiles, but it gathered a good deal of younger talent and, in the 'fifties, came as close as it ever would to constituting an intellectual force ranged against the conservative establishment. The absence of any formal structure was a productive advantage to the group, and Hans Werner Richter's guests, invited anew from meeting to meeting, had flexible tastes in genre and style. In 1950 the early *neoverismo*, best represented by Heinrich Böll (who received the group's literary prize in 1951) was being superseded by lyrical radio plays (bought for good prices by the broadcasting companies, which were still financially stronger than the publishers), and a renewed imaginative mode, well exemplified by Ilse Aichinger's "Spiegelgeschichte" / "Mirror Story," awarded the prize in 1952, and by the poetry of Ingeborg Bachmann (1953 prize). In the 'fifties other transformations were imminent: the modest gatherings of earlier years were rapidly changing into superparties attended by the major publishers, on the prowl for new talent, and a new generation of supremely gifted authors appeared, including Martin Walser (1953 prize) and Günter Grass (1955), Hans Magnus Enzensberger (1955), Uwe Johnson (1959), and Jürgen Becker (1960), who was to develop his experimental prose along rather different lines from the early commitments of the group. Politically, the group was more effective in the earlier 'fifties, when intellectuals and Social Democrats shared an intense aversion to rearming the country, than later in the decade, when the Socialists largely accepted Adenauer's policies. In the early years, the unified political activity of workingmen and intellectuals (that elusive dream of the 'sixties) was potentially within reach, but as the workers began to participate more fully in the industrial society and the Socialists were defeated in an important test vote on rearmament (1958), oppositional writers lost their hoped-for allies, and their own political undertakings, e.g., the founding of the Grünwald Circle (1956) to combat renascent fascism and of the Committee against Nuclear Rearmament (1958), lacked full resonance and were occasionally organizational failures as well.

Hans Erich Nossack (b. 1901), who came fully into his own in the 'fifties, combines probing metaphysical concerns, alien to the temper of the younger generation, with a sober language that leaned toward "reports," "records," and "observations" long before Uwe Johnson and his laconic contemporaries. Nossack himself suggests that his life as creative writer began when all his manuscripts and diaries were destroyed in the burning ruins of Hamburg (July, 1943), and his chronicle of the destruction of the city, written immediately after the carpet bombing but published later, suggests central motifs that reappear in his later narratives—the fearless confrontation with death omnipresent in life, his belief that "border situations" offer a chance to start life afresh, close to the essential, and his trust in women, whom he sees as better at understanding the ultimate tests of experience than men. In *Unmögliche Beweisaufnahme*, 1959 / *The Impossible Proof*, 1968, Nossack soberly records the court proceedings against an insurance clerk whose wife had disappeared without a trace after seven years of happy marriage. But the confessions of the clerk indicate that the court as a public institution is not the proper place in which to deal with the intense privacy of metaphysical experience: both husband and wife have long lived close to silence, death, and the absolute. One night they decided to depart together "into the uninsurable." The woman proved more courageous than the man and disappeared beyond the ken of normal human beings, but her husband, who pleads guilty for his cowardly return, was unable to relinquish his accustomed life, with all its compromises, security, and cheapened words; he asks the court to condemn him to perpetual self-scrutiny. Sartre had his reasons for praising Nossack as an exemplary German existentialist.

The writings of Franz Tumler (b. 1912) display traditional patterns paradoxically reversed. As a young man, Tumler (who comes from the southern border of old Austria) believed in the vital forces of landscape, tribe, and nation, but in the mid-'fifties he produced a spate of prose works that clearly indicated he was changing course. In the 'sixties he quietly joined those who were creating a German *nouveau roman*, stubbornly probing the process of narration itself. In his early story *Das Tal von Lausa und Duron,* 1935 / *The Valley of Lausa and Duron* he wrote about an unhappy group of *ladini*, trapped in their glen between warring Austrians and Italians, and praised the heroic virtue of belonging unquestioningly to an archaic community (an idea most welcome to Nazi cultural functionaries). For some time after the war he continued to concern himself with the divergences in Austrian and German life. But in his novel *Der Schritt hinüber,* 1956 / *The Step Beyond* he turns to private emotions, portraying the vicissitudes of a strong-willed and confused woman who is caught between her love for a dispossessed landowner and her promise to a young Russian officer (made to save two refugees) and yet returns to her husband, only to feel in the first embrace that she is no longer his, marked forever by the searing experiences of her other life. The landscape of upper Austria, under Soviet and American occupation, is barely suggested; Tumler concentrates solely on the discrepancies between what really happens and what people recount and tries to unmask the dubious imaginings that transform actual events into false plots, sequences, and meanings. It is the issue central to his later *Aufschreibung aus Trient,* 1965 /

Report from Trent, in which radical doubts and a sure literary performance balance each other splendidly.

Realignments of the 'Sixties

IN THE EARLY 'sixties the Adenauer government had to face up increasingly to many problems left unanswered in the period of hectic material rehabilitation. On September 17, 1961, a month after the building of the Berlin wall, general elections were held in which the CDU/CSU lost its absolute majority, and neither the subsequent coalition of Christian and Free Democrats nor the Erhard cabinet (after Adenauer retired from the chancellorship in 1963) was able to deal effectively with new issues of foreign policy, complicated by the conflict between the adherents of an "American" and a "French" orientation, the reemergence of vocal groups on both the right and the left inimical to the parliamentary system, and a sudden slackening of the *Wirtschaftswunder* that resulted in rising unemployment and a deficit in foreign trade. In February, 1966, came the first major confrontation between students and the police in Berlin, and in local elections in November the middle-aged nationalists of the National Democratic Party (NDP) made an unexpectedly strong showing in Hesse (7.9%) and in Bavaria (7.4%), the traditional strongholds of the Socialists and Catholics. The Grand Coalition of Christian Democrats and Socialists was first conceived as an emergency response to the many concurrent crises at home and abroad; and while it permitted the Christian Democrats to remain in office, not all rank-and-file members and intellectuals in the Social Democratic Party were unanimous in supporting the decision to share power with the conservatives rather than (as Günter Grass proposed) to go it alone. But in pragmatic terms the Grand Coalition (1966) began well: economic measures were rapidly instituted and successfully stemmed the recession, unemployment decreased, and in some local elections in 1968 the nationalists again lost some of their new strength, at least for the time being. The radical students, who have done much to hasten the necessary transformation of obsolete university structures, are beginning to feel the discrepancies between real social pressures and paperback ideologies: it is difficult to force a utopia in a less than revolutionary situation, and being deprived of effective allies in the trade unions, radical student groups have to seek the support of restive apprentices and high school students eager to turn the extraparliamentary opposition into an antiparliamentary force.

The Group 47 continued to meet in its accustomed way, occasionally staging its meetings abroad, but the increased publicity did not exactly counteract the symptoms of advancing age. Gifted new authors read from works in progress, including Alexander Kluge (1962), Reinhard Lettau (1962), and Peter Bichsel (1965 prize), but many observers, both favorably and unfavorably disposed, complained of a certain strained perfectionism, totally devoid of substantial experience. At the Princeton meeting (1966), frail Peter Handke (b. 1942) firmly pointed out the new generational abyss separating the young from their "grandfathers" who had established the group. In his lecture on the situation of the German intellectual (1962), Walter Jens had anticipated some of the mounting problems, at least by implication: German intellectuals, he suggested, were far less close to the workers than their French counterparts, and they were intensely reluctant to confront the world of the second industrial revolution—"the self-assertion of man in daily life and in uniformity." Other writers, particularly in the industrial Ruhr district, had recognized these deficiencies in recent writing for some years. They convened at the Dortmund Archives for Workingmen's Writing (*Archiv für Arbeiterdichtung*) to explore the traditions of socially concerned literature and to concentrate attention on daily experience in mines, offices, and steel mills. Max von der Grün (b. 1926), a researcher at the Archives, was joined by Walter Köpping, who wanted to compile a poetry anthology for miners, and an open discussion, on June 17, 1961, attracted many people anxious to discuss the issue of "Man and Industry in Modern Literature." Few of the writers who continued to meet and to publish as members of the new Group 61 were really workingmen, but most had had prolonged experience in industry; and while Group 47 and its "in" critics went *en masse* to the United States, their far less sophisticated competitors were publishing their first *Almanach* (1966), containing sentimental poetry and some first-rate prose pieces, including Klas Ewert Everwyn's "Beschreibung eines Betriebsunfalls" / "Description of an Accident at Work." Uneasily skirting the perils of maudlin factory verse and the abominations of Socialist Realism, the writers of Group 61 courageously confront central problems of contemporary literature.

The Grand Coalition and the radical students (who have taken the theoretical and practical initiative in politics away from intellectuals who must write a page a day in order to make a living) changed the options open to the left-of-center writers who, during the Adenauer era, had settled comfortably into their role as an institutionalized opposition. The Socialists are partners in power, the opposition has to regroup, and each writer has to decide whether he still believes that parliamentary government offers fertile opportunities or whether, following the radical student groups, he would prefer to see the parliamentary establishment destroyed in order to make way for other political systems. Günter Grass chooses the parliamentary system and refuses to join "the progressive conservatives," who in the afternoon "use Communism as a wine-red plush sofa to lie and dream on," but his fellow writers on the left are less unified in their views; there are, as Martin Walser mentions, the believers (like Peter Weiss), satisfied with an obsolete vocabulary, and the skeptical doubters (like Enzensberger), "who do not even trust the commitment which they demand of themselves." Frustration runs deep: in the summer of 1967 the political effectiveness of German Vietnam poetry was discussed in many periodicals, and after the French unrest of May, 1968, insistent questions were raised time and again on the fragmented left. I think that Hans Magnus Enzensberger (whose political assumptions I do not share) has characterized the underlying motifs of dissatisfaction more soberly than anyone else. He clearly recognizes the political *Ersatz*-function of much postwar German writing and speaks unhesitatingly of the "self-delusions" of the writers who think it possible to solve political problems by literary means. He suggests for the future an illusion-free, more modest view of the writer's social mission. I suspect that the process of sobering up will be a difficult one, for in countries with an undernourished parliamentary tradition delusions of public grandeur are the writer's hereditary disease.

But whether or not literature is dying, and whether it has a function in society, are questions which must be resolved by the act of writing; and every new work of art offers a new challenge to critical skepticism. Hubert Fichte's *Die Palette*, 1968 / *The Palette* [*Bar*] reveals a picaresque world hardly affected by any ideologies: the dropouts, dope peddlers, petty thieves, and amateur exhibitionists who habitually congregate in their Hamburg hangout have detached themselves from Society outside; and although they develop laws and value structures as rigid as those of the bourgeois squares (a *deux chevaux* is just barely permissible, recurrent VD infection a mark of distinction, and bisexuality *de rigueur*), they confront the city police as they comb the parks with as much condescension as the political organizers of peace marches. Fichte's text has (as Jeffrey L. Sammons suggests) a magnificent forward drive; yet everything happens in timeless splinters *now*, and the nearly interchangeable characters, perceived from a totally behaviorist perspective, exist only in their magical names and their professional argot; throughout, the past tense of traditional narration is carefully avoided. I am not convinced by Fichte's scattered attempts to imitate Günter Grass's word games and to "round off" his characters by introducing biographical materials in Alexander Kluge's "documentary" manner. Antifascist exercises in Pop *caves*, isolated from the less puerile world outside, strike me as futile folklore.

In his novel *Die Deutschstunde*, 1968 / *The German Lesson*, Siegfried Lenz (b. 1926), who began publishing in the early 'fifties, brings together his many gifts in an earnest and frank narrative about art and power in the days of Nazi Germany and after. Siggi Jepsen, a young man who attends a special school for problem children, writes his class essay on the topic his German teacher has assigned, "The Joys of Duty." Obsessively, he expands his composition to include his early days in the little village of Rugbüll, near the Danish border, and a portrait of his father, who silently imposed his immutable concept of duty on his family, his friends, and the village. Siggi's father, Jens Ole, was the local constable and fully identified his sense of performance with the demands of the Nazi state: he delivered his older son, who had mutilated himself to escape army service, over to the authorities and, on orders from Berlin, fought his own prolonged and fierce battle against his oldest friend, the expressionist painter Max Ludwig Nansen (perhaps a portrait of Emil Nolde), spying on him, taking away his paintings, burning hidden sketches. Lenz, once strongly influenced by Hemingway, does not believe in political melodrama; confrontations between his antagonists are muted by their long intimacy, the policeman Jens continues to represent the postwar German government, and the painter Nansen is considered by the postwar generation to be a mere "cosmic decorator." I am not sure whether Lenz fully avoids the pitfalls of allegory: the constable and the painter surely incarnate the repressive and creative traditions of Potsdam and Weimar, and the witness Siggi has a hard time blurring the allegorical scheme by presenting an epic surfeit of remembered detail. But I hesitate to push my objections too far because the principles of authoritarian discipline and intellectual creativity continue in different guises to determine everyday experience in both Germanies, and Lenz, in his own way, does not fail to deal with a central issue that has plagued many generations.

THE MOST ESSENTIAL decisions concerning German poetry were made by Goethe, Hölderlin, and other romantics toward the turn of the eighteenth century, and for a long time their achievements were considered canonical. There was no German Baudelaire (Mörike made a poor substitute), and the "modern" revolution, in the German context usually called "expressionism," impinged but fleetingly on the substance of poetry. Stefan George (1868–1933) and Hugo von Hofmannsthal (1874–1929), while responding firmly to the challenges posed by world literature, created islands of conservative form, and Rainer Maria Rilke (1875–1926) preserved the cohesive structure of the German poem, keeping at a considerable distance from the surrealists, futurists, or Mayakovski and his friends. During World War II, Rilke unexpectedly emerged as a lyric antagonist to Hitler: an entire generation of young people unwilling to lend active support to the National Socialists withdrew into Rilke's "inscape" of feeling; but precisely because they fled the scene of concrete conflict they soiled their hands while trying to keep them clean. After 1945 disillusionment came swiftly: returning soldiers and hungry prisoners of war were repelled by the "aesthete" who had surrounded himself with princesses and rare roses; they disliked his finely organized sensibilities, out of touch with their own experience, and rejected a noble idiom that was too far removed from their harsh and basic vocabulary. Yet in the later 'forties Rilke's position as secret king of German poetry had been assumed by Gottfried Benn, who in his mature poems and in his poetics combined sober despair with a principle of *l'art pour l'art* salvation: the world was empty, history totally unreal, and, in "the general decay of meaning," the "absolute poem," devoid of hope and "addressed to no one," contained the only possible significance. For a few years after the publication of his *Statische Gedichte*, 1948 / *Static Poems* in Switzerland (he was blacklisted by the Allies for his brief flirtation with the Nazis) until his death in 1956, Benn proved fascinating to the many younger intellectuals who had survived the war by the skin of their teeth. His collage technique, which, by juxtaposing incompatible vocabularies, expressed disgust with history, was imitated even by later poets who were completely at odds with his negation of social change. Young poets of the 'sixties writing Benn parodies still remain prisoners of his suggestive force.

In the years immediately following the war, poets attempting to redefine the function of man and art were opposed in their metaphysical orientation by other poets who concentrated instead on the consoling rediscovery of vegetative nature, landscape, and plant. The "nature poets," condescendingly termed "salamanders" by their adversaries, were united in their antipathies rather than in nuance: they all preferred the close detail of living nature to vast anthropological horizons, felt more at home in rustic hamlets than in asphalt cities, loved the seemingly insignificant and humble (whether a leaf of grass or an old farmhand), and were content to improve upon the four-line stanza or the ode, rather than to invest their considerable energies in corrosive experiment. Yet their achievements, which transcended political boundaries as well as generation gaps, remain distinctly individual: Wilhelm Lehmann (b. 1882) works with myth and plants, Peter Huchel (b. 1903) shows poor inhabitants of the spartan landscape of his native Mark Brandenburg, Karl Krolow (b. 1915) absorbs surrealist elements and strives for fragile and translucent effects, Günter Eich (b. 1907) integrates his nature emblems with thoughtful political commitment, Elisabeth Langgässer (1899–1950) and Heinz Piontek (b. 1925) combine attention to the vegetative with a distinctly Christian view of man's fate, and Johannes Bobrowski's childhood landscapes imply a bitter vision of Germany's political role in the East. In contradiction to the warning platitudes uttered constantly by Brecht's later disciples, the "nature poets" are able to contemplate trees without overlooking the uneasy life of men.

In the 'fifties a new pattern began to coalesce, in which were anticipated the conflicts and polarizations of the coming decade. Tensions between "metaphysical" and "nature" poets receded, and discussion centered on a second wave of experiments related to the past efforts of the surrealists and futurists, and on the renascence of Brecht's didactic verse dedicated to social change.

In the early 'fifties Hans Arp's early poetry was republished
(1953); the "Vienna group" studied dada; Ivan Goll's (1891–1950)
verse attracted new audiences, and Eugen Gomringer (b. 1924)
began to formulate the principles of concrete poetry as it was
then being developed in Europe and by the Brazilian *Noigandres*
group. Walter Höllerer's anthology *Transit* (1956) clearly illustrated the new attention to past innovations in language and
form. In his introduction Höllerer suggested that his anthology
was to "document the situation of the modern German poem
after expressionism, dada, and surrealism" and pleaded for a
poetry that responded to "the smallest detail of experience," fed
by a supraindividual memory. Paradoxically, these aesthetic
demands nearly coincided with the international comeback of the
playwright and poet Brecht, who believed that brilliant articulation of isolated experience was not enough; the entire world, as
the potential material of experience, had to be changed. But
Brecht's initial impact on the younger poets (who imitated his
ballads and the lean verse of his middle period rather than the
imagist style of his last years) was an ambivalent blessing. As
political revolutionary Brecht looked forward to a changed future,
but as didactic poet he went back to the plebeian songs of the
fifteenth- and sixteenth-century German marketplace, turning the
Lutheran idiom of psalm and church hymn to his own use. A
conservative poetic revolutionary, Brecht reinforced the inherent
traditionalism of the German poem and contributed in his own
way to the increasing isolation of the younger poets from the
world of Eluard, Yeats, Pessoa, and Pound. Hans Magnus Enzensberger, the first to face resolutely the contemporary social
scene, productively combined Brecht with Benn's collage technique, but other poets' submission to Brecht actually went against
their own poetic grain. I am thinking particularly of Erich Fried
(b. 1921 in Vienna) who, during his difficult development in exile,
at first derived much strength from the language of the German
fairy tale and from Biblical memories, later learning from Joyce
and Gerard Manley Hopkins to make his poems test the individual words stubbornly for hidden meanings and musical
potentialities. But in his more recent volume, *und Vietnam und*,
1966 / *and Vietnam and*, he has fallen among the other Brech-

tians. He has cut himself off from his own past style and, in an almost mystical act of self-effacement for the cause, has assumed a laconic tone that reveals little of his rich imagination.

In the 'sixties, experimental poets eager to liberate language from conventional grammar, and politically committed poets intent on changing the world rather than German syntax, confronted each other, their patterns of conflict nearly paralleling polarizations of public issues. Helmut Heissenbüttel, Franz Mon, H. G. Helms, and their allies in experiment are closer to Wittgenstein's analytical philosophy than to Hegel's myths, and their adversaries affect a polemical jargon in which "alienation" and "manipulation" are parroted as mechanically as Heidegger's "being of being" was thirty years ago. Peter Hamm's anthology *Aussichten, 1966 / Vistas* explores the poetic intent of the young left in practice and theory: turning against experimental art, Hamm deplores its lack of social concern, caused by an ideology of splintered time and suggests that avant-garde "texts" clearly "reflect the difficulties of the late bourgeois world in communicating." The new poets of the 'sixties, he firmly declares, are "realists" who, like their predecessors Enzensberger and Kunert, want to use enjoyable poetry to create critical attitudes. In Hamm's anthology, the work of the younger poets from the German Democratic Republic far surpasses the rather Alexandrian exercises of their contemporaries elsewhere: Volker Braun (b. 1939), Bernd Jentzsch (b. 1940), Karl Mickel (b. 1935), and Sarah (b. 1935) and Rainer Kirsch (b. 1934) articulate the feelings of a new generation of born socialists whose vital voices express their lust for life. They are all Brechtians, too, but they prefer the young Brecht and themselves write like his Baal, taking the sterile conflict between experimental and committed art in their swinging stride.

1. Nelly Sachs

NELLY SACHS (b. 1891) rediscovered her Jewish origins in Hitler's Berlin, and after she had been miraculously saved from persecution, she concentrated her aesthetic gifts into a poetic voice that had firmness, distinction, and intensity. Coming from an upper-middle-class family, she early found herself encouraged in her ambitions to write or to dance. As a fifteen-year-old she was deeply impressed by Selma Lagerlöf's *Christ Legends,* 1908, but when her own stories and legends were published (1921), they were hardly noticed by the critics, with the possible exception of Stefan Zweig. Her life and art changed totally when she witnessed the fate of the Berlin Jews but was herself permitted, upon the intervention of Selma Lagerlöf and a Swedish prince, to leave for Stockholm in the spring of 1940. "Death was my teacher and master," she said when looking back on these years; and after a period of shock and silence, she began writing during the winter of 1943–1944 as she had never written before, courageously reliving her experiences, recalling the dead, and trying to extract metaphysical significance from the continued sufferings of her fellow Jews. Constantly working on her poetry and loyally translating recent Swedish literature into German, she continues to live in a bleak Stockholm apartment house, and the Nobel Prize of 1966 (shared with the Hebrew writer Samuel Joseph Agnon) has done nothing to break her productive, self-effacing solitude. An American anthology containing many of her poems and plays was published under the title *O the Chimneys,* translated by Michael Hamburger and others (1967).

Nelly Sachs's poetry has often been described as a closed constellation of recurrent images, but it is more an evolving body of themes and modes that verge on mystical sayings, full of harshness, depth, and complexity. Out of her collections of the later 'forties, including *In den Wohnungen des Todes,* 1947 / *In the Habitations of Death,* 1967, and *Sternverdunkelung,* 1949 / *Eclipse of Stars,* 1967, emerges a dirge for the murdered children of Israel;

her personal requiem for her bridegroom blends with a chorus of clouds and winds deserted by the dead; and in the second volume, a survey sweeps from Israel's distant past, as represented by the great kings and patriarchs, to the happy future assured by a new generation of young people winning land from the desert: a memorial to death expands into the total history of the Chosen People. It is Job who most unforgettably suggests strength, consolation, and meaning: he, "the windrose of agonies," has his place "on the navel of suffering" and, though his voice "has joined the worms and fishes . . . one day the constellation of [his] blood shall make all rising suns blanch." In the volumes of the 'fifties and early 'sixties *(Und niemand weiss weiter,* 1957 / *And no one knows how to go on,* 1967; *Flucht und Verwandlung,* 1959 / *Flight and Metamorphosis,* 1967; and *Fahrt ins Staublose,* 1961 / *Journey into a Dustless Realm,* 1967) the dirge gives way to a comprehensive vision of a world undergoing constant spiritual transformation. Powerful images from the thirteenth-century mystical Book of Zohar fuse with memories of the German folk tales about Melusine and Genoveva, both of whom were rescued when all hope seemed dead. Nelly Sachs's formal strategies are changing, too; the musical ordering of lines yields to a surprisingly abrupt syntax and a more inclusive vocabulary that employs complex compounds and, occasionally, terms borrowed from the most modern technology. Among the poems of this decade, the "Landscape of Cries" (as Hellmuth Geissner suggests) most convincingly shows her new imaginative force: the world, a wounded woman, "tears open the black bandage" and "hieroglyphs of screams," dating from time immemorial to the days of the concentration camp of Maidanek and of burning Hiroshima, are "released from bloody quivers." History itself is transformed into "cells of prisoners, of saints," and the poet also utters only "an ashen scream from visionary eyes totally blind." But Nelly Sachs's poetry is always evolving; in her verse of the middle and later 'sixties, including *Glühende Rätsel,* 1964 / *Glowing Enigmas,* 1967, she prefers to use a more compact stanza of six or less three-beat or four-beat lines, close to the mystical sayings of old and yet admirably fitted to articulate a vision which, starting with fragments of daily experience (be it a walk in Stockholm or laundry day), explores the frontiers of individuality in prebirth and afterlife, makes the small things—in contradiction of Rilke—visible by words, and restlessly searches for an elusive divine force that may "turn away" and yet prophesy in "pale lightning on walls of ashes." These sayings are almost devoid of traditional syntactical signs; what we hear are fragments of ecstatic utterance almost beyond language.

Seminal images are essential to the poetic world of Nelly Sachs, and her bare root words (stone, cry, star, ashes, fog, blood, finger, hair, tree, breath) lend themselves to a shifting complex of recurrent metaphors that document the development of her vision. These images are more resistant to change than the stanza organization and the rhythmical patterns, and when they do change, they indicate essential shifts of attitude. In her early verse, as Werner Weber has pointed out, the dominant image of sand connotes an ambivalent universe embodying both suffering and hope: there is the sand of the Egyptian desert and of the fields reaching up to the gas chambers, sand on the path of wanderers, exiles, the condemned, the poor. Implications of departure, time, haunted humanity relate consistently to a concatenation of accompanying images of steps that lead to love, to death, or to prayer, and of shoes, old, new, worn, trampling on the worms of the earth. But beyond the trying sands, there is Jehovah's salt: the most holy and cursed of all the minerals because it points to God's punishment of Lot's wife and yet, in its blessings, to a thirst that is religious as well as physiological. There are evil fingers turned to salt and sterile landscapes—yet salt is something blindingly archaic, something in the bones of the earth and the heart of the waters, something that drives thirsting man to seek after the boldest fulfillments: "Israel, a rose of salt." In Nelly Sachs's later poetry, the image of the fish, common to the iconography of many religions, implies the terrible condition of man: "twitching between water and land, robbed of his scales," floating belly up on the streams, and again and again "bleeding from his gills." Mystical images fuse, and Nelly Sachs speaks in nearly Christian terms of the fish on the Cross.

The imagery of Nelly Sachs tends toward visionary scenes reminiscent of theatrical fragments or ritual plays. In *Eli: Ein Mysterienspiel vom Leiden Israels*, written 1944–1945 / *Eli: A Mystery*

Play of the Sufferings of Israel, 1967, Nelly Sachs tells the story of a revenge without revenge: the war has ended, a little Jewish community in eastern Europe is being rebuilt by those who chanced to survive, and Michael, the local cobbler (and one of the thirty-six just of the earth), sets out to find the soldier who killed the boy Eli, who, when his parents were being dragged away, desperately blew his shepherd's pipe to invoke God's aid. On his pilgrimage to hunt down that "piece of skin in which all the putrescence of earth congregates," Michael crosses over to the other country and confronts Eli's killer, whose only child has just died of a sudden fever; and the killer literally turns to dust when he stares into Michael's face, from which emanates the awful radiance of God Himself. *Eli* has often been discussed and translated but is surely not among the most convincing of Nelly Sachs's poetic plays: adhering too closely to the traditional stage (with minor characters and Hassidic folklore treated realistically, as well as gauche attempts to imitate everyday idiom in verse), it inevitably fails to realize its own potential. Nelly Sachs's most perfect play is *Abram im Salz / Abram in a Landscape of Salt* (begun as early as 1944); it symbolically suggests, in a kind of phenomenology of the spirit, man's growing thirst for transcendence. In a primeval landscape, luminous with salt (that religious element), King Nimrod, clad in red fur and celebrating the zodiac, is worshiped by his followers as a godlike hunter; but he regresses into a time without future, while young Abram, who was to be sacrificed in the cave of death, frees himself from the shrouds, heeds the call of a ram's horn (the *shofar*), and accepts the summons of the highest God. His parents call him back, but he, "the bud of salt," has decided to serve the other voice: "All horizons have I torn like my shrouds . . . I come!" The author of *Abram in a Landscape of Salt* has come a long way from her early imitations of the legends of Selma Lagerlöf. Her early plays (except *Eli*) and her verse of the 'fifties and 'sixties are among her best, surprisingly masculine, achievements. She convinces most when she moves confidently along the thin linguistic line conjoining old romantics and new surrealists, ignoring the crude pressures of contemporary technology and feeling secure in her mystical haven, which combines elements from the

Book of Zohar, from the Christian thought of the German baroque, and from the Neo-Platonic ideas that preceded and nurtured both. It is a translucent world as eclectic as that of W. B. Yeats, and as indestructible.

2. Johannes Bobrowski

IN HIS QUIET WAY, Johannes Bobrowski (1917–1965) was a man of striking contradictions: rustic and scholarly, deeply conservative and excitingly modern, a Christian citizen in a Communist state who was unwilling, as he said, to be considered by Western observers a "Daniel in the lions' den." Bobrowski was born in Tilsit, a small town on the border of East Prussia and Lithuania, spent much of his childhood on the farm of his grandparents, and went to school in Königsberg, where he began to read Herder and the "magus of the North," Johann Georg Hamann (1730–1788). In the late 'thirties he moved with his parents to Berlin-Friedrichshagen, where he studied art history and joined a Protestant youth group. When World War II broke out he served in Poland, France, and Russia, was taken prisoner, worked as a miner in the Donets region while attending antifascist training courses, and returned to Berlin-Friedrichshagen in 1949, where he was active in East German publishing houses and participated for some years, as a member of the East German Christian Democratic Union (CDU), in the political life of the German Democratic Republic. Bobrowski's first poetry was published during the war in *Das innere Reich*, the periodical of the "inner emigration," and when he returned from forced labor in the Soviet Union, he was encouraged by Peter Huchel, who printed a selection of his poems in *Sinn und Form*. Bobrowski's most productive years extended from 1959 to his untimely death: he prepared three collections of verse (*Sarmatische Zeit*, 1961 / *Sarmatian Time; Schattenland Ströme*, 1962 / *Shadowland Rivers;* and *Wetterzeichen*, 1966 / *Storm Signals*) as well as two novels dealing with racial and national tensions in the East, many excellent short stories, and outstanding translations of Boris Pasternak and the Czech poet Konstantin Biebl, hounded by the Stalinists to suicide. An English anthology containing poems from Bobrowski's first

two collections was published under the title *Shadow Land* by
Ruth and Matthew Mead (London, 1966).

Bobrowski often denied being one of those "nature poets" who
ignore the social aspect of man, but many of his best poems,
including "Kindheit" / "Childhood," "Winterlicht" / "Winter
Light," and "Wagenfahrt" / "Carriage Drive," are reverent hymns
to the forests, rivers, and plains of East Europe. His is a pastoral
world recollected in poetic idiom: "Evening, / the river resounds,
/ the heavy breathing of forests. / Sky, by screaming birds
covered, / shores / and darkness, old." There are the familiar
trees of his childhood: poplars, willows, and alders; bees, birds,
and fish abound; and in the flickering light of memory, smug-
glers, shepherds, fishermen, hunters, gypsies, and horse traders
go by in the night; with "his little carriage / the grey Jew" passes,
hawking his wares. Bobrowski time and again returns to the
rivers and streams that cross the eastern plains and, intoning their
magical names in German, Lithuanian, and Old Prussian, recre-
ates idyllic monuments to an indestructible love: "A trace of
smoke, / over the shoal / where untiring were / embraces, always
/ the river alive." But Bobrowski's pastoral does not suggest a
timeless Arcadia: space turns into time, geography into history,
and probing the brooding beauty of "Sarmatia" (his symbolic
landscape extending from the Finnish lakes to South Russia),
Bobrowski seeks "the traces of people lost" and ponders the cruel
chronicle of battles and betrayals, of entire nations threatened
and crushed by merciless invaders, whether Teutonic knights or
the Nazi armies to which he himself once belonged. The plains
of Sarmatia, alive with the specters of Old Prussians, Lithuanians,
Poles, Russians, gypsies, and Jews are, to him, the vast spaces
of German guilt.

In his "Pruzzische Elegie" / "Elegy on the Old Prussians"
(published in his first collection in the German Democratic Republic but deleted from the volume when republished in West
Germany), Bobrowski suggests what happened to the archaic
bliss of an old tribe when its lands were invaded by the Teutonic
knights, crusading against the "heathens" of the East. Written
history no longer records these acts of destruction, and the poet
has to read the faint traces left in the landscape and listen to

the fading songs of old women who have at least preserved a shabby echo of epic events. The Old Prussians lived happily in the "dark forests" among "the slowly meandering rivers," but when the armies of the Teutonic Order advanced, their happiness changed into a dance of death, and an "alien Mother of God" triumphed over "their burning huts." Intimately related to this elegy, in which Bobrowski as a German and a believing Christian ponders the crimes of his Christian fellow Germans, are other poems: early ones in which he looks upon the burning Russian villages, churches, and cathedrals along the path of the advancing armies in the spring of 1941; a few poems alluding to the fate of the gypsies who once roamed the plains before they were killed by "the men with leaden eyes"; and three important poems dedicated to Else Lasker-Schüler, Gertrud Kolmar, and Nelly Sachs, who have recorded in German verse the heritage and sufferings of the Jewish people. My theme, Johannes Bobrowski once said, is "the Germans and the European East . . . a long tale of unhappiness and guilt ever since the days of the Teutonic Order. Perhaps not to be eradicated and atoned for, but worthy of hope and an honest attempt in German verse."

In several major poems, placed strategically throughout his collections, Bobrowski himself touches on his basic artistic principles, his loyalties to poets of the past, and his productive admiration for some of the writers of our time. His first "taskmaster" was Friedrich Gottlieb Klopstock (1724–1803), whose capacity for making language come alive by exploring its full musical and metrical potentialities he early admired; and later he suggests an affinity that goes beyond technique. In a grammatically and syntactically obscure poem dedicated to Klopstock, Bobrowski announces his determination to grasp "the reality" (*das Wirkliche*) of stream and forest landscapes, though his senses may be wrapped in darkness; articulating "the shadowy tale of guilt and atonement," he has no other language but that of his own "forgetful people"—yet he dares to trust their fragile idiom because Klopstock before him did likewise: "Down into the winters / I say, wingless, of rush / their words." In another poem, "Immer zu benennen" / "Always to Name," Bobrowski emphasizes his loyalty to a poetic tradition extending backward from Georg

Trakl to Hölderlin and Klopstock, and defines the blessings and dangers of the poetic act: "Always to name, / the tree, the bird flying / the russet rock where the river / runs, green." To name the "real," to summon up memory, is to create order; but the poet suspects his naming involves a dubious element of the arbitrary that works against pure order: "Signs, colors, it is / a game . . . it might end in injustice." Naming is both sacred and playful, ·and the poet is searching (as Bernhard Boeschenstein suggests in his skillful analysis) for a higher force which will ensure that the act of naming does total justice to the things named. Yet the search proves vain, and in the absence of any higher force the poet's only recourse is to accept the painful paradoxes of poetry as a sacred game. Bobrowski's verse comments on poetics should, however, be read in the larger context of other poems about the figures to whom he feels particularly close: Villon (portrayed as a kind of Baltic *picaro*), Marc Chagall, the mad Hölderlin in his tower, the Polish romantic Mickiewicz, the Finnish poet Alexis Kivi "writing his name in forest air," and the Czech rebel Petr Bezruč who "stands above the place of trial / dark, in the mountain gate." There is much to be learned, Bobrowski implies, from the poets of the European "East," long ignored by German readers.

When Bobrowski died, his achievements were praised by official Marxist critics as "exemplary Christian contributions to the development of the socialist literature of the nation," and a good deal was made of his activities in the East German Christian Democratic Union and of his indubitable efforts to build bridges to the Slavic East in consonance with the ideas of the theologian Hans Twand, cofounder of the Prague Peace Conference. The critics were surely right that many things had helped make Bobrowski feel at home for years in the closed society of the German Democratic Republic, but they had not read his late poetry. Bobrowski wholly agreed with governmental policies toward the Slavic nations of his poetic Sarmatia (he never said a word against inhuman Soviet policies in the Baltic states), and, as a man of reflection, he found East Germany more tranquil than the industrial societies of the West; in remarking on the elections to the People's Parliament he suggested that he found homely gatherings at which neighbors discussed local roads closer to his heart than the crass commercialism of electioneering in the United States (of which he admittedly knew very little). But Bobrowski did not share the official belief in the direct political impact of literature and left no doubt in his last poems that something essential was missing from the lives of the neighbors for whom he was writing. Bobrowski's sense of the tragic was daily offended by the cheap optimism of the cultural establishment, and when his friend Peter Huchel was removed from the editorship of *Sinn und Form* (1963), promptly to disappear from the intellectual life of the GDR, Bobrowski wrote a series of poems allusive in tone to Huchel's last published verse. It was clear that he was feeling more and more like a speechless stranger among his people. In his last poem, "Das Wort Mensch" / "The Word Man," published posthumously on June 8, 1966, he confessed to his disgust for a society that prided itself on repeating mechanically the empty vocabulary of humanitarianism without ever being truly humane: "Where love is lacking, do not / utter the word."

I do not question Bobrowski's Christian commitment as believer and citizen, but as poet he was closer to an all-embracing myth of nature such as can be found in German poetry of the later eighteenth century, and to an idea of an earthly community of neighbors who keep their mutual love alive by invoking memories of gory "Sarmatia." Unlike most of his contemporaries in either German republic, he fully accepted the glorious traditions of the ode, hymn, and elegy; but while preserving their selective diction and harsh inversions, he developed his own unobtrusive mode of free verse that is driven, as John Flores shows in his penetrating study, from a bare "stuttering" of nouns at the beginning of each poem to a final cry for communication. In love with a green world alive with Lithuanian water sprites, and distrustful of Brecht's theories, Johannes Bobrowski believed that future poetry would, once again, derive its force from magic conjuration.

3. Ingeborg Bachmann

INGEBORG BACHMANN has always had more friends than adversaries among her critics: she had the good fortune, rare among younger writers, to be awarded the coveted Group 47 prize (1953) and to be at the same time highly praised by conservative Hans Egon Holthusen for deriving poetic strength "from the sources of primordial life." Born in provincial Austria (1926, Klagenfurt), cosmopolitan and highly educated Ingeborg Bachmann has lived in Vienna, New York, Rome, and Berlin. In her theoretical studies she has concentrated on the neopositivists, on the critical reception of Heidegger (the subject of her doctoral dissertation), and on Wittgenstein. She has often provided the composer Hans Werner Henze with texts for ballets, songs, and operas, but while most of her contemporaries hesitate to alienate the rewarding mass media, Ingeborg Bachmann's narrowly circumscribed achievements rest proudly on a few volumes of poetry and prose. They are searching and intense, occasionally impaired by a gauche combination of high polish and utterly sentimental *Kitsch*.

In her first volume of poetry, *Die gestundete Zeit*, 1953 / *On Borrowed Time*, Ingeborg Bachmann fused linguistic and emotional strains welcome to both the older and the younger generation. Older readers raised on Hölderlin and Heidegger appreciated her lean new version of German classical language and her existentialist images of a threatened world; and the younger, socially committed critics, who in the early 'fifties were just emerging as a compact group, welcomed her controlled experiments with verbal collage and the few hard, dry poems in the manner of the older Brecht; hers was clearly a mode that expressed a central moment of intellectual transition. With tender stoicism, her lyrical self confronted a world both radiant and somber; there were jubilant assertions of surf, cloud, and sun ("the best thing is / in the morning . . . to stand up against the immovable sky"), but merciless time and a correlated syntax of *yets* and *buts* limited all potential triumph of feeling, and (as in Günter Kunert's poetry) each ascending movement was offset by an image of falling, withering, and decaying: "How long, how long / will this crooked branch resist the storms?" Moving restlessly in harsh patterns of rhymeless verse, Ingeborg Bachmann's sensibility roamed hungrily from one sphere of the imagination to the other: a Mediterranean, "positive" landscape (reminiscent of Gottfried Benn's visions) unfolded: Mt. Hymettus, oil and salt, olives, simple jugs, honey, ships—yet again, her jubilantly assertive landscapes bordered on "negative" lands of mists, marshes and night, ice and dead fish. Her poetic self inevitably sought a final haven in the landscapes of its intellectual origins ("Grosse Landschaft bei Wien" / "Great Landscape near Vienna"), but only to face crumbling ruins devoid of meaning, an expanding steppe, and sweetly withering art close to Hofmannsthal's earliest verse.

Ingeborg Bachmann's *Anrufung des grossen Bären*, 1956 / *Conjuration of the Great Bear* almost instinctively repeats the basic pattern of jubilant praise (Parts I and III) and despair (Parts II and IV) that is deeply ingrained in her view of human existence. But in contrast to her sociologically committed contemporaries, she here advances into a realm of private memories, fairy tales, and pervasive myths. The starry image of the Great Bear, suggested in the central, often-anthologized poem of the collection, deals with the grizzly, the permanent threat to humanity: akin to Rilke's giant angel, the mighty old bear of the cosmic forests may break through the underbrush of the stars, as the first stanza suggests, at any time, and endanger human beings who are fascinated and frightened by his overwhelming majesty. In the second stanza of the poem, the bear himself speaks to humanity below: to him, the earth is nothing but a fir cone which he playfully pushes in front of himself, tests between his teeth, bats with his paws. Compiling a catalogue of Biblical allusions, Wolfgang Rasch has tried to show that the poem implies a theological message; unfortunately, he does not admit that Ingeborg Bachmann, in the third stanza, clearly affirms that established religion can no longer aid man against the threat hanging over all beings; whether or not people pay their tithes in church or pray to a blind God does not alter their potential fatality and the great bear's freedom to rip all fir cones, all worlds, from the trees of the universe. Yet in spite of her boldness of imagery, Ingeborg Bachmann develops many of the poetic concerns of the second volume in consonance with German tradition; in the initial sequence of assertive poems, borrowed time has become a secret blessing, for it yields unforgettable memories ("Borrowed time / time left to us! / What I forgot touched me with radiance"), and precise images of a Carinthian childhood appear in compact stanzas combining the *a b a b* rhyme pattern of the *Volkslied* with a deceptively simple series of paratactical lines with four or five stresses ("The cripple yields / his hunchback to our touch / the village idiot reveals his dreams"). These poems of the Austrian landscape come close to achieving Georg Trakl's translucent ease.

Ingeborg Bachmann's popular radio play *Der gute Gott von Manhattan*, 1958 / *The Good God of Manhattan* develops her fundamental concern with the absolute in a loose string of lyrical scenes. Jennifer and Jan, two star-crossed lovers (actually a Radcliffe political-science major and the young European intellectual she happens to pick up when her train pulls into Grand Central Station), hunger after infinite fulfillment; and while they move from one Manhattan hotel room to another (from a dirty cave below street level to cooler and loftier rooms on the seventh, thirtieth, and fifty-seventh floors respectively), their love too rises to higher and purer intensity. But their ascent toward the absolute is closely watched over by the good God of Manhattan, and precisely because Jennifer and Jan come close to ecstatic triumph over time, they are condemned to death by the good God who, eager to sustain social order, convention, and the inevitable relativity of human existence, cannot tolerate the rise of the young lovers to timeless perfection of feeling: against their explosive passion he employs his usual weapon and destroys Jennifer with a gift-wrapped bomb. Jan, who (in a last gesture of permanent love) has canceled his return ticket to Europe, escapes death because on his way to the hotel he stops in a bar to relapse for a few minutes into his old, autonomous, lonely self; and Manhattan's good God, who secretly admires absolute lovers, has nothing but skeptical predictions for the finite and shabby possibilities facing Jan in the future. Ingeborg Bachmann has an exquisite feeling for the tropical luxuriance of the Manhattan summer, but her lovers are saccharine puppets who constantly indulge in pseudometaphysical *blague* rather than in making love. Behind the fake sophistication of *The Good God of Manhattan* lurks massive immaturity.

But Ingeborg Bachmann is not easily deflected from her goals. In her collection of short stories *Das dreissigste Jahr*, 1961 / *The Thirtieth Year*, she again returns to characters in stubborn revolt against the limitations of conventional life: a man of thirty years explains his thirst for the absolute; a musically talented *bohémienne* invites lesbian experiences because she wants to transcend the limitations of her sex; a judge breaks down because he wants to know the "real" truth in a murder case; and in "Alles" / "Everything," a story of considerable power, a young father hates his son because the child (in whom the world was to have been reborn) accepts things as they are, but he resigns himself to being a "square" father when the child is killed in an accident. Recurrent desires, recurrent failures; but these characters are far more alive than the lovers of Manhattan, and their world (Austrian, sharply outlined, contemporary) reveals conflicts more adult than those suggested by a mechanical contrast of convention with the infinite.

Hermann Broch once suggested that the true romantics are those who, in our relative world, are obsessed with the absolute; and in Broch's sense, Ingeborg Bachmann is surely among the most resolute romantics of the new consumer society. In a programmatic speech she once stated that we all feel the desire to transcend the limits which are our destiny, and that we all direct "our glance toward the complete, the impossible, the unattainable, be it that of love, of freedom, or any other greatness." Her poems are restless attempts to push language (the limitations of which she adamantly defined in her Frankfurt Lectures on Poetics in 1960) beyond the confines of temporality; and her prose continues the relentless drive. The trouble is that the open structure of narrative prose does not compel her, as does the lean poem, to control her sentimentality, which combines curiously with her intellectual thirst for absolute fulfillments; in spots, she does write as if from an unmade bed, and offers the untrammeled confessions of a feline soul rather than more impersonal art. Her poetic capabilities are far ahead of her narrative voice, and the divergences between them may help explain why, to the regret of many, she has been publishing less and less in recent years.

4. Paul Celan

PAUL CELAN was born Paul Antschel, in what was then (1920) the Rumanian town of Czernowitz, and his decision to change his name to something ornate and aesthetically pleasing reveals much of his resolution to counter the harsh limitations of a coarse world by undertaking acts of poetic choice. While in his early verse the counterstatement was of the melancholy and musical kind, he has since come to distrust language itself, and his resistance against it was extended to breaking up sentences, idioms, and individual works into an assemblage of private splinters on the brink of silence. Spending his youth in a small Rumanian border town may have isolated Celan from literary developments in European centers of discussion and innovation, but it also helped open his sensibilities to strands of many traditions: Hassidic, German, Rumanian, Russian, and French. When in 1941 German and Hungarian troops occupied the town, Paul Celan's parents were taken off to the death camps, but he himself survived in a Rumanian labor detachment. When the Soviet army drove out the Germans, he was able to continue his studies; and after the war had ended, he left for Bucharest and Vienna, where he published some of his early poems in *Plan*. In the late 'forties he finally settled in Paris, completed his language studies within a few years, and accepted a lectureship at the Ecole Normale Supérieur. His seven collections of poetry are *Der Sand aus den Urnen*, 1948 / *The Sand from the Urns*; *Mohn und Gedächtnis*, 1952 / *Poppy and Memory*; *Von Schwelle zu Schwelle*, 1955 / *From Threshold to Threshold*; *Sprachgitter*, 1959 / *Language Grilles*; *Die Niemandsrose*, 1963 / *The None Rose*; *Atemwende*, 1967 / *Reversal of Breath*; and *Fadensonnen* 1968 / *Thread Suns*. Celan is also a distinguished translator of modern French poetry and of the difficult Russian verse of Alexander Blok, Sergei Esenin, and Osip Mandelstam, to whom he feels particularly close. It is a pity that English translations of Celan's poetry are scattered through many different anthologies; American publishers evidently like their German poets either explicitly political or not at all.

Celan's *Poppy and Memory* contains many of his first poems and clearly represents the earliest stage of his developing art. In the postromantic and symbolist tradition, Celan speaks of love and death, incorporating into his stately lines the musical possibilities of the German folk-song stanza; his language, utterly devoid of contemporary technical or political idiom, concentrates anachronistically on the noble, the "beautiful," and the ceremonious. Celan delights in combining *fin-de-siècle* echoes (carpets, roses, hair, vines, swords, and hearts) with Georg Trakl's palette of blues, browns, and black. The murmuring music if soft and pleasing; genitive metaphors, some startling, some vague, abound; and only a few images (the human-eye image, for instance) and a few poems (such as "Ewigkeit" / "Eternity") anticipate in their compact lines and harsh compounds the future transformations of his verse. James K. Lyon rightly suggests that the "Fugue of Death" ("Todesfuge"), the most famous poem in recent German literature, stands, with its concrete theme and paradoxically fluid, unpunctuated structure, distinctly apart from Celan's other early verse; there are two other poems quietly alluding to the death of his mother, but the "Fugue of Death" is the only one explicitly concerned with the world of the concentration camps. In this poem Celan manipulates a few motifs in recurrent and changing combinations, to confront the life of the imprisoned Jews (the collective speakers of the poem) with that of the German *Kommandant* of the camp, who writes letters home to his blonde Margarete, and in his blend of aesthetic inclinations and cold brutality closely resembles Reinhard Heydrich. Daily foretasting death in the "black milk of the morning," the Jews have become slaves; the *Kommandant* orders one group to dig its own graves while another is to play a dance. The fateful incompatibility of the two worlds is revealed in the final epigrammatic pairing of motifs: "Thy golden hair Margarete / thy ashen hair Sulamith." But the aesthetic success, or rather the haunting suggestiveness of the poem (in which the lilting, dactylic rhythm complies with the *Kommandant*'s order that his Jews dance), may be a highly problematic achievement; against the writer's intent, metaphorical stylization and pure musicality make the poem attractive to those who would ignore the ugly realities, seeking, rather, an escape in literature from troublesome reflection. In West Germany (where, according to the revised statute of limitations, concentration-camp murderers who did not act from base personal motives can no longer be prosecuted), Celan's "Fugue of Death" has become a popular textbook piece, and one of the academic commentators admonishes the classroom teacher to stick to the text, lest "student discussion deviate from the work of art to the persecution of the Jews."

In the middle and later 'fifties, Celan's poetry changes rapidly, and the collection *Language Grilles* suggests the intensity of the transformation; as one of Celan's interpreters suggests, the image inherent in the title may imply both the barred windows through which prisoners or monks speak to their visitors and also the idea that language itself imposes an iron pattern on reality. To "turn against" means to renounce, to concentrate, to take the narrow path; and Celan turns against not only the tender surfeit of his early poetry but also against language as a false means of communication: to continue writing is merely to record individual encounters with scattered words. Musicality has given way to razor-edged stanzas fascinating to the reader's eye; long and ornate verse yields to irregular three- or four-beat lines in disjointed syntactical patterns; genitive metaphors are replaced by bold compounds. Celan dehydrates his poetic landscape: stones and rocks circumscribe the horizon, and a sterile plain threatens with "mud, flint, sand, pebbles, lava, and basalt." Life, or what is left of it, resides in the eye, which, enhanced (if not inflated) to inhuman proportions, hovers over infertile wastes, its anatomical parts almost obscenely revealed: retina, lid, lashes, and eyeball, a hungry vortex waiting to swallow up everything. The world, once rich with roses and courtly words, has been reduced to a terrifying encounter between bloodstained eyes and merciless rocks. To be silent constitutes the new rite of true unity.

In *Reversal of Breath* Celan pushes his search for the absolute essence of poetry even further, and finds himself caught between the extreme demands he makes on idiom and his diminishing hope of communicating his search; the farther he goes in his relentless quest, the more exclusively he relies on a tortured language all his own, fiercely disregarding the capacity of any reader. Celan's longing for the indestructible core of poetry and his instinct for poetic articulation are at odds; individual poems consist of broken stanzas of a few words, and an increasingly obsessive concern for compounds burdens the line with a chain of kenning-like riddles ("cheektower," "ashneedle," "clipperbliss," "nipplestone") or creates verse of resounding if totally incomprehensible charm. Celan sees himself going to the verge of utterance: "In the rivers north of the future / I cast my net," he says of his pursuit of something "northerntrue" and "southernclear" that does not represent anything or anybody but his own poetic intent, "even devoid of language," if need be. The poem "Accumulation of words, volcanic" moves cautiously, as it were for the last time, within the confines of human communication: in a planetary landscape of geological transformations the poet sees himself cast against "a floating mob of anti-people" who concentrate intently on the mere copies and imitations that comprise their lives—yet these efforts come to an end when the poet creates his "wordmoon" which causes an ebb tide, baring hitherto hidden "heartshaped craters" testifying to forgotten primeval events, "the birth of the kings." The cosmic images have harsh edges but do not entirely obliterate the vision of the romantic poet boldly creating a luminous and enduring counterworld of his own.

Paul Celan rarely defines his poetics, and his oft-quoted speech upon receiving the Georg Büchner Prize in 1960 reflects a transitional phase of his work, superseded by his later more radical practice. But essentials are suggested: his resolve to continue Mallarmé's thought to the bitter end, his belief that modern poetry is moving toward silence (suggested a decade before Susan Sontag), as well as his insistence that the successful poem must balance on the borders of its own existence: in order to be, the poem must constantly pull itself back from the realm of the "never again" into the sphere of the "as yet." Harald Weinrich, who has written the most illuminating essay on Celan, suggests that the increasing autonomy of the poet's idiom leads to a kind of "meta-language." Yet, restlessly hovering on the borders of potential communication, Celan's poetry does encompass a good many explicit concerns, literary, political, and religious. Celan has no qualms about openly criticizing fellow poets for becoming excessively involved in conveying social messages before they have tested their language; in "Huhediblu" he rages against "the empty skins of the vigilante poets" who produce toadlike sounds (*Geunke*) from their facile "fingerguts" (*Fingergekröse*) or mere "holiday dessert." Yet in Celan's earliest poems, filtered memories of his own political commitments appear; in "Shibboleth" thoughts of past defeats that destroyed the hopes of his particular generation are articulated in poetic allusions to the Austrian civil war between the socialists and the conservatives (February, 1934) and to the defense of the Spanish Republic against Franco: "February. No pasarán." He does show his generation's distrust of metaphysical engagement; in a poem dedicated to Nelly Sachs he recalls a conversation with her about her "Jewish God," against whom he argued then; now he admits that she may be right to say that theological questions do not require definite answers. Heaven and earth are reversed in their hierarchies; the sky is covered with "pocks" and "pustules," like the skin of a sick man; and in a moving poem about the Umbrian landscape of Francis of Assisi, Celan expresses doubts about the blessings of traditional Christianity: "Splendor that does not console, splendor / those who are dead Francis / still beg." But elsewhere glimpses of transcendence appear, and in one of his most recent poems Celan in almost mystical terms suggests the presence of a more than human force of "light" and "salvation."

In pushing his allegiance to the European symbolists too far and in pressing his search for an ultimate language structure, unsullied and permanent (the Platonic idea of the poem), Celan has become a prisoner of the inevitable dilemma confronting the poet intent on unremitting experimentation. He wants to say something absolutely pure but finds himself far ahead of those whom he might wish to address; and discovering "songs sung beyond humanity," he cannot avoid the danger of singing to himself alone. But he does not shrink from the monologue uttered in a harsh landscape of rocks and stones; refusing to use something that has been used before, he proudly accepts the role of the no-sayer and sets his sights on the final "noem" ("Genicht") in which language is stripped to its bare bones: "deepinsnow / eepino /ee i o." Increasingly estranged from the baffled reader, he is sacrificing his high gifts to keep future poetry new and strange.

5. Helmut Heissenbüttel

HELMUT HEISSENBÜTTEL resolutely continues along the lines of the traditional avant-garde, but the critics disagree on whether his poems, or rather "texts," should be described as abstract, concrete, or simply meaningless. Such divergences of opinion, as well as the occasional bewilderment of his interpreters (myself included), attest to his stubbornness and verve. Heissenbüttel was born in 1921 in Rüstringen/Wilhelmshaven, spent his youth in his native North Germany, was wounded early in the war on the eastern front, subsequently studied literature, architecture, and art history, and now works as editor for the South German Broadcasting Corporation. It would be inaccurate to characterize him as an *homme de lettres*, for he is really a man of all media; he has developed a wide range of linguistic and aesthetic interests and can discuss the record of the month, Wittgenstein, the Russian formalists, Marshall McLuhan, and recent trends in the arts, including painting and photography, with knowledge and sober precision. He himself does not want to be ranked among the producers of poetry, but I do so anyway because his movement toward a variety of experimental modes derives largely from his turning against the vestiges of romanticism in his own verse; and even in his most insubstantial gestures of protest I sense a sharply personal concern with the syntactical order and symbolic message he left behind in his abandoned poems. Matters are complicated because, except for a few reworked fragments, we do not know Heissenbüttel's earliest poems. His published verse collections, *Kombinationen*, 1954 / *Combinations* and *Topographien*, 1956 / *Topographies*, show him well on his way to total disengagement from the romantic mainstream of German poetry, and in his six *Textbücher*, 1960–1967 / *Textbooks* he productively advances his artistic exercises beyond the limitations of the established genres and allies his verbal structures with the graphic arts. I often like his theoretical essays better than the practical results, and I am sure that his collected articles in *Über Literatur*, 1966 / *On Literature* are of absolutely key importance for our critical understanding of future developments in the arts.

In his *Combinations* and *Topographies* two opposing forces clash: a pensive imagination still concerned with the summer afternoons, little railway stations, and long-forgotten songs of his "buried childhood," and a harsh constructivism striving to reorder fleeting memories in almost mathematical formations. Step by step and in chronological sequence the traditional poem, often represented by echoes of Rilke, breaks apart, and the individual lines are fitted together in rigidly numbered stanzas, series, and incantatory repetitions; as punctuation progressively disappears, inherited syntax dissolves, and the isolated elements of language are united in patterns no longer grammatical. Heissenbüttel still looks back on his salad days, but with "mocking desire," and older poets are of little help; alluding to T. S. Eliot and, indirectly, to Gottfried Benn, Heissenbüttel speaks of "the spiders that circle / around the heart, the dead stone." Rather than participate in their tradition, Heissenbüttel wants to compile inventories of words, hoping thereby to rediscover the visible immediacy of things; in his poem "Fensterinhalte" / "Contents of Windows," a backyard with trees, laundry lines, and balconies offers its "consolation of the visible," and in the first section of the *Topographies* Heissenbüttel creates a new kind of "thing"-poem *(Dinggedicht)*, in order to set the image of places especially dear to him free from the inherited burdens of communication and to show them as they really are. The romantic ego recedes, and the "Tautologismen" / "Tautological Exercises" that conclude the volume are designed to demonstrate the final liberation of the word from the bondage of grammar. It is almost as if Heissenbüttel were intent upon showing us the most intimate record of his transformation from "poet" to "demonstrator" of words.

But Heissenbüttel does not belong to an obsolete avant-garde stumbling upon the achievements of yesteryear. He perceptively remarks that he belongs within a tradition of experimental writing that extends as far back as the visual poetry of the baroque; among his more recent ancestors he mentions Mallarmé (1842–1889), Arno Holz (1863–1929), Apollinaire (1880–1918), the dadaists, and Gertrude Stein (1874–1946). He also stresses the

importance of Filippo Tomaso Marinetti's *Manifesto tecnico della
letteratura futuristica* (May 11, 1912) which, for the first time in
the history of European literature, sharply articulated the demand
for the destruction of ossified grammar, the exclusive use of verbs
in the infinitive (to indicate a limitless stream of energy), the
abolition of adjectives and adverbs, and the substitution of
mathematical signs for punctuation. Heissenbüttel argues that
after Georg Trakl two conflicting traditions within the development of German writing—the symbolist and the experimental
—inevitably clash, and that any writer today has only the choice
of working within the symbolist context like Paul Celan, of
negating tradition in aggressive parody, as do writers from Benn
to Enzensberger, or of participating in the effort to liberate communication by opposing the law and order of grammar. Historically, Heissenbüttel sees the antigrammatical tradition as continuing the fight of the late-eighteenth-century angry young men,
the *Sturm und Drang* writers, who questioned the rules of genre
because they felt that they throttled the new possibilities for vital
experience; the experimenters of our own century combat the
rules of grammar because these imply an ordered world which
has long ceased to exist. For Heissenbüttel, the antigrammatical
resistance is preparing the second revolution against the establishment in literature.

Explicating possible approaches to his own texts (which cause
considerable difficulties for readers trained exclusively on poems
of the other tradition), Heissenbüttel suggests three critical norms
that separate the "old" poem from the "new." (1) The poem in
the grammatical tradition insists on personal originality; the
"new" poem consists of montage of previously used materials,
and it is not spoken by an irreplaceable individual but rather
by a consciousness existing in its speech. (2) The poem of the
older tradition continues to assert its meaning in a symbolic way,
opening up views of the great universals; in the "new" poem
the linguistic materials are freed from the syntactical context that
was sapping their life energy and now radiate restored vitality—
Marinetti's idea of *parole in libertà* resurrected. (3) "Old" poems,
Heissenbüttel claims, exist in an atmosphere of festiveness and
solemnity (*Feiertäglichkeit*) and run the risk of becoming mere

decorations unrelated to the rapid changes in the world; the "new" poem constitutes an exercise of the poet's combinative abilities—it corresponds to the search by writers for a variety of methods with which to respond to the "irritations" of modern life. In the agrammatical poem "the word has changed its status" and (he hopes) now substitutes the diversified force emanating from the "fields" of new combinations for what has been lost along with syntax.

In his *Textbooks* Heissenbüttel makes use of many methods that go far beyond Eugen Gomringer's "concrete poetry," and, fully aware of the danger inherent in the isolation of verbal materials from their grammatical context, he develops a principle of cyclical composition, within the individual publications as well as within the entire sequence. Potentially, all six *Textbooks* should be considered one inventory of the author's irritations with the world. As in his earlier publications, older materials are constantly absorbed and redeployed in the new setting: the new pieces include funny stories told by murdered Indians or by mere geometrical lines; explorations of linguistic meaning reminiscent of Joycean punning ("Ein Satz / Einsatz / Einsätze" = "A sentence / pledge / entrance [of musical instruments]"); excellent notes on a conversation with doctrinaires that reveal the mechanics of ideological utterance ("I speak I have opinions no opinions several opinions many opinions . . ."); and, of little consolation to believers in political progress, a "Politische Grammatik" / "Political Grammar" consisting entirely of recurrent variations on the verb "to pursue": "Pursuers pursue the pursued But the pursued become pursuers And because the pursued become pursuers the pursued become pursuing pursuers and pursuers pursuing pursued . . ." (Heissenbüttel has been particularly influential among Czech poets who have grown tired of prescribed messages). In his "Sprech-Wörter" / "Speech-Words" Heissenbüttel scatters a few nouns, infinitives, *ands*, and *buts* attractively across the white page, and from the encounter between the reader's eye and the optical order of the words emerges a new challenge to the aesthetic sensibility; the combination of words in one of the patterns ceases to imitate flying doves and sea gulls and instead rhythmically suggests the presence of their

restless flight. But Kurt Leonhard is right in saying that Heissenbüttel's "Gedicht über die Übung zu sterben" / "Poem on Practice in Dying" thus far represents his most compact and solid
achievement. Combining some highly personal memories with
scraps of past conversations and advertising copy, ceaselessly
moving from place to place, a modern consciousness here reveals
experience totally made up of speech, at once infinitely rich and
extremely limited. It is one of the rare German poems that can
compete with Ezra Pound's finest.

It would be easy to praise or condemn all of Heissenbüttel's
work from the vantage point of either the grammatical or antigrammatical tradition, but quality is not necessarily identical with
either the old or the new. Heissenbüttel is an educated and highly
self-critical writer who is dissatisfied with the mechanical experiments that are mushrooming now—fifty years after dada—in the
little magazines; he wants to evaluate soberly the advantages and
deficiencies of the methodological alternatives which he presents
to contemporaries with rational and constructivist leanings. He
rightly asks whether words which have acquired much of their
force within grammatically ordered utterance can be lifted easily
from the syntactical sequence and profitably shifted to other
contexts without a grave loss in energy and the power to express
complex interrelationships, but I am less sure that Heissenbüttel
is fully aware of another fundamental paradox implicit in his
work. Words are to be liberated from the fetters of grammar, and
yet, since aesthetic appeal requires an order, a grouping, or a
context, they must be reassembled again in new patterns (often
taken from the visual arts) and thus submitted to another form
of discipline—e.g., the attractively firm contours of Heissenbüttel's typographical blocks of printed words in *Textbook* 4. One
discipline replaces the other, and Heissenbüttel and his allies,
while speaking of new freedoms, may well be devising new forms
of enslavement. Perhaps art cannot live without these ambivalent acts of liberation.

6. Günter Kunert

IN HIS POEMS Günter Kunert (b. 1929) combines an intense drive to capture almost cosmic spheres of bliss with a bitter knowledge of human frailness. Kunert has studied the Marxist classics, but since he is one of the burnt children who have experienced racial discrimination, the war, and, during the Stalinist period, the triumph of the official system of untruth, he writes poetry that is elegiac rather than hymnic, bitter rather than sweet, and hardly sustained by the robust certainty which the rulers of Ulbricht's Germany expect of their subservient poets. He has learned from Brecht and from Kafka and speaks in the low voice which always challenges totalitarian regimes because it implies hesitation, insight, and compassion. In the 'fifties Kunert's poems were praised as "consecrated to new activities and aspirations"; ten years later they were condemned as "direct affronts" to the socialist state.

Kunert's *Tagwerke*, 1961 / *Works and Days* includes much early dross but also states persuasively his personal dialectic: rising hope undercut by the confining limitations within which man has to live out his destiny. In the programmatic opening poem Kunert "sings his thirst," which cannot be satisfied "by the air from the mountains" or "the moist breath of southern forests," but only by absolute happiness; in a sweeping gesture of universal sympathy, he calls on geologists, pilots, teachers, poets, and women to grant him of their abundance, to bestow on him the "swimming glances" needed for fulfillment. Like Victor Hugo, the poet roves in infinite spaces of hope and future time; inevitably, the image of the pilot, surveying vast distances, carrying the expectations of mankind, recurs in many variations; there is even a poem on Gagarin and the Russian space dog Laika. Kunert has taken his image of the pilot from Brecht, who uses it in some of the didactic plays, as well as in *The Good Woman of Setzuan*. But from Kunert's "Gesang für die im Zwielicht leben" / "Song for Those Who Live in Twilight" and other related poems emerges a merciless counterimage: man, like a snapshot, dives into the light "for one hundredth of a second / from dark eternity"; he is divided between memory and hope (like Germany), a being with "whitish skin . . . filled with bowels, bones, and some brain," of "short memory," surviving only because he knows how to conform: "A crippled tree / stretching out his contorted branches, dripping with rain." If cosmic hopes crystallize in the image of the pilot, Kunert captures his awareness of man's limitations in the image of the quest for El Dorado, appearing both in his prose and his verse. The poet, exemplary of searching mankind, is like a last survivor of a group of buccaneers who goes staggering on his lonely way but is killed by a panther "before he steps out of the belt of forests / to see El Dorado, as it was promised." The image of the voyage, inseparable in Kunert's early verse from the idea of social change, has become dark and foreboding; and pilot and buccaneer are archetypal emblems of an imagination divided against itself and seeking a final moment of serenity: "To feel nothing but warmth / to hear nothing but the surf / To believe / between heartbeats: now there is peace."

In his *Erinnerung an einen Planeten*, 1963 / *Memories of a Planet* we find another strain which separates Kunert from his dogmatic contemporaries. He is unsentimentally in love with Berlin. He walks "under wet trees," thinks of tender chance encounters in subway stations, observes children playing in crumbling apartment houses, feels the astonishment of night and silence, "as if somebody had deciphered / by accident / a trace, obliterated, on an old map / the discolored indication / there is a city here." In his Berlin poems Kunert sometimes draws on the early expressionists, but the experiences that torture him are those of his own age. In the past and in the depths of the city are the dead: Jews, Germans, Soviet soldiers who fought in the streets; in the "ovens" (more clearly than elsewhere) "whisper voices / so terribly familiar and yet so alien"; in "houses / trains, / cars / on the bridges and towers" people are busy "forgetting, forgetting, forgetting." It is, perhaps, the recent history of Berlin which robs Kunert's Marxist perspective of the obligatory optimism; he cannot forget the past as easily as do the planners of the future. He continues staring into the dark: "Over the city, a cloud gathers: / the past. Flowing away / irresistibly, again it returns." Out of Kunert's increasing skepticism about human affairs, particularly about those in the Republic of Peasants and Workers, grow the parable poems and verse expressing radical doubts about the meaning of history itself. In the parable poems a seemingly distant event is recounted in four or five sparse lines, and an ingenious alternation of past and present tenses dryly invites the contemporary reader to draw parallels closer to home: in "Kansas City" the governor leaves his citizens alone but reserves for himself the right to think; and in "Unnötiger Luxus" / "Unnecessary Luxury" King Tharsos of Xantos, himself totally blind, prohibits by law the production of what people call lamps, thus metaphorically anticipating the cultural directives of more recent government functionaries. Kunert's *Verkündigung des Wetters, 1966 / Announcement of the Weather* attests to the growing conflict in him between continued commitment and an increasing sense that all historical change is meaningless. Man has only a fragile chance, like a raindrop or a snowflake, "of arriving somewhere in the dawning," to make a fresh beginning again and again.

In spite of his personal concerns, Kunert has not yet been willing to leave behind the traditional forms of German literature; he rarely ventures beyond the *Volkslied* stanza, an occasional sonnet (on Hiroshima), and his favorite mode, the lean, unrhymed verse Brecht used for his parables and didactic discourse. Kunert enjoys working for the modern mass media, but he does not go far beyond the established pattern of the *Lehrstücke* Brecht wrote in the 'thirties; the trouble is that the contemporary political events he explores with Brecht's formal tools prove peculiarly resistant to the abstractions of the "Marxist oratorio" style. Kunert's "Denkmal für einen Flieger" / "Monument to a Pilot" (in *Tagwerke*) reads like an updated version of Brecht's *Badener Lehrstück vom Einverständnis;* Kunert's good pilot, an American from Detroit, dies rather than deliver an atomic warhead to U.S. troops stationed in West Germany; "Fetzers Flucht" / "Fetzer's Escape" (also in *Tagwerke*) presents the case of eighteen-year-old Harry Fetzer who decides in a West German refugee camp to return to the GDR and face an investigation of his possible implication in the death of a border guard; he sees his decision as the only way to regain his integrity as a human being. I much prefer Kunert's television opera *Der Kaiser von Hondu, 1959 / The Emperor of Hondu,* a sophisticated spoof on American military governments in the tradition of "The Teahouse of the August Moon." Kunert may incline to conservative and tested forms, but in his interest in Edgar Lee Masters, in whose *Spoon River Anthology* "the dead speak with the voice of truth," in the Peruvian poet César Vallejo (1893–1938), and in the Polish writer Zbigniev Herbert (b. 1911), Kunert keeps himself responsive to the constant challenges from abroad. In a closed society this melancholy Marxist continues to search for the open word.

7. Hans Magnus Enzensberger

WHEN HANS MAGNUS ENZENSBERGER first published his poems he was immediately cast in the welcome role of the angry young man, but the fixed public image has tended to obfuscate the changing concerns of a highly gifted intellectual. He is more learned, cosmopolitan, and restless than any of his contemporaries; essentially unwilling to settle down in any place or way of thought, intent on radical doubt, he does not participate in collective stances for very long. Enzensberger was born (1929) in the small South German town of Kaufbeuren, spent most of his childhood in Nuremberg, studied at the universities of Erlangen and Hamburg, and at the Sorbonne, and received his Ph.D. (1955) for a brilliantly argued dissertation on the romantic poet Clemens Brentano (1778–1842), from whose poems he derived a central concept of his poetic theory. In the mid-'fifties he, like anybody else of his generation, did a stint with a broadcasting company, but soon he set out on his voyages—to the United States, Mexico, Scandinavia, the Near East, and the Soviet Union—as well as on his chimerical trips to find Arcadian bliss on isolated islands, whether Tjöme in the Oslo Fjord or, more recently, Cuba.

Enzensberger, like Brecht, wants his reader to think, and it is difficult to isolate his poetry from his bitter polemics against the German mass media (including the august *Frankfurter Allgemeine Zeitung*), from his translations, and his editorial projects. His three volumes of poetry, *verteidigung der wölfe,* 1957 / *in defense of the wolves; landessprache,* 1960 / *language of the land;* and *blindenschrift,* 1964 / *writing for the blind,* relate chronologically and thematically to his political analyses and to the few literary essays in *Einzelheiten*, 1962 / *Details; Politik und Verbrechen*, 1964 / *Politics and Crime;* and *Deutschland Deutschland unter anderem*, 1967 / *Germany Germany inter alia*, as well as to his anthology of modern poetry and his translations of William Carlos Williams (whom Enzensberger considers the patriarch of independent American writing). The first American anthology of Enzensberger's verse suggests in its title (taken from a subdivision of the German original) that Enzensberger offers *poems for people who don't read poems* (1968) and likes his writings to be used by those who want to transform a world that offends their sense of fairness.

In verbal strategies and thematic interests, Enzensberger's first two volumes of poetry differ somewhat from the more subdued tone and the lean economy of the third volume. In his *defense of the wolves* and *language of the land* Enzensberger demonstrates an impressive richness of linguistic techniques, stanzaic patterns, and modes of speech. These collections include aggressively ironic attacks against all power, property, and technology; luminous love poems in a soberly contemporary idiom; and a pensive, almost elegiac poem articulating his most intimate longing for an existence of pastoral happiness, quiet, and peace. In the well-known early poem, "counsel at the highest level," he rages against the sexually impotent "makers of history," whom he advises to jump off their jets, ironically defends the "wolves" in power against the unthinking victims who blandly watch television and have given up any thought of changing the world, identifies the greedy consumers with hooked fish, dangling from the lines of cynical fishermen in the rich societies of America, Russia, and West Berlin, and coldly condemns the dead souls who live out their sham lives in the midst of red tape, accumulated files, and rustling IBM cards. In his gathering of nonpeople congregate generals, managers, consumers, functionaries, professors, mendacious researchers, rubber merchants, and "fat widows" who, all unmoved by the German past, wallow in their commercial, technological, and military "things," amassed to stifle life: bonds, telegrams, warships, tennis courts, checks, real estate (*not* on idyllic islands), cars, movies, golf, eau de cologne, barracks, department stores, and radar screens. But Enzensberger's fine sensibility is oppressed not only by industrial goods and people without memories; what he hates most is the crude force imposed upon him by the perpetual production processes of the industrial world and by media and ads that assault his eyes and ears, catching him in a net of data, sounds, commercial offers, and threatening him with the disgusting secretions of smoke, smog, soot, and foam, all anticipating the lethal radiation that some day will seep from anonymous laboratories.

To the relentless pressures of the military-industrial complex the poet (not the social critic) Enzensberger responds in a rather traditional German fashion, appealing to the quiet fortitude of animals and plants, seeking escape in the miraculous depths of the sea, and longing to merge with the elements of the earth: his "organic" refuge distinctly if paradoxically implies that he places little faith in historical progress and in definite transformations of society; his poetic utopia resides in an unchanging nature, from which all cruel struggles between strong and weak, all lethal fungi, and all poisonous growths have been carefully removed. Enzensberger likes his nature alive with rare animals that have aesthetically pleasing names (otters, seals, salmon, sables, owls, and albatrosses) and with humble, hardy plants. In many of his best poems (not all of which are included in his American anthology) he sings the glories of the white cherry blossoms which make the thunder hesitate and cause butchers to hide, fearful of "the wild yes" of innocence. He extols the lowly celery, which does not participate in the inhumanities of man; in a later volume he writes of the northern lichen that quietly survives all the vicissitudes of man. Goodness is to be found only far from people, perhaps even nowhere on the surface of the earth, and the poet eagerly follows oysters and fish into the deep or speaks as a diver who, at the bottom of the sea, finally finds happiness in solitude, in dark and undisturbed silence. Most revealingly (at least for the earlier Enzensberger), in his poem "voices of the elements," the world, with its newspapers and daily social responsibilities (including unpaid bills), is of unmitigated evil, and happiness resides only in partaking of "the tender dialogue of the resins," salts, and alkalines, and in sinking "into the soundless monologue" of the substances at the dark heart of being. Sometimes the angry young man flees rather far.

Enzensberger's third collection of poems, *writing for the blind,* stands a little apart from his previous verse. Lines and stanzaic patterns are lean, there is less self-indulgent play with mannered paradoxes and surrealist *confiture* (or rather, secondhand Jacques Prévert), and while some of the earlier motifs recur repeatedly, a personal record emerges of Enzensberger's attempt to withdraw to a Scandinavian hideaway of water, stone, moss, and tar (and a rustic life with his family); the intellectual tries to find his haven in remote nature, and inevitably fails. In contrast to his earlier verse, too, world and counterworld are suggested less in abstract terms ingeniously polarizing nature and technology; now people and issues have individual and particular names (there are poems about Theodor W. Adorno and Karl Marx), and the alternatives of commitment and withdrawal confront each other within the pastoral experience itself. There are the simple house, the water, and the jug (one of Rilke's blessed "things"), but there are also letters, telegrams, and the "red knob on the transistor radio" blaring news about Caribbean crises and Dow-Jones averages; there is geographical distance and yet a modern conscience filled with painful knowledge ("bouvard and pécuchet . . . pontius and pilate") and, as Walter Benjamin early suggested, with reproductions of reproductions ("of images of images / of images of images of images"); gentle friends gather in the evening, alive with "light laughter and white voices," but the poet increasingly feels that there is social irresponsibility in his semblance of bliss: "fearless therefore ignorant / quiet and therefore superfluous / serene therefore without mercy." In "lachesis lapponica" ("lapland lot") the pressures of conflicting demands turn the poem itself into a dialogue between the romantic admirer of northern plains and the ardent partisan of Fidel Castro, committed to political action: the two speakers, whose utterances are printed in different type, duly impress each other, but the discussion is left in ironic abeyance and there is little likelihood that either of them will totally prevail.

Enzensberger is at his best when he balances his erudition with his sense of quality and does not try to display his considerable bag of tricks in one poem alone. In his theoretical essays he almost makes himself out to be a late disciple of Edgar Allan Poe, and his aversion to any idea of inspiration, his scholarly awareness of the literary past as a constant challenge to the modern writer, and his philosophical and constructivist inclinations place him closer to Ezra Pound, W. H. Auden, or Gottfried Benn than the social critic Enzensberger might wish. From the work of Brentano, Enzensberger derives for his private poetics the central idea of linguistic *Entstellung* (displacement), a technique that counteracts the tendency of language to ossify in clichés and mechanical turns of phrase; I am not certain how Enzensberger's *Entstellung* differs from the "alienation device" (*priëm ostranenija*) which the Russian formalists, eager to define the de-mechanization of language, discovered in futuristic poetry. Enzensberger knows how to write romantic tetrameter and to play with the inherited techniques of the surrealists, but fundamentally he wants to shock by skillful and occasionally affected combinations of incompatible elements of rhythm, vocabulary, and idiom; while carefully exploiting, rather than negating, tradition, he avoids rhyme as well as the rules of capitalization, but secures unity of the poetic texture by means of nets of alliterations, assonances, and recurrent vowel patterns ("mokka / coma / amok / NATO"). He loves oxymora that unveil the conflicts within social reality, delights in extensive series of asyndeta that link contradictions, and handles proverbs, idioms, and quotations, made slightly disreputable by microscopic changes, with devastating meticulousness. Within the individual poem he arranges with force and determination his linguistic confrontations of the most disparate technical and professional vocabularies, and many younger poets, dissatisfied with the inherited literary idiom, have followed his lead. Few, if any, try to emulate his sober, pensive, and graceful love poetry.

Enzensberger manages to combine, with wit, urbanity, and ease, a bit of Bukharin and Lord Byron. "The blacks call me white / and the whites call me black," he says of himself; as a social critic and the editor of *Kursbuch* (1965–), the most intelligent publication of the radical German left, he may aspire to change the entire world, but as a poet he appears much more concerned with himself than with the perspiring masses anywhere; he despises the high and mighty but is equally disgusted by the little people he sees in the streets, toiling, colorless, docile, and ugly.

In an illuminating essay Paul Noack has called Enzensberger a conservative anarchist, but I wonder whether this clever label quite covers the productive intellectual who loves cherry trees, old books, and a future universe free of oozing machines and terrifying sounds, inhabited by a select few who suit his egocentric, exacting, and fastidious tastes. Most intensely of all, Enzensberger does not want to suffocate in precast thoughts and cemented ideologies; and when Peter Weiss recently asked him to declare himself unequivocally for the underprivileged and to "sacrifice his doubts and his reservations," Enzensberger replied sharply that he preferred his doubts to mere sentiments and had no use for views free of internal contradictions. Fortunately, Enzensberger wants a world no less open, changing, and paradoxical than his verse.

8. Wilhelm Lehmann

WILHELM LEHMANN (1882–1968) once said that his moment between "not yet" and "not again" was very brief. Public recognition came to him late and for an inconclusive span of time; in the 'fifties and early 'sixties, after he had written narrative prose and verse for more than forty years, middle-aged audiences began to appreciate the high quality of his craftsmanship, but young readers felt little inclination to tolerate an old man who stubbornly went on praising the climbing vine, the fragrant dill, or the little cloud. Lehmann's is essentially a botanical world of "narrow surfeit"; the National Socialists had despised the lonely schoolteacher who indulged in his private poetry of watercress and salamanders (but did not betray his Jewish friends), and the young generation of the 'sixties studiously ignores the craftsman who does not explicitly deal with the public events of Hiroshima, Auschwitz, and Vietnam. I suspect that Brecht and Lehmann are the only true antagonists of recent German poetry, together constituting its fundamental dialectic and paradoxically sharing an intense commitment to humanity, the one speaking of changing history, the other of cyclical nature.

Wilhelm Lehmann was a teacher all his adult life. From the early 'twenties until his retirement (1923–1947) he was schoolmaster at Eckernförde, Schleswig-Holstein. He was born in Venezuela but, as he relates in his brief autobiographical report *Mühe des Anfangs*, 1952 / *Pains of Beginning*, he came to Germany as a little boy and, under his mother's stern eye, grew up in Wandsbek near Hamburg, attended the universities of Tübingen, Strassburg, Berlin, and Kiel, and wrote a dissertation in older Germanic philology (1905). In Berlin he met Moritz Heimann, the editor of the avant-garde publishing house S. Fischer, and also came to know Gerhart Hauptmann (1862–1946) and the pensive Silesian novelist Hermann Stehr (1864–1940), whose anti-Semitism he considered "a sin against the world's being"; he was possibly the only student of his generation who, demonstrating astonishing sensitivity, set out for England to meet W. B. Yeats. Lehmann first wrote stories and novels of high autobiographical and lyrical if not expressionistic intensity and received half of the Kleist Prize for his novel *Weingott*, 1921, the other half being awarded to Robert Musil (1923). He was fifty-two years old when he published his first collection of verse, *Antwort des Schweigens*, 1935 / *The Response of Silence;* and five more collections were added in subsequent years: *Der grüne Gott*, 1942 / *The Green God; Entzückter Staub*, 1946 / *Charmed Dust; Noch nicht genug*, 1950 / *Not Yet Enough; Überlebender Tag*, 1954 / *Surviving Day;* and *Abschiedslust*, 1962 / *Joy of Parting.* He convincingly combined German and English (and occasionally Gaelic) traditions to articulate his "organic" vision of the world. Lehmann himself often suggested that he owed much to the older Goethe and to his friend Oskar Loerke (1884–1941), a poet of distinction; but he was more reticent about the impact of Annette V. Droste-Hülshoff (1797–1848), who certainly preceded him in the harsh precision of her nature imagery. He always was lavish in praise of Gaelic myth and English poetry, which he knew in considerable detail, including John Donne and the lesser metaphysical poets, as well as Gerard Manley Hopkins, T. S. Eliot and, above all, Robert Graves. Lehmann cherished English because, more than any other language, it offers "an inexhaustible richness of expressions for things present, for density and the tangibility of things"; for

Lehmann's linguistic sensibility the English tongue served as a happy antidote to the fatal abstractions of the traditional German academic idiom.

Almost alone among English-speaking critics, S. S. Prawer, showing delicate understanding, tried recently to delineate Lehmann's poetic evolution from a style close to expressionism to a later mode of lean concentration, but he had to admit that there were hardly any startling developments. There may be changing nuances: an increasing stress on the melancholy of old age, a sparser line consisting of only two or three words, a harsher juxtaposition of "natural" and "mythological" elements; Lehmann's poetry, like nature, lives by gentle recurrence rather than irrevocable change. From his early to his later verse, Lehmann responds to a sylvan world with few historical implications. "I say moon" he begins an early poem, "Mond im Januar" / "Moon in January," and immediately attempts to give the most precise account of the visible sublunar "events": the radiance on a crow's nest, the trembling of a lonely spot of water in the cool light, the freezing pond, the glimmer on a snail's slow path over some wooden wall. Yet his delicate account of momentary refractions deepens into the timelessness of myth; and as the moonlight glides over the wintry landscape, the poet's personal reaction to the lunar moment merges with an archetypal response in which mankind itself answers to moon, and sky, and earth: "Diane her body opens to / Endymion." The impeccable two stanzas of the poem "Oberon," which still belongs to Lehmann's early work, most clearly suggest the blissful intersection of "nature" and "myth" in an unforgettable instant of fragrant presence. A modest "overgrown path, cut into the warm red loam" with "pimpernel and beggar-tick" has absorbed the most distant past: "Oberon was riding here / grasshopperquick." In the presence of the summer and the movements of the plants, nothing has been lost; and although Oberon, the king of magic transformation, may have slipped back into the past, there still resounds a marvelous echo "as from his golden / spur / when the winds in the quivering grasses / stir." Then and now are one, and the precise implications of pimpernel and beggar-tick (in the original German: *Lolch*), suggesting healing and endurance, betray something of the permanent consolation inherent in a moment of high noon.

I find many of Lehmann's "nature" poems no less political in their final implications than his few topical poems (e.g., "Nach der zweiten Sintflut" / "After the Second Flood"), because he fully shares the instinct of the great realists to discover dignity and meaning in the humble, the forgotten, and the "proletarian" corners of nature that totally lack melodramatic importance or heroic splendor; it is only a step (as we have learned from Walt Whitman) from singing the praise of grass to the poetic triumphs of the underprivileged. The poem "Entzückter Staub" / "Charmed Dust" suggests much of his fundamental intent. Again a scene set between late winter and early spring, somewhere in northern Germany: humble willow trees, a few patches of dirty snow, shabby bushes, and the noise from the road penetrating to the barren fields. But the genre "scene" elaborates an essential tension of low and high, forgotten and meaningful, colorless and radiant: in a mudhole, under "wounded twigs of thorn," the reflection of heaven can be discovered; a turkey, on a forgotten farm, proudly displays his many colors and, while running across the yard, resembles Cleopatra's barge as it once emerged from Shakespeare's play. There is brittle laughter resounding through the sterile landscape: "A handful of dust ascended" high into "the gaping mouth of the icy wind." It is "the hymn of the larks" that voices, weightlessly and safely, what the silent and tortured earth cannot say.

A few of Lehmann's later poems skillfully fuse echoes of German romantic verse, the pensive irony of the old man, and a conversational "middle" style reminiscent of English traditions from Pope to W. H. Auden. I do not mean the weak poem "Antibes," overrated by German anthologists because it seems so close to Gottfried Benn's collages, but more relaxed and graceful verse like "In Solothurn," 1950. In the mind of the aging poet, who has just arrived in the small Swiss city of Solothurn, memories of restless wanderings and the sense of the blissfully present moment in the shadow of old churches and fountains melt into each other. Resting on the steps ascending to the cathedral, he watches the people in the town square, coming and

going: "Hôtel de la Couronne. In golden patterns, balconies /
A car just stopped. Did she get in? / Adieu! Her shawl caught
by the wind." Remembrance, recognition, and renewed loss, but
as the fountains go on flowing, the personal memories of the poet
again merge with older memories of other lovers, other voices,
and art and experience, past, present, and future combine: "The
waters speak / of us poetically a hundred years hence . . . /
of me, Pierre de Provence and you, fair Maguelonne." It is a
graceful and erudite fusion of romantic irony and an urbane *vers
de société*, extremely rare in the German tongue.

Karl Krolow (b. 1915), Lehmann's talented and occasionally
reluctant disciple and ally, once argued that Lehmann's poetic
world, because of the predominance of plants and animals of the
lowest order, was sometimes endangered by progressive dehumanization. Krolow fails to admit that Lehmann, confronting
depraved humanity, prefers to be intensely human by remaining
reticent about people; Lehmann does not construct self-sufficient
verbal patterns but "expressions of a maximum of existence,"
in order to make the dehumanized lives of his readers more
human again. In speaking of the evident arcana of nature Lehmann does not aim at a reproduction of "life" but, as he himself
stresses in his collected essays *Dichtung und Dasein, 1952 / Poetry
and Presence*, at a most intense "being present" (*Dasein*); and while
"life" (*Leben*) may feel at home in the sham idiom (*Schein-Sprache*)
of the communication industries, the happier moments of "being
present" call for a language (*Sprache*) of analogous intensity and
substance. Lehmann seeks (as does Herbert Marcuse) to combat
manipulated, diffuse, careless, and mechanized living, and, believing almost heroically in the efficacy of the word, tries to
restore a Goethean "meaningful presence" of the world to verse;
he seems totally immune to the ontological gap between chestnut
trees consisting of wood and leaves, and those consisting of
words and printer's ink. In his inevitable nominalism Lehmann
dislikes ideological universals but, unlike his philosophical con-
frère, the Austrian novelist Heimito von Doderer (1896–1966),
distinguishes clearly between the necessary "abstraction" of
scientific methodology and the fatal "derivatives" spawned by
advertising, television, newspapers, radio, and the movies. He

suggests that the poet should "complement" scientific universals by reminiscences of individual nuances (poets prefer the specificity of cherries to the generality of fruits) and argues passionately against the linguistic clichés of "managers, professors, and fast travelers"; indeed, he considered himself a "revolutionary, an anarchist," and a "member of a resistance group" who fights against manipulated idioms. Lehmann has often been condemned for his willful playing with mythological figures and his obsessive returning to almost endless chains of botanical terms, but it is precisely his search for the concrete (*das Gegenständliche*) and the underived that, paradoxically, drove him to speak of Merlin, Oberon, or Blanscheflur, and to insist not on indefinite flowers but on aconite, darnel, and pimpernel. These names and terms imply primeval and "true" responses to the concrete world: in a mythic name, language still lives "in the sensuality of expression," and in the inherited and precise botanical term humanity still responds to the essence of the plant. The Latin term *nasturtium*, for instance, relates to Greek *mnastorgion* and thus etymologically articulates the essential vitality of a plant "desirous of humidity." In the old term, the plant, as it were, "speaks itself for itself, and human egotism falls silent"; language still protects the real as the skin protects the flesh.

During the 'sixties Wilhelm Lehmann was increasingly forced to defend his poetry against the activists. He made a fundamental distinction between revolutionaries, who want to change the world, and poets, who want to look at it in order to make people feel more of the world in their verse. Stressing the poem's intent of looking long and lovingly at creation, Lehmann came closer to young Marx than his adversaries of the New Left usually suspect: young Marx too, in his *Economic and Philosophic Manuscripts* (1844) suggested in his restless and tortured language that it was the final aim of all historical development to enable man to look disinterestedly, that is, aesthetically, at the things of the world. Young Marx believed that the aesthetic stance of admiring meditation would be possible only after the final social revolution; Lehmann implied that the perfect poem enables sensitive people to dwell loyally on nature, independently of and before social change; the poem anticipates, as it were, the aesthetic results of social revolutions. I am not particularly convinced by Lehmann's idea that innocent Nature (as revealed by good poetry) may counteract human feelings of moral impotence in our age of terror; such an argument, I fear, rashly identifies the organic and the moral spheres and conceals the abyss between the moral neutrality of trees and flowers (outside history) and the guilt and innocence within the human and historical realm.

But Lehmann's impeccable poems are superior to his theoretical principles formulated in self-defense, and perhaps more efficacious, too. He was an extremely resilient writer who imposed upon himself severe technical and strategic limitations in order to expand man's narrow sensibilities; and by combining the noble tradition of the German *Naturgedicht* with English patterns, he successfully refined an important strain of German writing in a highly urbane way. Within his own selective sphere, he created a body of lyric work rich in variety of tone and attitude, from which the political is not wholly excluded; and the recurrent reproach that he refrained from speaking out on public issues does not discredit his unerring craftsmanship, his intellectual scope, or the exquisite quality of his work. Lehmann once anticipated the possibility that passionately moral activists would cease to read his poetry, and he added sadly that such people might turn out to be moralists without being human. It is a thought worth pondering.

KENNETH TYNAN HAS suggested that Germans use their theater as a public library and museum, but I should add that they have long expected the stage to fulfill the tasks of both church and parliament; and ever since Friedrich Schiller demanded that the German theater serve as a "moral institution" (1784), few revolutionaries have had the courage to insist that theater has something to do with a game, or, in fact, a "play." After May, 1945, German actors and producers were busy rehearsing the European and American repertoire from which they had been isolated by the National Socialists, who had cared mostly for textbook classics and Viennese operetta. Thornton Wilder's *Our Town* [1938] and *The Skin of Our Teeth* [1942], and Jean Anouilh's *Antigone* [1944] were performed nearly everywhere in the western zones of occupation, and their freedom from naturalist stage conventions impressed both audiences and writers; in Switzerland Thornton Wilder had been performed in 1938/39 and 1943/44 at the Zurich *Schauspielhaus* (the only important free German-speaking stage on a continent held captive by Adolf Hitler) and had set Max Frisch and Friedrich Dürrenmatt on their separate courses. Wolfgang Borchert's *Draussen vor der Tür* (written 1946) / [Outside the Door] *The Man Outside,* 1952, first staged on November 21, 1947, articulated the feelings of the returning soldiers and demonstrated that expressionism could not be revived; if after World War I young playwrights had hymnically affirmed the essential goodness of man, Borchert asked shrill questions that reverberated among the ruins. His play drew its strength more from its central metaphor than from its latter-day expressionist structure: "outside," the returning soldier, hungry, deprived of wife and son, searching for the meaning of his life; and "inside," former officers and recent profiteers who, seated at tables representing their new security, offer pat answers that convey no meaning at all to their petitioners. Yet Borchert's social critique was connected with his existentialist concerns: the experiences of the returning soldier are set in the frame of a morality play, in which a helpless God accepts the triumph of Death, a sated undertaker to whom people have become mere black flies. Borchert's soldier asks Job's question, but his God is a tired old man isolated from the fate of man.

Carl Zuckmayer, Max Frisch, Fritz Hochwälder, and Friedrich Dürrenmatt dominated the stage of the early 'fifties, but later in the decade there emerged conflicting theatrical currents that were related to the comeback of the playwright and producer Brecht (East Berlin production of *Mother Courage*, January 11, 1949) and to the increasing influence of the "absurd," or rather ontological, theater emanating from Ionesco's *Bald Soprano* [1950] and Beckett's *Waiting for Godot* [January 5, 1953]. Brecht chose not to return to a country suffocating in Socialist Realism; instead he sought asylum in a place where the courageous artistic experiments of the Weimar Republic seemed to be in favor among Hitler's inveterate enemies. It was an ironic coincidence that very soon after he had settled in East Germany the situation changed rapidly: relative tolerance was replaced by strict regimentation, and Brecht could rescue his new establishment only at a price. But the third version of *Galileo* [1955] made even his compromise with Socialist Realism artistically productive, because it transformed the brittle, undramatic discussions of the Hollywood text [1946] into more theatrical situations and created genuine characters imbued with believable drives. There were other consequences, too: precisely because Brecht time and again submitted to the demands of the government, he created a protective screen, behind which he could continue to develop his scenic craftsmanship and educate his disciples; thanks to his tortuous accommodation to the regime, younger playwrights were able to devote their talents to the epic theater and occasionally avoid a doctrine which in practice amounted to a renewal of the stage techniques of Sardou, with a dash of Stalinism added. In the German theater it was difficult to contest Brecht's genius and his theatrical elegance, and the playwrights of the absurd, who wished their poetic images to indicate man's alienation as something totally irreparable, had less resonance in Germany than elsewhere; perhaps it was also true that a society just emerging from hell had little call to opt for a world without meaning, time, or hope. For many playwrights, including Max Frisch, Friedrich Dürenmatt, Peter

Weiss, and Günter Grass, the theater of the absurd offered a moment of challenge or confusion, but it was Wolfgang Hildesheimer (b. 1916) who most explicitly came to the defense of the theatrical tradition extending back through the surrealists to Alfred Jarry's *Ubu Roi* [1896] and the nonliterary art of the clown, the acrobat, and the mime. In a penetrating discussion (1960) Hildesheimer admirably defined the boundaries separating the theater of the absurd from the theater of social commitment, but in his own plays he developed uneasily from near social satire in his *Spiele, in denen es dunkel wird,* 1958 / *Blackouts* to his *Nachtstück,* 1963 / *Night Piece,* 1967 which reveals a more piercing vision of culture as a recurrent nightmare that deprives any sensitive man of his sleep. The substantial difficulties facing the German followers of Ionesco emerge most clearly from Martin Walser's plays, which try in vain to pursue a historical examination of moral failures past and present, working with a scenic vocabulary based on "absurd" rather than social interests. In *Eiche und Angora* [1962] / [Oak and Angora] *The Rabbit Race,* 1963, method and issues work at cross-purposes: Walser wants to show a panorama of German history since 1945, and assembles a motley crew of chameleonlike Nazis, castrated concentration camp survivors, and frustrated women, but he cannot fuse the separate conventions of literary and nonliterary theater. His committed sensibility, literary in nature, is totally at odds with the wordless art of the clown; and his recent attempt to formulate a "new realism" for the theater constitutes but a brave apology for his own entanglement in incompatible contradictions.

In the late 'fifties and early 'sixties younger playwrights amply demonstrated how difficult it was to cope with a theater that paradoxically was supposed to be realistic without a trace of realism. Increasingly impatient with Brecht's parables of distant inhumanity in a make-believe China and with the poetic world of the "absurd" theater, they wanted to make contact with the social realities; yet they were unwilling to take the road of John Osborne and Arnold Wesker, on whom they looked down with a condescension that would be hard to surpass. Brecht's disciples in the German Democratic Republic used the rational methods of the epic theater to analyze their own environment and promptly found themselves in conflict with the functionaries who, as far as contemporary affairs were concerned, insisted on emotional empathy with positive party heroes, rather than a cool and critical audience. Peter Hacks was fired from his theater job and pushed into a politically less effective career of writing adaptations; Heiner Müller (b. 1928), whose *Der Lohndrücker* [1958] / *The Scab* dealt frankly with industrial conditions in the GDR, was ordered to revise the text, and turned in discouragement to reworking Sophocles; and Hellmuth Baierl (b. 1927) chose ideological submission and showed that his *Frau Flinz* [1961] was capable of developing from a Mother Courage figure into a politically correct collective farm manager. The documentary play, concentrating on public events of social import and often deriving its dramatic strength from the tensions of a trial scene, offered another possibility for theater with overt contemporary relevance. But the practitioners of the documentary theater differ considerably in political views and basic techniques: conservative Rolf Hochhuth, who triggered the entire trend in 1963, closely documented his first play but later came to feel that gaps in documentation were more telling than any archival source; Heinar Kipphardt's *In der Sache J. Robert Oppenheimer* [1964] / *In the Matter of J. Robert Oppenheimer*, 1968, used documentary materials dexterously arranged to correspond to television requirements; and Peter Weiss recently (1968) defined his documentary plays as replies to the lies and manipulation by means of which the mass media keep the unthinking masses in subservience. He wants his documents "unchanged in content but reworked in form" (as if changes in form did not alter content) and suggests that the surfeit of material be organized according to a "partisan principle" of selections, cuts, and montage. We are invited to jump out of the frying pan of the mass media into Peter Weiss's Leninist fires.

In the late 'sixties came a period of restless experimentation and few impressive plays. Older authors were rewriting their early scripts, and Brecht's literary grandsons stubbornly refused to follow established epic, absurd, or documentary patterns, insisting on doing their own thing, if possible all alone. Self-taught Martin Sperr (b. 1944) turned instinctively to a popular

mode reminiscent of Odön von Horváth (1901–1938), and his
Jagdszene aus Niederbayern [1966] / *Hunting Scenes from Lower Bavaria*
and *Landshuter Erzählungen* [1967] / *Landshut Tales* doggedly pursue
the truth of what really takes place in small-town offices and
bedrooms. Others, perhaps in closer touch with the cultural
revolution sweeping Europe, reexamine the essentials of the
theater, expanding or negating its inherited possibilities. Bazon
Brock (b. 1936) aims in his "theater of position" at liberating the
stage from literary lethargy, but he burdens the proposed "happening" with nearly twenty-five pages of closely argued theory.
Peter Handke (b. 1942) takes the elements of the theater neatly
apart, and his *Publikumsbeschimpfung* [1966] / *Dressing Down the
Audience* employs four speakers (advised to train their rhetorical
style by listening to the Rolling Stones, the Catholic liturgy, and
a cement mixer), who mercilessly attack the foolish expectations
of the audience. Handke is obsessed with an as yet unrealized
theatrical method-to-end-all-method and wants to make our
consciousness "absolutely precise"—if necessary by calling us
"Nazi swine" and "sop faces." His way of continuing the German
tradition of educational theater is to show us few carrots and
a big stick.

1. Fritz Hochwälder

FRITZ HOCHWÄLDER (b. 1911) belongs to those writers of the middle generation whose development was shaped, if not partly obstructed, by the burdens of exile. Hochwälder comes from a Viennese family of Jewish craftsmen and was trained to take over his father's workshop; the official document confirming that he was a qualified master upholsterer was among the few possessions he managed to take across the Austrian border in the spring of 1938. With other refugees, he first worked in Swiss detention camps and was later permitted to settle in Zurich, where he continues to live as a patriotic Austrian expatriate. In Vienna, he had sketched out a drama of incest [1932], but only after he had met Georg Kaiser, the relentless logician among the German expressionists, did Hochwälder make his "hobby" (as he says himself) into a vocation and write a few plays which after 1945 swiftly made their way on the international stage. For ten or fifteen years Hochwälder was among the best-known playwrights in the German language, but the generation emerging after 1955 cares as little for his plays as for those of Carl Zuckmayer. I suspect there are a number of reasons for his change of fortune: the triumph of Brechtian theater and of the "absurd" may have obscured his legitimate (traditionalist) achievements, but it is also possible that the inner discord of his dramatic world has become more apparent as the years went by.

Hochwälder's most famous play, *Das Heilige Experiment* / [The Holy Experiment] *The Strong Are Lonely*, 1954, first performed in Switzerland [1943] and, after the end of the war, on many other stages, demonstrates impeccable scenic craftsmanship; within the confines of the Jesuit College of Buenos Aires and a few hours of the fateful day of July 16, 1767, the forces of the sword and of the believing mind fatefully clash. Jesuit missionaries have built, among the Indios of the Paraná region, a state founded on communal work, spiritual togetherness, and human dignity, but the Spanish Crown cannot tolerate their achievement, because the men in power fear that the Jesuit state (a welcome haven to Indio slaves thirsting for freedom) may one day endanger the entire Spanish Empire on the South American continent. Don Pedro de Muira, the Spanish commissioner, orders Alfonso Fernandez, the Jesuit superior, to transfer the administration of the mission state to the Crown and to withdraw all Jesuits from the region. Fernandez refuses to submit, only to be told by a legate secretly sent from Rome by his own spiritual superiors that he must bow unconditionally to what the Crown requests because the South American successes of the Jesuits have weakened their position in Europe; and in order to save the order, already banished from France and Portugal, the mission state has to be sacrificed. Fernandez (who knows that the rule of the Spanish Crown means the brutal enslavement of his one hundred and fifty thousand Indios) cannot but yield to his superiors and orders the administration of the mission transferred to the Spanish; trying to make peace between the belligerent Indios, led by the disobedient Jesuit Oros, and the Spanish, he is mortally wounded. The trouble with Hochwälder's Jesuit superior is that he behaves like a hero in the German tragic tradition, for four acts subordinating his "subjectivity" to the "objective" demands of the order, but revealing before he dies in the stern finale that he is a constitutionally split character, wrecked by psychological uncertainties and unresolved tensions. He has not come to "will" what he "must"; but (an erring man closer to Georg Kaiser's rather than to Schiller's dramatic universe) he atones for his guilt by stepping into the path of a bullet fired against the Spanish by one of his beloved Indios, or maybe by Oros, his other self.

The other vital strain of Hochwälder's gifts emerges from his "modern mystery play" *Donnerstag* [1959] / *Thursday*, which he was commissioned to write by the directors of the Salzburg Festival. Hochwälder tries to transform medieval Everyman, or rather Dr. Faustus, into a bored professional in the consumer society: his Niklas Manuel Pomfrit, a successful architect who feels dead in his heart, finds himself the center of a pitched battle between the satanic powers of "Belial, Inc., " represented by a disingenuous little Viennese devil named Wondrak, and the transcendental, in the shape of poor Estrella and the beggar-monk Thomé (who, unlike Alfonso Fernandez, does not submit to the orders of his superiors). Wondrak promises Pomfrit that he is to enjoy in three days' time the highest blessings, including the best average middle-class home, an illuminating space trip, and the embraces of the sex-kitten Amalia, but after Pomfrit has been teased by preliminary intimations of these supreme rewards, he discovers on Thursday, his fatal third day, that he still feels stirrings of hope and love in his heart; he cannot be deprived, by any force, of his human privilege to choose freely. His fate remains in abeyance; only from afar does Death suggest that from his absolute despair may spring renewed belief: "Did not the world come too from nothingness?" Hochwälder convinces, not by this second-hand Christian existentialism, attuned to the Mercedes sensibilities of the Salzburg audiences, but by his extraordinary scenic exuberance taking up the conventions of the magic operetta popular in early nineteenth-century Vienna; if in *The Strong Are Lonely* Hochwälder relied on a lean prose, expressive in pregnant silences rather than in articulated statements, in *Thursday* he derives a good deal of theatrical strength from his native Viennese idiom, the absurd prattling of plebeian characters concerned with high philosophical speculation (above all, the servant Birnstrudl, directly lifted from popular traditions) and a quick sense of the funny and the grotesque that link the "mystery" to farce and the circus rather than to the literary stage. It is first-rate theater without really being an important play.

In a revealing lecture (1959) on his work, Fritz Hochwälder said that he considered himself a "Catholic" playwright in the sense of being a late heir to baroque sensuality, the sprightly *commedia dell'arte*, and the imaginative enchantments of the Viennese popular theater; he was not, he asserted, one of those "Puritans" who, by indulging in intense rational analysis, endangered the theatrical element of "show," movement, and color. (Whether the Protestant "Puritans" can be as readily identified with the avant-garde as Hochwälder suggests may be a different question.) In his practice, Hochwälder has unfortunately ignored much of his penetrating self-definition and, instead of working with his "Catholic" gifts, often strained hard to outdo the "Puritans" in dialectical exploration of irrevocable ethical decisions. In *Esther*, 1940, revised 1960, an Old Testament fairy tale in Viennese idiom; in *Die Herberge* [1955] / *The Inn*, a symbolic play about the ambivalent force of greed; and in *Thursday*, the "Catholic" element certainly predominates, but in many other plays, such as *Meier Helmbrecht* [1946]; *Der öffentliche Ankläger* [1948] / *The Public Prosecutor;* and *Donadieu* [1953], Hochwälder deals with strictly "Puritan" questions of responsibility, revenge, and justice. Against his grain he strives to be Georg Kaiser's successor instead of accepting the formidable task of being a distant and craftsmanlike cousin to Ferdinand Raimund or Carlo Goldoni.

2. Max Frisch

THERE IS SOMETHING constantly alive and open about Max Frisch's mind and work, and after more than thirty years of writing he continues to convey a distinct feeling of youthful energy, endless sympathy, and occasional naïveté. Frisch strikes me as a writer of renewed beginnings rather than of radical change: he does not sacrifice his interests easily, preferring rather to explore a few questions (involved with the essentials of modern human consciousness) in changing moods, figures, and genres; and if he does discover an answer, he is apt to reject it quickly in order to push his explorations still further. Much of his achievement consists of the revised and the tentative; fascinated by the vagaries of human life and often unconcerned with aesthetic structure, he will often pursue an analogous theme in a diary note, a story, a novel, or a play. His individual works are imperfect, but individual imperfections are less important than the intense continuity of his search. In our century it is more difficult than ever to be a Swiss romantic.

Max Frisch was born in 1911 in Zurich, of German, Austrian, and Swiss stock, studied German literature and art history at the University of Zurich, but, after his father had died, turned to journalism in order to make a living; there seems to have been ample time for creative roaming in the Balkans and for publishing a novel (1934). Within three years Frisch decided to resume his studies, duly went through the prescribed courses at the *Eidge-nössische Technische Hochschule* (Federal Institute of Technology), acquired his diploma in architecture, opened his own office, and tried to combine the tasks of the architect with those of the writer, alternating his work in Zurich with protracted travels in the United States and Mexico, to which he was to return often. The publication of *Stiller*, 1954 / *I'm Not Stiller*, 1958, almost coincided with important private decisions: Frisch, separated from his family, moved to a rural community (where he often met Dürrenmatt) and decided to concentrate on his literary work. But he was soon on the move again; he went on extensive trips to Mexico, Greece, and the Near East and, after his divorce, made a new beginning and settled in Rome (1960–1965) and later in Berzona, in the Swiss Ticino, where he continues to write today. It remains to be seen whether the public image of Frisch still has any pertinence; perhaps many audiences are inclined to prefer the image of the "relevant" political writer to the real man, who is essentially concerned with the uncertainties of the troubled and transitory self.

But it is easier to ask than to answer questions about the real Frisch, for his literary development oscillates curiously between genres and forms, or between private concerns and public issues; with almost protean cunning he changes the direction of his work midway, only to return to his beginnings and to start all over again. Separating those of Frisch's works which are concerned with the intimate vicissitudes of the self from those that deal with public issues of war, fascism, and power, I should like to suggest a sequence of four groups of plays and novels in which private and public interests, at least at first sight, alternate almost regularly. In his early prose and in the play *Santa Cruz* (written 1944), Frisch created a world of *fin-de-siècle* people longing for order and yet tempted by the more distinct wonders of infinity seized in moments of aesthetic fulfillment. When his early solipsism was shattered by his confrontation with destroyed Germany (as his *Diary* attests), Frisch wrote three "public" plays (1945–1949), including the first version of *Die chinesische Mauer* [1946] / *The Chinese Wall*, 1961, seeking to define a new concept of political civilization that differs from mere aesthetic "culture" alien to

moral passion. In the 'fifties (1951–1957) the "political" Frisch
turned to exploring the self once again, and in his plays *Graf
Öderland* [1951] / *Count Öderland*, 1962, and *Don Juan oder Die
Liebe zur Geometrie* [1953] / *Don Juan, or The Love of Geometry*, 1967,
as well as in his novels, including *I'm Not Stiller* and *Homo Faber*,
continued the more intimate search of the late 'thirties and early
'forties—only to reverse his course by writing *Biedermann und die
Brandstifter* [1958] / [Biedermann (Mr. Regularguy) and the Ar-
sonists] *The Firebugs*, 1963; and *Andorra* [1961] / *Andorra*,
1964—once more appearing to the world as the politically committed writer he had been immediately after the war. In terms
of chronology, periods of private search (1934–1944 and 1951–
1957) alternate abruptly with years of courageous if highly personal statements on public issues (1945–1949 and 1958–1961);
recurrent reversals, renewed beginnings, protracted contrasts
time and again. Of Frisch's three public plays of the immediate
postwar period, *The Chinese Wall* deserves ample consideration;
other plays, including *Nun singen sie wieder* [1945] / *Now They Are
Singing Again*, a requiem for the war dead, who want reconciliation, and *Als der Krieg zuende war* [1949] / *When the War Was Over*,
1967, dealing with a strong-willed German woman who loves a
noble Soviet colonel and hates her husband for his involvement
in the mass killings, did not survive on the stage for long. Walter
Jacobi has related *The Chinese Wall* (first version 1946, revised
1955) to dadaism; but it impresses me rather as an architectoni-
cally well-ordered attempt to combine Brecht's *chinoiserie* with
some of Thornton Wilder's techniques in order to construct an
inclusive stage able to express the restless human mind, which
teems with memories of historical figures and reminiscences of
fictional characters. The Chinese Emperor Hwang Ti claims to
have defeated all enemies beyond the borders of his mighty
empire and arranges a festive party to celebrate the final victory
of his "Great Order" and to reveal his plans for building a wall
that will protect his empire against all future change; he does
admit, however, that he has yet to deal with his last enemy within
the land, a certain Min Ko, who is called "the voice of the people"
and threatens stability by writing bitter satires that are passed
from mouth to mouth. The emperor's guests, including Colum-

bus, Napoleon, L'Inconnue de la Seine, Don Juan (who sketches the program of Frisch's later play), Philip of Spain, Pontius Pilate, and many others, gather on the terrace; the Man of Today warns Napoleon and Philip against returning, because uncontrolled power in the age of the atom may be fatal to all mankind, but he is far less outspoken when confronted with the power of Hwang Ti himself. Mee Lan, the princess, refuses to marry Prince Wu Tsiang, the victorious general (because "he wants to be happy through power"), and offers her love to the Man of Today, who speaks a good deal about the necessity for action but time after time fails to act. A deaf young peasant (who said nothing when the triumphal procession passed him by) is arrested, and a show-trial is ordered for the suspected "voice of the people." But the emperor's rule has come to an end, for Prince Wu Tsiang, offended by the princess's refusal, takes command of the popular revolution sweeping through the city; the revolutionaries break into the palace, rape the princess, and finally destroy the entire stage set. There remains the bare machinery of the theater, and the raped girl and the hapless modern intellectual embrace in a black happy end; in the meantime, the famous guests of the emperor again swarm over the stage and suggest, by repeating the opening passages of the play (which happen to consist of a pastiche of Shakespeare and Frisch), that history is a farce and everything will start again from the beginning.

It is not against the emperor but against the intellectual of today that Frisch aims the full force of his self-critical blow. A good deal of *blague* and constant lack of involvement; four times (my count is based on the revised version) the intellectual fails to act: he obediently calls for the show-trial of Min Ko when the emperor raises his dagger; he cynically delivers a rich vocabulary of useful political terms to denote the enemies of power not as honest people but as "agitators, spies, terrorists, and elements." "He merely shrugs his shoulders," Mee Lan says, "and lights another cigarette when they torture a deaf man and make him scream"; and he finally accepts the privileged role of court jester and official poet. In defending himself against Mee Lan, the intellectual reveals much of the private core of the public play: he accuses her of constructing a heroic image of him for herself, in order to indulge in cheap admiration; she sins against him by creating an image not true to his real being (as will many figures in Frisch's discussion of marriage conflicts). Yet the intellectual does have to admit that he had failed, and adds that nothing remains to the intellect (if it wants to create history) but to sacrifice itself, because the immediacy of involvement destroys critical distance and impartiality. In Frisch's view, both Mee Lan and the intellectual have erred, and yet there is final hope, or something close to hope, in their embrace, for it creates a unique and irrevocable moment that shatters the repetitive cycle of human history. Frisch's *The Chinese Wall* may be a play dealing with public issues of power and the intellect, but I doubt that it is a political play in the strict sense of the word. It offers, behind the veil of brilliant theatricality, a terrifying glimpse of maliciously repetitive history, isolated and inactive intellect, women mistakenly creating false images of their mates, and the impotence of the enraged common people; the only meaning is in the utterly private gesture of love. As in young Brecht's *Drums in the Night*, the questions are of public relevance, but the answer does not transcend the intimacy of a man and a woman.

In his work of the 'fifties, Max Frisch (as if aware of the insistent "private" element of his public plays) willingly returned to his exploration of the self and, after considering once again the traumatic conflict between life caught in daily routine and instinctive longings for timeless joy in his ballad of *Count Öderland*, came back to defining the ego and the pressures of the world in "internalized" if not psychological terms. In remarkable contrast to the melodramatic and occasionally crude ballad of *Count Öderland*, Frisch's *Don Juan, or The Love of Geometry* reveals a rare lightness of touch, analytical intelligence, impeccable elegance of language, and lean economy of construction. Some of Frisch's characters are trapped, in an almost material sense, by castle walls or repetitive schedules, but his Don Juan (like the artist Stiller) recognizes that it is far more dangerous, if not fatal, to spontaneity to be trapped by the images which people create; the individual's fight against the fetters of "space" and "geography" turns into a battle against the finer but stronger bonds of "myth" or what people say about each other. Frisch's Don

Juan is not frigid, but he complains, as does his cousin in G. B. Shaw's play, that he is the pursued rather than the pursuer; he occasionally stoops to women and instinctive nature, but these moments, he says, are unrelated to his true personality. He pays tribute to the flesh (the stage is indeed littered with dead fathers and offended husbands) but actually cherishes more abstract enjoyments; even his own father is afraid that there is something wrong with him because when taken to a bordello he plays chess. Don Juan loves geometry more than women: he likes the purity of geometric space, the neat correspondence of shape and technical force, the timeless validity of theoretical axioms, a soberness that comes close to being holy; he obviously has his own dreams of attaining fulfillment on an island of geometrical abstraction. His true life differs essentially from the myth of Don Juan, and he wants to escape the myth by pushing it to its final, theatrical conclusion: he suggests to the Bishop of Córdoba that he is willing to stage his descent into hell, with brimstone and all, before an audience of thirteen seduced ladies, if the Church will offer him asylum in a lonely monastery afterwards. The Bishop of Córdoba turns out to be merely another deceived husband in clerical disguise, but Don Juan proceeds with his plan, the astonished ladies witness the coming of the Commandant (played by a prostitute with a golden heart), and Don Juan finally withdraws from his public image, known all over Spain. But he has totally misjudged the ironies of life: taking refuge in the Castle of Ronda and studying geometry, he discovers that he loves the duchess (the former lady with the golden heart), recognizes that "male" geometry cannot offer a substitute for the wholeness of life, and does not seem surprised when told that he is going to be the father of the duchess's child. He has wisely failed: his "myth" will endure in spite of his efforts, and while he has strained to define his true self in abstractly geometrical terms, the vital exuberance of existence has irrevocably caught up with him.

To the private plays of the 'fifties, exploring the metaphysical and psychological claustrophobias of the self, Frisch's novels *I'm Not Stiller* and *Homo Faber* are intimately related. In spite of its allusive richness, *I'm Not Stiller* (discussed in the chapter of

Switzerland) belongs to the nineteenth-century German tradition of the *Bildungsroman*, in which a sensitive man of artistic leanings usually tries to define his authentic self against society, daily life, and political institutions. *Homo Faber* takes an important step beyond tradition: for the first time Frisch is not worrying about Switzerland, and we move swiftly through an expansive and cosmopolitan world (the Mexican chapters belong to the most brilliant pages of recent German writing). Walter Faber's difficulty is that he has defined his self-image in exclusively technological terms; separating himself from the fullness of being, he inevitably challenges the forces which he ignores to take their ironic revenge (his constant craving to use his electric razor to combat the blind forces of growth is as symptomatic of him as his mechanical way of filming sunsets). Fifty-year-old Faber pays a high price for his blindness to life. On shipboard he encounters Sabeth, a young girl with a blond pony tail; he half ignores, half suppresses, circumstantial evidence suggesting that she may be his own daughter, travels with her in France and Italy, becomes her lover, and, after a night on the shores of the Greek sea, carries Sabeth, who has been bitten by a viper, to an Athens hospital where she dies of an undiagnosed hemorrhage. Faber once more restlessly crosses the ocean and, while spending four days in pre-Castro Havana, finally comes to realize that to be human means to be involved in bliss and guilt, beauty and terror; and with a fervor reminiscent of Thomas Mann's Aschenbach in *Death in Venice*, admires handsome shoeshine boys, the strong white teeth of dark-skinned prostitutes, and the radiance of the sun on ancient stones. These are the days of his final euphoria, for his stomach pains return, and, preparing for an operation, he senses that he is not going to live; the engineer who has been in love with geometrical turbines approaches the cancerous threshold of death wishing for a single moment of life and light in which time and eternity would be one. Frisch's novel (or rather Faber's report) has many outstanding literary virtues: the consistency of the personal viewpoint, implying the self-defense of a narrow managerial mind with whom fate is catching up; an impressive net of proleptic motifs (including Mexican vultures and Faber's moribund professor, reminiscent of the beggar in

Flaubert's *Madame Bovary*); and, finally, Frisch's skillful handling of Faber's last transformation, reflected in his vocabulary's slowly acquiring sensibility and verve. But I doubt that Frisch has handled the antithesis between the rational Faber and those still in touch with the depths (whether nature, art, history, or death) with sufficient narrative tact and wealth of nuance: he pushes the tension too often into a merciless opposition between the technological and the humanist "cultures"; Faber's counterfigures (the young artist in the jungle and Sabeth's mother Hanna, who, as an archeologist, knows the hidden dimension of being) are apt to form an all too compact group; and sometimes there emerges an almost allegorical contrast between sterile rationality (engineers and managers) and existential wisdom of death and life (artists and archeologists). At its best, *Homo Faber* brilliantly shows a limited mind suddenly confronted with infinite life; but at its worst, Frisch sets "fate" and "feeling" against the lucid intellect.

I confess that I am among those who are dissatisfied with Frisch's *The Firebugs* and *Andorra,* which once again offer public statements, in contrast to the intensely private search of the immediately preceding novels and plays of the early and middle 'fifties; in *The Firebugs* Frisch relies on a style not entirely his own, and *Andorra* comes close to obscuring rather than analyzing the aberration of anti-Semitism. *The Firebugs* presents a tightly constructed parable of terror unresisted: Biedermann, a bourgeois Regularguy, does not oppose the firebugs who cunningly and blatantly force their way into his house. In his cowardice and foolishness, Biedermann actually helps two firebugs set up gasoline barrels in his garret; the third member of the group seems less dangerous, because he likes fires for strictly ideological reasons and opposes those who burn out of pure lust. Biedermann, believing that it is best to make friends with the terrorists, offers them roast goose and good drinks, but they proceed according to plan, and after he has given them his matches as a special sign of confidence, his house and the surrounding quarters go up in flames. In a postlude written for German performances, the firebugs are revealed as devils who shut down hell because Heaven has granted too many pardons to real sinners, and Biedermann and his wife praise the fires because the destroyed cities are rebuilt in glass and steel.

Like Brecht in *The Resistible Rise of Arturo Ui,* Max Frisch argues against the resistible triumph of the firebugs but concerns himself with the perverseness of interpreting history as fate and the moral deficiencies of those who want to resist. It is the Chorus of the Fire Brigade which (contrary to theatrical tradition) constantly debunks the idea of fate in human history as pernicious nonsense and reminds us that rational man should be able to analyze a political situation critically in order to act decisively. The chorus knows the difficulties of obtaining the facts in an age when the mass media are constantly regurgitating precast messages, but it continues to exhort Biedermann to shed all the irrational fears that result in blindness and to resist the temptation to call everything that happens "fate." Interpreters of the play often forget that Max Frisch gives a moral, perhaps existential, dimension to Biedermann's failures: precisely at the moment when he has rallied his courage against the firebugs, his own resolution is sabotaged by the results of his moral failure and his own lack of humanity. This is the function of the Knechtling motif: Biedermann's poor employee Knechtling (father of three children) has invented a hair tonic, but his boss Biedermann wants all the profits for himself and dismisses the man from his job; hapless Knechtling thereupon commits suicide in his kitchen. Just as Biedermann wants to expel the firebugs from his house, the news of Knechtling's death arrives, a policeman asks unforeseen questions about Biedermann's former employee, and Biedermann (in a crucial moment) tells the authorities that the barrels under his roof contain hair tonic rather than some other highly flammable stuff. Those who want to resist the totalitarian firebugs, Max Frisch suggests, should solve their own problems of human and political behavior; if they fail to do so, their ability to resist will be marred if not totally broken by their bad consciences and the skeletons in their closets. Biedermann's piercing cry of despair, "Do you expect me to be scared every single minute?" reveals the complexity of this emblematic situation which can never be fully exhausted by one-dimensional interpretations.

Frisch's "didactic play without a doctrine" has been historically related to President Beneš's failure to resist the Czechoslovak Communists (a reading supported by a note in Frisch's *Diary*) or the unwillingness of the German middle classes to resist the Nazis (interpretations not mutually exclusive), but I am troubled by the way in which Frisch suddenly tries to write like Dürrenmatt, Brecht, or the contributors to the famous Zurich cabaret *Cornichon*. Moving into the political sphere a step beyond his private world, Frisch uses an alien style as his crutch; he sounds an extremely effective warning to resist political terror, but the warning is uttered in an antiseptic lend-and-lease style, indicative to my mind of a moment of ebbing creative force.

Andorra is meant to discuss anti-Semitism but, returning to Frisch's personal problem of spontaneous self and imposed image, does not really face up to questions of power and history. In Andorra, a little country bordering on a hostile *Reich*, a fierce schoolteacher has a son by a *señora* from the other side of the border; to keep his secret, he tells the community that he has rescued the little Jewish boy Andri from persecutions in the other country. The Andorrans at first like their little "Jew" because they want to show that they differ from the people in the other country, but as Andri grows up and the enemies threaten to invade Andorra, the people of the community start to speak disparagingly of his being different. Proud Andri responds by assuming exactly the character which the community assigns him; he has had his moments of happiness, but when pushed into the job of a salesman by his boss (who says that Jews like money), he chooses to incarnate what people call Jewish character traits, gestures, and gait, and interprets his fate as that of the scapegoat. In vain Andri's father tries to tell his son that he is not Jewish at all, but Andri does not want to listen any more; and when the enemies invade Andorra and the community submits without a shot being fired, Andri is taken away, and his father (perhaps the real tragic figure of the play) hangs himself. Critics have been rightly irritated by the many incompatibilities that counteract the intent of the play, and I do not mean that most basic incompatibility of mobilizing mere words, props, and stage lights to evoke the mass murder of six million people. I doubt the dramatic analogy: in Andorra, a young masochist obsessed with the idea of being a Jew is taken away, but in the concentration camps millions of real Jews were killed; in history, being Jewish is not a matter of mere projected images but of shared vicissitudes and religious substance. The truth is that Frisch has tried to raise his private question of self and image (which he discusses in *I'm Not Stiller, Don Juan,* and elsewhere) to public relevance, but has inevitably failed to "psychologize" historical events. His pro-Jewish play without a real Jew provided, as Robert Brustein suggests, "wet whips for a Germany repellingly eager to flagellate itself."

Frisch's own idea of his art comes close to asserting "private" priorities in their public functions. He admits that he writes out of personal necessity, not because of social demands; in the act of writing, the will to endure the world coincides with the desire for communication and the thirst for other people. It is not, primarily, a matter of message and instruction; Frisch makes fun of those audiences which, in the hallowed German tradition, expect the poet to be a pseudo priest, marriage counselor, or youth leader, and he dislikes critics who cannot tolerate a man who writes plays simply because he happens to enjoy writing plays. But the priority of the private concern does not imply lack of social function: public responsibility "catches up" with the writer, "slips into" his work, forces itself upon him. Frisch's key term characterizing the writer's public function is *zersetzen* ("dis-integrate"); this term, often employed by the Nazis against the intellectuals, is made a badge of honor. Being absolutely and unconditionally loyal to what is alive and therefore filled with contradictions, the writer hopes to dis-integrate the abstract and monolithic conflicts dominating the world; and, speaking of the writer's "combative resignation," Frisch believes that his precise and loyal concern with the individual as it really is will provide an answer to the prefabricated arguments of power. But in devoting himself to the restless individual, Frisch has often been inclined to explore the claustrophobias of the infinitely sensitive ego caught in a world of restrictions. To *be* means to be imprisoned, and the prison walls may take on many colors and shapes; there are castle walls, snowdrifts, melancholy fogs, or merciless rows of filing cabinets, and, perhaps more fatal, the lifeless images which people construct for each other, and, the most deadly prison of all, haughty time itself. In a basic stratum of Frisch's works people believe that in a life beyond the walls there is more happiness; and they are incessantly pursuing their quest for distant islands of blue and white, rich in fruits and abundant in light (Hawaii, Öderland's Santorin, Pelegrin's and Faber's Cuba); on a higher level of consciousness, Don Juan and Stiller come to recognize that it is more dangerous to be imprisoned by images made by others, and to suffocate within the walls erected in the minds of man. But the essence of the "geographical" or "psychological" prison is time, which the living cannot escape; and with the true stubbornness of tortured souls they all search, on the blue islands and beyond the ossified images, to experience the unspeakable bliss of a unique and paradoxical "moment of eternity," beyond time and repetition. Romantically obsessed with searing intensity of experience, and eager to escape repetitive life and the nightmares of cyclical history suggested in *Santa Cruz*, *The Chinese Wall*, and *Count Öderland*, they are dilettante mystics in a universe without God, seeking final redemption from time in a burning moment of piercing, if only aesthetic, delight.

I suspect the literary distinction of Frisch's later novel *Mein Name sei Gantenbein*, 1964 / *Let My Name Be Gantenbein* closely relates to his continued fight against burdensome determination by space and time. In *I'm Not Stiller*, the protagonist (who could not deny a close family resemblance to Frisch himself) was still inextricably involved in the net of images projected by society and political institutions, but in *Gantenbein* the narrator's imagination easily and weightlessly soars above the pressures of the spatial and temporal order and, like Fichte's philosophical Ego that posits the world, programmatically breaks the oppressive links of "story," "character," and "experience" constituting the traditional novel. Inventing his own kind of *nouveau roman* in analogy to those recent films in which the restlessly shifting camera creates and explores meaning, the narrator seeks to confirm his idea that every "I" invents his own "role," builds himself a number of identities, tries them on for size, and discards them at will: whether he sketches, for himself, the role of Gantenbein, a man who pretends to be blind in order to see how people really are (and marries the inconstant actress Lila, who may as well be a *contessa* as a housewife); or chooses to be, for a moment, the intellectual Enderlin who does not want to go to Harvard because he believes that he has only one year to live, or the bearish architect Svoboda, his "roles" are far from final and are constantly reformulated, corrected, or modified by first-rate subsidiary stories, which Gantenbein, or somebody else, tells to an inquisitive call girl or the barman. Hardly anything happens, but definite patterns of experience emerge; and hiding as well as revealing his anxiety about old age and bitter jealousy, the narrator artfully triumphs over inert mass, suffocating space, and the fetters of temporal sequence. In remarkable contrast to Robbe-Grillet and, sometimes, Uwe Johnson, Frisch's "new novel" successfully shows that courageous narrative experiment need not lack irony, sympathy, and compassion with the human lot.

As an artist, Frisch has never looked for the easy way out; he has paid for every success with a near failure. He began, a generation ago, as a traditionalist who was impressed by Strindberg and, in his prose, by his compatriots Gottfried Keller and Albin Zollinger, but contrary to other German writers, he moved steadily on to exciting and occasionally futile experiments; there are at least a hundred years of literary history between his early prose and *Gantenbein*. As a craftsman of the stage, Frisch has learned from Thornton Wilder, Brecht, Büchner, and, in less happy moments, from Dürrenmatt; and although he is often considered a disciple of Brecht, he derived most of his "epic" techniques from Wilder's plays before he came to study, meet, and admire Brecht. In spite of his strong feeling for public concerns, Frisch is a writer of the private sensibility; if his private problem and the public issue coincide, he succeeds in writing a first-rate play, as *The Chinese Wall*; if not, more dubious products result. Of his plays, *The Chinese Wall* (because of its productive tension of sophisticated theatricality and abysmal skepticism) and *Don Juan, or The Love of Geometry*, the most lucid of recent German comedies, belong among his most distinguished achievements; and as a novelist, Frisch has steadily advanced from *I'm Not Stiller*, deeply related to the nineteenth-century tradition, to *Gantenbein,* which skillfully fuses structural experimentation with human sympathy. Perhaps it is Frisch's deepest secret that he is basically a lyric poet whose songs of the self are, in our age of prose and commitment, cunningly hidden behind the mask of his novels and plays.

3. Peter Weiss

PETER WEISS's plays are the objective correlatives of an intense internal drama in which the artist clashes with the revolutionary, intent upon changing an unbearable world; and his "documentaries" are exercises in the self-effacement of a deeply troubled sensibility. To Weiss (b. 1916) isolation came slowly, inevitably, and mercilessly: while the Nazis marched in the Berlin streets, the boy was told that his father was Jewish, and the subsequent years of exile in London, Prague, and Stockholm were a period of more than geographical separation from his happier past. Obsessed with adolescent thirst for romantic self-expression, he painted, wrote poetic prose (for some time in Swedish) and withdrew from a world in which the allied armies were fighting the Germans and the fires burned in the concentration camps. Analyzing and judging his experiences in piercingly sincere autobiographical narratives, Peter Weiss hesitatingly returned to his native tongue and pondered whether or not he was guilty of inhumanity because he had indulged in the vagaries of the private self while others suffered and died. In *Marat/Sade* [1964] / 1965,* the conflicting voices of the introvert and the activist failed to answer the fundamental question, but in the mid-'sixties Weiss formulated a firmer response to the challenge of his past. In his "Ten Working Points of a Writer in a Divided World," first published on September 1, 1965, in a Swedish newspaper (and later translated into many languages), Weiss committed himself to the Leninist forces of historical change, above all those exemplified by events in the "Third World," combined his in-

* *Die Verfolgung und Ermordung Jean Paul Marats, dargestellt durch die Schauspielertruppe des Hospizes zu Charenton unter Anleitung des Herrn de Sade / The Persecution and Assassination of Jean Paul Marat as Performed by the Inmates of the Asylum of Charenton under the Direction of the Marquis de Sade.*

vestigation of the Auschwitz concentration camps with a simplified interpretation of fascism and, in the late 'sixties, developed
his own kind of documentary theater in the tradition of *Agitprop*
and early Piscator; in his revolutionary masques *Gesang vom
lusitanischen Popanz* [1967] / *Song of the Lusitanian Bogey*, 1968, and
in his *Viet Nam Diskurs* [1968], monolithic political arguments,
more likely to strengthen the believer than to convince the skep-
tic, are charged with the theatrical force of chorus recitations,
group movements, and ingenious pantomime.

In his autobiographical reports *Abschied von den Eltern*, 1961 /
[Taking Leave of My Parents] *The Leavetaking*, 1962, and *Flucht-
punkt*, 1962 / *Vanishing Point*, 1968, Peter Weiss returned to the
villas and gardens of a pampered childhood, to the loneliness
of a boy who had lost his sister in a car accident, and to the
recurrent but fruitless attempts of the exile to find friends, be
loyal to many women, and create expressive works of art. In the
prehistory of Weiss's conversion to social commitment, the basic
metaphor is one of closed, narrow, suffocating space, with voices
from the outside calling to distant fulfillments; and when the
walls of the family are destroyed by time and death, the young
man finds himself in the deeper prison of tense introversion,
protracted years of psychological impotency, and obsessive concern for his paintings, which he considers a private answer to
brutal history. There is a rare moment of bliss in Hermann
Hesse's Swiss landscape of mountains and love, but exile in
Sweden (a frigid country of ossified middle-class conventions)
pushes the groping artist further into his "monologue in the
void." His radical friend Hoder (i.e., the well-known socialist
physician Max Hodann) speaks of the necessary dedication to
changing the old world, but, reading Kafka, the young painter
responds by discussing the vicissitudes of experimental art in
the Soviet Union; and after his friend's death, he vainly tries to
escape, in true romantic fashion, into the mindless life of inarticulate lumbermen in the vast Swedish forests. Yet transformation
comes slowly and in many thrusts: he discovers Henry Miller's
Tropic of Cancer, breaks with Franz Kafka's world of threatening
authorities, and, watching the first movies showing the corpses
in German concentration camps, confronts the hell in which

many of his friends had perished. In a first act of decisive liberation he leaves Stockholm for Paris and, in an extreme moment of "absolute freedom," suddenly discovers in the streets of the city that he is ready to face realities other than those created by his own imagination and "to participate in an exchange of ideas" far beyond his private self.

In the chronicle of his exile Peter Weiss says that many critics characterized his early paintings as imitative, and I would add that his early German plays (published 1968 in the two-volume collection of his theatrical writings) are those of an epigone, trying in his isolation to combine what has been developed in many arts by others. There is a good deal of Strindberg, whom Peter Weiss has translated, and Franz Kafka; and in later plays a strong fascination with surrealist shock techniques as developed in Alfred Jarry's *Ubu Roi* and filtered through the movies of Buñuel and Vigo. *Der Turm* [1949] / *The Tower*, 1967, a poetic parable in the mode of Strindberg's *Dream Play*, shows the life and death of the circus artist Pablo (a distant cousin of Kafka's Hunger Artist), who excels in breaking fetters and chains. Compulsively returning to the mystical tower from which he once escaped in body rather than in soul, Pablo insists that he anticipates freedom while chained, again wants to demonstrate his skills, and (symbolically acting out the playwright's obsession with the burdens of his past) strangles himself while disentangling the ropes; escape from bondage is one with death. *Die Versicherung* (written 1952 [1966]) / *The Insurance*, an entertaining collage of nineteen chaotic scenes alive with screams, color, and crudeness, explores the theatrical heritage of the surrealists and prefigures German concern with the "theater of the absurd" by almost ten years: at a bourgeois party reminiscent of George Grosz or Elias Canetti, guests and dogs devour a fat goose; the chief of police (whose bedroom wall has been damaged by a bomb) wants to buy complete insurance against all possible pitfalls of history; occasional lovers make out behind coal stacks; the revolution comes like a spring shower; and in the end, rotating parasols and buzzing sewing machines triumph in dadaistic vitality. But Peter Weiss has never been entirely happy with artful exuberance; his *Nacht mit Gästen* [1963] / *Night with Guests* resolutely checks surrealist surfeit by returning to the techniques of a somber puppet play sustained by a story of robbery, rape, and murder, told in doggerel verse of intentional coarseness; and employing a highly impressive chorus of children who, totally unmoved by gore and violence, delight in choral rhythms of "ene mene eia weia / ache wacke weck." Driven by his early distrust of resplendent art, Peter Weiss opts (as does Thomas Mann's Adrian Leverkühn) for the archaic, but I wonder whether he realizes how closely allied the archaic is to the barbarian.

In his *Marat/Sade* Weiss has reached an essential turning point as playwright and critic of society; while observing the rehearsals of the play on the stage of the Rostock Theater (German Democratic Republic), he moved closer to identifying himself with the radical figures of his imagination. *Marat/Sade* basically consists of a play within a play: it is aging and obese De Sade who produces his own script about Charlotte Corday's murder of Jean Paul Marat, for the edification of both patients and authorities at the Charenton insane asylum; and in a complex time pattern involving the day of the actual murder (July 13, 1793), the moment of the commemorative performance (July 13, 1808), and the hour of the present-day theatrical experience, history itself emerges as counterforce to mere theatrical concerns. De Sade, who has been committed to Charenton for political reasons, does not have an easy task: discussing life, death, and revolution, he steps into his own play in order to answer Jean Paul Marat (played by a paranoiac) while, as producer, he must continually defend his text to Monsieur Coulmier, the director of the institution, who is disinclined to tolerate radical formulations because they unmask the discrepancies between the revolutionary rhetoric and the bourgeois practices of the triumphant liberal regime which he represents. In Weiss's revised text (1965) De Sade mockingly laughs at his inability to discipline the fury of the patients whom he has paradoxically provoked by his therapeutic play: stamping and shouting "Revolution Revolution / Copulation Copulation" they rush forward, are beaten by the nurses at Coulmier's command, and only the falling curtain of the real, not the fictive, theater rescues the modern audiences from raging chaos. We, the new accomplices of Coulmier, are to be attacked by the final thrust as well.

In the discussions of the marquis and the tribune of the people Peter Weiss touches upon fundamental concerns of the modern intellect. The antagonists rarely speak to each other, but they do articulate two cohesive views of humanity: De Sade sustained by romantic self-pity, "existentialist" solipsism, and a circular view of history; Marat incarnating the abstract rhetoric of the revolution, a scientific view of mankind, and an unhesitating belief in productive action. De Sade rages against the indifference of a nature that does not impart sense or meaning, blindly killing in bleak monotony (an "individual" death is therefore a great achievement); Marat believes that it is De Sade's personal apathy which prevents him from intervening to halt the social evil of the world. But De Sade rejects the idea of man's acting beyond himself: since man is largely unknown to himself, he should concentrate on exploring his own ego and consider the impersonal issues of the moment (be they patriotism, nationalism, or the turmoil of the masses) inconsequential specters; Marat asserts that it is imperative to live by acting in the historical moment and that the particular moment demands that the revolution be defended against the middle class, which lives by exploiting the fourth estate; a second stage of the revolution is necessary. The marquis does not see any meaning in the first or second stage of any historical development: to him history is but a blind alley and a frustrating "again and again": the real prison to be shattered is that of the introspective self, and wherever these invisible prison walls are not destroyed by copulating flesh, revolutions are mere prison mutinies easily betrayed by corrupt fellow prisoners. Alternating monologues formulate De Sade's narcissism and Marat's commitment; the question is whether these alternatives do not in fact anticipate the views of the radical socialist Jacques Roux, who, a premature Leninist, interprets the revolution strictly in economic terms, demands concrete measures for distributing the means of production, and insists, in an idiom devoid of enlightened rhetoric, on well-aimed and violent action *now*. But for all its increased relevance, Peter Weiss's *Marat/Sade* suffers from considerable handicaps and demands an ingenious and vital director who is willing (in Artaud's tradition of "total theater") to enhance the theatrical potentialities of a play in which lively pantomime must replace dramatic movement, and scenic confrontations almost hide the absence of a truly forceful and precise language. There is not a single memorable line in the entire score of this spectacle, brilliantly sustained by the most "culinary" riches of the modern stage.

In the early summer of 1964 Peter Weiss attended the Frankfurt trial of the administrators and guards of the Auschwitz concentration camp and, drawing on actual source materials, transcribed what he heard in his *Die Ermittlung* [1965] / *The Investigation*, 1966. Unspeakable suffering and mindless henchmen are once more confronted, and the dramatic event, freed of theatrical dross, turns into a fierce and sober ritual that keeps alive the memory of those murdered in camps, ditches, cellars, and prisons. Rather than produce facts, the playwright compresses the monstrous realities of the courtroom with unobtrusive energy: he successfully transforms the legal procedures into a dirge, in which the killers judge themselves. The eighteen accused retain their individualities (because they retained their names in the camp), while the nine witnesses, or former "unpersons," are assigned mere numbers and articulate what hundreds of others actually said before the judges. Weiss asserts that he is simply offering a "concentrate" of the court proceedings, but he actually does much more: he has changed the prose statements of the court session, as preserved in the stenographic record, into a consistent free-verse line of three or four beats that seems to shun equally everyday idiom and heroic five-beat blank verse, and he conducts his investigation in an effectively structured way, first leading his listeners into the camp (Cantos 1-2), then exploring the daily hell of the prisoners (3-4), symbolically confronting one of the victims with one of the killers (5-6) and, in the second part, building up a terrible sequence of annihilations: death by shooting at the black wall (7), death by injected poison (8), death by hunger (9), death in the gas chambers (10), and death in the fiery ovens (11); if this is theater, it is one of "total drainage of emotion" (Adolf Klarmann) rather than of alienation or empathy. In his thoughtful and highly personal essay *Gespräch über Dante* [1965] / *Discussion about Dante* Weiss reveals the fundamental source of his formal intents: the thirty-three parts of his investigation relate to the structure of Dante's *Inferno,* and the mystical number itself emerges as a sign of involvement and despair. Dante created his universe thinking of Beatrice, and his late heir thinks of the fate of a Jewish girl whom he might have saved from the camps by acting more resolutely on her behalf. His structure of thirty-three parts, giving form to the most infernal matter in human history, implies his cry for forgiveness, and the most impersonal cipher (as so often in his work) hides his most personal plea.

But Peter Weiss pushes his artistically sharpened investigation beyond reestablishing the facts and in his own way suggests a definite interpretation of the concentration camp system. He places the statements of Witness 3 in such a structural context that they inevitably dominate. Witness 3 has more of a personal past than the others, and describes himself as a physician who was politically active long before being sent to the camps; precisely because he had been concerned with political theory he was able to see the continuities linking the camp "society" with the society outside the barbed-wire fences. What he discovered was a world ontologically no different from that outside: the attitudes within the camp were potentially present in the competitive society outside and only more fully "realized" in the death mills; many captives (he is evidently thinking of the German Jews) once shared national and acquisitive aspirations with those who later became guards: their functions are, within the acquisitive system, interchangeable. Peter Weiss takes great care to let these analyses go practically unopposed: Witness 5, who suggests a kind of "existentialist" interpretation of the camps by saying that they radically differed from society outside, unwittingly supports Witness 3 when she describes the "radically different" laws as those of theft, brutality, and expropriation. The only people who directly oppose Witness 3 are the murderers themselves or their defense attorney. Yet I cannot entirely agree with Witness 3, for my mother, who died in a camp, was not a potential Nazi guard; and while I am certain that Witness 3 rightly stresses the later collaboration of important German industries with the camp administrations (established beyond doubt by the Nuremberg Tribunal), I suspect that he is totally unaware of concerted economic efforts by the SS which resulted after 1939 in its establishing an economic empire of its own; planning to monopolize power, the SS tried to build a production system that would undermine private industry—called "liberal" by the SS newspaper hacks—and the competing strength of Hitler's party organization. In economic practice and intent (though often counteracted by other orders), the policies of the SS *Reichswirtschaftshauptamt* in the later years of the war closely resembled the operations of the Stalinist Secret Police Ministry, which staffed vast construction and goldmining industries with slaves guilty of being Polish or Estonian. Old-fashioned concepts of capitalist exploitation certainly do not suffice to explain the origin of the German or any other camp system, nor the shabby sadism of the guards; and by asserting that the prisoners were but potential guards, Witness 3 takes the invisible dignity of dying away from the dead.

Peter Weiss's development as a playwright has been difficult because he took his time freeing himself from Hermann Hesse, Strindberg, and Kafka, protractedly dispersed his talents in the graphic arts, movie-making, and lyric prose, and hesitated long in deciding whether to write in Swedish or German. He arrived late, but brought to the stage his sweeping views of history and great technical ingenuity; and although his language is flat (and for that reason admirably effective in *The Investigation*), he often compensates for his lack of a personal idiom by displaying a forceful scenic imagination that challenges the most intelligent directors of our time. Repelled and attracted by images of sickness, flagellation, torture, and death, and darkly obsessed by his awareness of his own past failure to combat inhumanity, Weiss has tried harder than any of his contemporaries to fight the introspective middle-class *bohémien* in himself by concentrating his energies on social aims independent of his vulnerable sensibility. Moving tensely between absolutes, he has chosen total commitment rather than total self-concern. In his Charenton play De Sade compares Marat in his bathtub to an embryo swimming in the amniotic fluids that protect it from the confusing world outside, and regrets that the people's tribune, transfixed in rigid thought, can no longer be affected by unpredictable reality. To both lonely Marat and self-tortured Peter Weiss, revolutionary ideology had become another protective womb.

4. Peter Hacks

PETER HACKS (b. 1928), Brecht's most sophisticated disciple, was educated in West Germany, but after his first success as a playwright he decided to move to the German Democratic Republic, at a time when the first, fragile "thaw" (1955/56) had raised hopes that literary experimentation might again be possible. Like Brecht, Hacks was born into an upper-middle-class family and studied the theory and history of drama with Artur Kutscher of Munich (1878–1966), who had been one of Brecht's reluctant teachers forty years previously; unlike Brecht, however, Hacks completed his graduate studies and received a Ph.D. for his dissertation on Biedermeier theater (1951). The erudite Hacks does not have the poetic fury that surges from his master's early plays; and although he theoretically sympathizes with Brecht's sensuous Baal, his dry and brittle talent strikes me as the Alexandrian kind, more readily provoked by printer's ink than by living flesh. Enjoying his role as Ulbricht's theatrical gadfly, Hacks likes to challenge the petit bourgeois tastes of the ruling Stalinist functionaries by his irritating lack of respect for anything or anybody, his calculated display of sensuality, and his theoretical (if occasionally snobbish) intelligence. His better plays usually cause prolonged discussions that never fail to touch upon questions of intellectual and political relevance.

Hacks began with imitation, parody, and adaptation. His *Eröffnung des indischen Zeitalters / Onset of the Indian Age*, first performed in Munich in 1955, tells the story of Columbus, following the lines of Brecht's *Galileo:* Columbus, as fascinated as Galileo by new scientific discoveries, and with the liberating call of the open seas, introduces, by tirelessly asking questions and doubting established concepts, the popular "Indian Age" in which reason and the underprivileged are to be close allies. Other early plays are exercises in debunking romantic ideas of the German past by showing how small people make their own decisions, or skillful adaptations of theatrical texts reaching from Aristophanes to the German *"Sturm und Drang"* writers; among the more successful ones I would certainly include Hacks's parody of the German medieval Duke Ernest chapbook (written 1953), in which Italian merchants plotting the Crusades are not sure whether they should dub the new venture the "Blessings-and-Brocade Corporation" or "Christ-Export"; an adaptation of John Gay's sequel to the *Beggar's Opera,* in which Polly Peachum marries a noble savage of the American West; and the clever reworking of Offenbach's operetta *La Belle Hélène.* In Hacks's version, Venus, a rather disreputable but revolutionary goddess who makes slaves into free men, increasingly irritates Jupiter, who is unwilling to change his conservative administration of human affairs.

In the early 'sixties, Peter Hacks's political play *Die Sorgen und die Macht* [1960] / *Of Problems and of Power,* which dutifully explores the industrial relations of two neighboring factories, challenged the functionaries, who, once again busy disciplining the restive intellectuals, immediately fired those involved in staging the play and brought up its implications at a stern party conference. The functionaries did not have to find fault with Hacks's condescending criticism of the Hungarian revolution, but they were enraged by his image of man, as well as by his application of Brechtian alienation techniques to a presentation of contemporary economic problems. Hacks suggested a world without a positive hero: his glassworkers and girls are people, "turbulent, fleshy, sensual, eating, drinking, and breeding" (Walt Whitman), but minus and minus equals plus, the playwright implies; the many egotisms effectively counteract each other and contribute beneficially toward the final aims of socialist society. Party critics suddenly discovered that Peter Hacks was of bourgeois origin and had therefore dangerously underrated the role of the party in leading the toiling masses; more revealingly, they asserted that *Of Problems and of Power* was a "cold" play because of its use of alienation effects which endangered the audience's potential commitment to and emotional identification with the cause of progress. Brechtian alienation was obviously useful enough for unveiling the internal contradictions of distant Chicago or of Hitler's *Reich*, but as soon as matters of immediate economic interest and the Communist state are touched upon, a coolly reasoning audience may be of some disadvantage to the regime, and the writer does better to return to "culinary" plays, old-fashioned illusion, and traditional empathy.

But Peter Hacks is as clever as he is stubborn and, while beating the functionaries with their own theoretical stick of "realism," continues to set his theatrical aims very high. His blank-verse comedy *Moritz Tassow* [1965], his best play so far, possibly borrows its material cue from Erwin Strittmatter's (b. 1912) novel, *Ole Bienkopp*, 1963, which created a considerable stir when it appeared. Strittmatter's "Ol' Bee-Head," an inarticulate, Baal-like fellow in alliance with all forces of nature including the procreative one, establishes a peasant commune on his own, against the directives of the party, only to be vindicated later when the party decides to reintegrate the small holdings—created by breaking up the large estates—into more efficient units; the former "deviationist," persecuted by the Stalinist political machinery, turns out to be a prophet, for he has instinctively seen the true light of developing socialism. While Strittmatter (who on Brecht's suggestion used blank verse for a political comedy [1954] on agricultural questions) insists on a neat contrast between Stalinist inflexibility and the new vitality of the regenerated post-Stalinist organization, Peter Hacks explores the conflict in a more dialectical fashion, and by cunningly changing the character of the protagonist, he raises questions of more than agricultural relevance. Hacks's Moritz Tassow shares Ol' Bee-Head's sensuality, but he happens to be an intellectual; he spent the twelve years of the Nazi *Reich* in silence and meditation as a swineherd and, after the small village of Gargentin is liberated by the Soviet army, he comes forth as a liberator of the poor; he immediately dispossesses the lord of the castle and, proclaiming the instant and total revolution of mankind, takes over the large estate, with the help of a few village paupers and a tramp. Inevitably, he clashes with the party administrator Mattukat, whose task it is to divide the estate according to the current party directive into small individual holdings, although he himself feels

that at some point in the future big, integrated "communes"
might be more efficient. Hacks avoids all melodramatic contrast:
Mattukat, a sober and somewhat pedestrian man who has been
in a concentration camp, sincerely believes that the new law of
land division expresses relevant revolutionary experience and
tries to act as the concrete situation requires; Tassow, who likes
to speak in grand poetic images, fastens on the ideal of an instant
and utopian transformation of humanity. Mattukat seeks reasons
for acting here and now, Tassow mockingly asks whether Lenin
made the revolution according to laws, and deplores the "daily
changing eternal truths" which the functionary follows in his
administrative actions. Mattukat has his temporary victory, for
the instant commune, in spite of Tassow's fine speeches, does
not work, and the land is subsequently divided among the more
expert farmhands. Moritz Tassow, though beaten in the agricultural field, decides to become a writer and to continue to challenge the functionaries by his irresponsibility, his noble speeches,
his many carnal desires, and his ideas, far more imposing than
daily tactical adjustments. Mattukat and Tassow will continue
to clash, for action and intellect are not identical; the functionaries, Hacks implies, would be lost in the thicket of daily exigencies if the irritable poets did not go on searching for utopia
and spontaneity.

In his sprightly "Versuch über das Theaterstück von morgen,"
1960 / "Essay on the Theater of the Future" Peter Hacks reveals
some recent assumptions that partly diverge from his Brechtian
loyalties. Hacks speaks as condescendingly as did the young
Brecht about the "hills" (not summits) represented by Ibsen and
Hauptmann and mocks Hofmannsthal's "stupid Viennese.
melancholics," but these iconoclastic gestures cannot conceal his
desire for a new "proletarian classicism" including, surprisingly,
a revival of the old heroic blank verse, now throbbing with "the
rhythm of progressive nations." Proletarian classicism no longer
needs any "high" figures, for in socialism everybody (even a
swineherd or writer like Tassow) may be involved in problems
of more than private significance: thus, Hacks asserts, proletarian
classicism is the first classicism completely devoid of conservative
elements. But in spite of his provocative antitraditionalism, Hacks

cannot thrive without the heritage of the past; and even his Moritz Tassow (the final *w* is not pronounced in local idiom) would be far less alive if his author were not carried forward by his polemic against Goethe's poet *Torquato Tasso* (1790), who has his own struggle with that man of action, the diplomat Antonio. I am not sure whether Brecht would sympathize with Hacks's predications about the proletarian virtues of heroic blank verse, but he would certainly enjoy the cunning idea of building the foundation of a new theater upon a Hegelian *Aufhebung* of Goethe's finest play.

5. Rolf Hochhuth

I CAN CONCEIVE of the self-tortured intellectual Peter Weiss apart from his various writings, in which he tries to answer his private questions in increasingly impersonal terms, but I am unable to separate Rolf Hochhuth from his plays: he is completely one with the fiery rage, the restless drive, and the grand and noble simplicity of his old-fashioned drama that has recently changed the theater, publicly reminded us of our sins of silent complicity with evil, and challenged establishments old and new. Hochhuth was born in 1931 in the small Hessian town of Eschwege on the Werra River and shared, for some time, the daily experiences of his Protestant, upper-middle-class contemporaries. He early felt, as he said in a lucid interview with *Partisan Review,* "history as a fatality," holding sway over nearly helpless people. Hochhuth was educated in the prescribed *Gymnasium* after the war but decided against taking the traditional qualifying examinations for the university and worked instead in academic bookshops in Munich, Heidelberg, Marburg, and later in a publisher's office, meanwhile reading voraciously and trying his hand at autobiographical prose experiments and an abortive family saga in the epistolary mode. He is a largely self-taught man who, I believe, suspects his intellectual compatriots of coldness of heart; his wide-ranging if disordered reading combined conservative historians and observers of the German past, including Bismarck and Theodor Mommsen, with Thomas Mann, Robert Musil, George Bernard Shaw, Ernst Jünger, and Gottfried Benn, whose best poems he continues to place above Brecht's. It was Erwin Piscator, the grand old man of the political theater, who first produced a much-cut version of Hochhuth's *Der Stellvertreter / The Deputy* [1964] on February 20, 1963, in West Berlin. Reviews were mixed, but Hochhuth's charge against Pope Pius XII was vehemently discussed by Berlin students, Cardinal Montini responded on the part of the Vatican in an open letter, and subsequent productions in Basel and New York had to be protected by detachments of police in the streets; in Paris alone *The Deputy* was performed more often than in all (reluctant) West German theaters taken together. In his second play, *Soldaten / Soldiers* [1968], first performed on October 9, 1967, in West Berlin by Piscator's successor, Hochhuth continues to press his relentless search for unassailable truth: treating Churchill's alleged complicity in the death of the Polish premier Sikorski and in the fire-bombing of German cities in World War II, he asks fundamental questions about individual responsibility in any technological war and challenges the British authorities, the veterans of the German *Luftwaffe*, and, by implication, American bomber pilots in Vietnam as well. Discussion continues, and the modest playwright nearly vanishes behind the dust and fury of the universal and largely subliterary fray.

In his first play Hochhuth accuses Pope Pius XII of coldly ignoring his Christian duties and dramatically contrasts this deputy of Christ on earth who fails to speak up for the dying Jews with the young Jesuit Riccardo Fontana, who voluntarily takes the Pope's ordained place among the suffering and joins a transport of Roman Jews destined for the Auschwitz death camps. Hochhuth takes great care to build his play in a succession of conflicts gradually leading to Riccardo's confrontation with the Pope and his martyr's death. In Berlin (Act I) Riccardo Fontana meets the papal nuncio Cesare Orsenigo, who does not want to infringe on diplomatic conventions, and Kurt Gerstein, a member of the Protestant opposition working within the SS, who informs the Church authorities about the mass murders in the concentration camps. In his father's house in Rome (Act II) Riccardo clashes with the cardinal, who, representing the political circumspection of the Church authorities, refuses to listen to his young subordinate and quickly relegates him to a minor job in Lisbon. But Riccardo returns to Rome where (Act III) the Gestapo is rounding up the Jews. Together with his father, who has come to share Riccardo's sense of moral urgency, he presents to Pope Pius XII his demand for a politically effective protest addressed directly to Hitler. The Pope passionately discusses revenue problems, the power vacuum in Italy after the fall of Mussolini, the necessity of reestablishing a political balance in Europe, and then affectedly dictates a highly stylized document in elegant prose totally devoid of concrete support for people dying in the concentration camps (Act IV). Riccardo pins the yellow star of the Jews on his cassock, joins a transport and, in Auschwitz (Act V), defends his courageous and despairing stand against the satanic doctor who rules the death mills. He turns down his opportunity to leave the camp and is shot by an SS guard before he has a chance to kill the doctor.

Hochhuth's implacable rage and his restless verse precariously hold together a ragbag of theatrical styles, including elements of the old morality play, Schiller's (and Racine's) magnificent confrontations of noble antagonists, a good deal of naturalism (the Nazi functionaries in the tavern derive from Carl Zuckmayer's *The Devil's General*), Shaw's polemical stage directions, and a few stanzas of expressionist poetry (Act V, Scene 1). Willy Haas has suggested that Hochhuth has written a historical play with a theological core, but I suspect that the play is structured the other way around: in his first act and the last act, increasingly dominated by the devilish doctor (replete with ludicrous black-silk cape, quotations from Stendhal and Valéry, and a metaphysical hatred of life), the playwright constructs a metaphysical frame consisting of ontological issues of humanity and history, good and evil. In the center (Act II–Act IV) he creates a historical play which sometimes deteriorates into cheap melodrama and adolescent cops-and-robbers games. Hochhuth rightly argues against Paul Celan's all too beautiful concentration-camp poetry; yet Hochhuth's blonde Helga, against a backdrop of Auschwitz smoke, teasingly puts on panties adorned with SS runes. The trouble is that the diverging tendencies of the morality play and the historical drama coincide with Hochhuth's divergent moral and historical arguments, which tend to counteract rather than to enhance each other. His charge that for moral and religious reasons the Pope should have clearly and vehemently protested against the persecution of the European Jews has not been fully answered even by the most ardent admirers of Pius XII; but his historical argument that such a protest would have been politically effective and would have saved the lives of many people comes close to being a dubious predication in retrospect, for it assumes, among other things, that Hitler's *Reich* was a monolithic structure with unified and foreseeable responses. It was, on the contrary, a jungle of conflicting warlord interests.

The issues are troublesome; and I for one cannot agree with the belated moral absolutism of those who proclaim that the Pope should have protested *no matter what*, because I know that for those really involved the life of a single Jew was more important than an ineffective gesture of highly abstract import. We Gestapo prisoners of 1944 must have been a sadly irreligious lot; I can remember no one who asked questions about the Pope, but many who were impatient with the Allies for not bombing the Nazi communication installations. Hochhuth's Jacobson, who asks why the Allies do not destroy the railways leading to the concentration camps, articulates a pressing question which was then on the minds of many.

Walter Kaufmann, who admirably defends Hochhuth as a playwright, suggests that "he has tried to write a tragedy" with a "truly tragic" hero, and inevitably concentrates on showing that Riccardo Fontana, confronted with the satanic doctor and the burning corpses, "loses his faith" and implies, in his last words, that he dies a repentant sinner; we are to believe that the ardent young Jesuit abruptly fails in his faith. Yet it is difficult to demonstrate from the text that Riccardo is a hero who fails and that *The Deputy* is a true tragedy in the traditional sense of the word. Hochhuth tries hard to present Riccardo as a highly sensitive, irascible, and emotional human being (at one point Riccardo even suggests that the Pope be killed and the SS made responsible for his murder), but Riccardo does not yield to the doctor, who wants to break his faith; to Riccardo, the evidence of absolute evil confirms the necessary existence of God. After he has been working for ten days burning corpses at the doctor's demand, he does wearily raise his voice, like Job, against a God "who devours his young," but when offered a chance to escape decides to stay because he has become Christ's real deputy "who represents the Church" and asks that his father be told that he has found fulfillment in the death camps. In this context his last words ("Call me in the hour of my death") do not imply the repentance of a sinner but the resilient humility of a Christian whose beliefs have undergone the most cruel of tests. We are in the presence of a constant martyr who wants to save the honor of the Church (as he himself says) and gives us little reason to believe that he is a failure or, as other critics assume, that Hochhuth has written a straightforwardly anticlerical play.

In *Soldiers* Hochhuth takes up a question which emerged briefly in his first play. He examines that other unforgivable act of inhumanity in our time—the fire-bombing of enemy cities which resulted in the murder of burning and suffocating noncombatants in exploding cellars, melting streets, and tumbling houses. Many critics believe that Hochhuth has weakened the scenic impact of his argument against bomber pilots turned criminals by combining his views about the devastation of the residential areas of Coventry, Hamburg, and Dresden with a theatrical investigation of the case of Polish Premier Sikorski, killed under mysterious circumstances in an airplane accident near Gibraltar on July 5, 1943. The issues are matters either of historical record or, in the case of Sikorski, mere suspicion, but Hochhuth's play takes a curious introspective turn because he uses a dramatist who, like Weiss's De Sade, presents his own play within the play. The theatrical producer and writer Peter Dorland, a former bomber pilot and wing commander of the Royal Air Force, is dying of cancer and, a modern Everyman, wants to explore his personal responsibility in an inhuman world; he hopes that this play, entitled *The Little London Theater of the World*, which he was commissioned to write for a festive convocation at Coventry celebrating the centenary of the Red Cross convention, "will foster the idea, both within his own generation—his enemies, his fellow pilots from World War II—and his son's generation, that the convention concerning aerial warfare drafted by the Red Cross for the protection of the cities should be given the status of international law." In the *Prelude* (preceding the dress rehearsal of *The Little London Theater*) ideas and obsessions dominating Dorland's mind emerge in shifting visions of air-raid victims and devastations, speeches of a West German air force colonel who was decorated in the years between Guernica and Stalingrad, a dialogue with his son who serves with NATO, and the "dream partner," Air Marshal Harris, who happened to be responsible for the final order sending Dorland over the city of Dresden. The three parts of the play itself (rehearsed against the ruins of Coventry Cathedral) center on the towering figure of Churchill, who finds himself caught in the dialectics of his struggle against Hitler, and exercises his power "on the level of his enemy": Dorland (and with him Hochhuth) insists on Churchill's fundamental implication in the fire-bombing of noncombatants and the prearranged death (murder) of Sikorski. It is Lord Cherwell (wearing a black silk coat like the Auschwitz doctor) who elaborates the plans for Operation Gomorrah, projected to eradicate the center of Hamburg and to transform the city into a maelstrom of fire. Churchill, against the advice of his soldierly chief of staff, approves the operation because he thinks of it as the next best substitute for the "second front" long demanded by an impatient Stalin. But the war alliance is endangered (Dorland/Hochhuth telescopes chronology) for other reasons, too: the Poles, led by Sikorski, distrust the Russians and want to extract a guarantee of their eastern borders by using the discovery of the Katyn graves of thousands of Poles massacred by the Russians. Sikorski presents his expectations to Churchill, who advises him to accept political realities; and when Stalin breaks with the Poles and Sikorski comes between the Allies, Lord Cherwell by indirection develops a plan for doing away with the Polish general. Churchill, eager to save the alliance, by silent gesture rather than explicit assent, agrees to Cherwell's idea; Sikorski is thereupon killed in his plane. In the final part of Dorland's play, Churchill, the man of power, has to confront the Bishop of Chichester, who accuses him of using the abominable methods of his enemies, and of changing soldiers into criminals who do not even see the people they kill. But in the *Epilogue* Peter Dorland (now once again the producer rather than the wing commander) refuses to pronounce final judgment on Churchill, who has won the war against Hitler. He has explored his past and done his share in redefining what constitutes "a criminal deed," but his case against Churchill is left in abeyance.

The German critic Siegfried Melchinger believes that Hochhuth's play suffers from the deficiencies of combining a "visionary" frame with a harshly "realistic" core, but I think that the twofold structure effectively expresses the restlessness of Peter Dorland's mind, slowly emerging from its obsessions and moving toward an intense, sharply contoured encounter with the man of power; Dorland's vision must differ, in degrees of reality, from Churchill's massive, public world. It is the essential virtue of the play that Churchill emerges as a firm, fleshy, powerful character (a first-rate part for a great actor with infinite resources). In contrast to the polemical simplification of the figure of Pope Pius XII, Hochhuth's Churchill radiates greatness, rage, vanity, courage, sadness, and resilience, and while preparing his case against the prime minister, Hochhuth, with growing insight into the pressures of a historical situation, offers an apology for the towering man who shoulders the most odious responsibilities in order to win the battle against the inhuman enemy who fired the first shot. Hochhuth, who *writes* history (of a kind), cannot escape utter fascination with the man who *makes* it; there is, of course, Lord Cherwell with his satanic claptrap again, but he pales beside the mythical figure of the prime minister, whom Hochhuth likens to Neptune or Atlas carrying the universe on his back. He clearly agrees with Heinrich Mann, who said that Churchill was "a hero out of Corneille wearing the mask of our time." Hochhuth's man of power grows into an almost tragic figure, who, accepting his agonizing responsibilities with open eyes, sadly realizes that history consists of disparities between plans and results and that he is leading his country to victory—and future decline. Churchill as "central personification of the war drive" confirms the dramatic unity of *The Little London Theater* because his decisions concerning the bombing and Sikorski's fate are related politically and dramatically: in order to strengthen and save the alliance, Churchill unleashes Operation Gomorrah and accepts Cherwell's

scheme to have Sikorski killed in a fake accident; and the death
of the Polish general visibly exemplifies (as does the apparition
of the woman burned to death in Dresden or, in *The Deputy's*
third act, the Jewish family) what abstract orders imply for the
individual. Hochhuth's historical play, which gravitates toward
clashes in high places and yet does not want to disregard the
victims down below, cannot do without the most precise picture
of individual suffering; inevitably, *veranschaulichen* ("to make
visible") is one of the recurrent key terms and basic techniques
in Hochhuth's theater, for he desperately wants us to see the
afflictions of a concrete human being.

Hochhuth's individualism relates closely to the existentialist
mood of the 1950s in Germany rather than to the collectivist
1960s; he has little in common with the youngest crop of intellectuals who draw on Hegel, Theodor W. Adorno, and Herbert
Marcuse, or with Peter Weiss, who has come to believe in the
historical forces emanating from economic and social change.
Hochhuth's view of history is far from monolithic: an almost
Manichaean vision of the world as a battlefield of good and evil
(incarnated in his many allegorical figures and in the metaphysical frames of his plays) enters into an uneasy union with his
belief in the great men who create and yet are the captives of
the historical process that kills millions of silent victims rarely
mentioned by the historians in more than one laconic sentence.
At the historical core of his plays, Hochhuth clings to his heroic
antagonists but, passionately concerned with the sufferings of the
many, finds himself as a playwright in the difficult position of
having to bring to the circumscribed stage vast concentration
camps or burning cities. He desperately attacks the technical
boundaries of the stage, courageously risks melodramatic or
amateurish solutions (as in Act V of *The Deputy*), and finally has
to content himself with the illustrative example of the suffering
individual (condemned by uncomprehending critics as lacking
a specific function) or with the traditional messenger who reports
what the age-old decorum of the theater does not tolerate. Perhaps his concern with the "visible" accurately expresses his
despair with the limitations of a stage still unfit to encompass

the millions of people dying, burning, suffocating, slaughtered.

Riccardo, Gerstein, Churchill, Dorland, and the Bishop of Chichester all agree that history is cruel: it is an "airstrip strewn with corpses," a heap of tears and destroyed loyalties, a horde of lemmings in search of death, or, in Riccardo's and Sikorski's recurrent image, "a meat-grinder" (*Fleischwolf*) that crushes living human flesh. Hochhuth shows his lingering existentialist outlook when he refuses to accept easy and superficial consolations such as those offered by philosophers like Hegel and instead resolutely asserts man's dignity against the black horizon of the historical process; he may be Camus's last German disciple. Strangely enough, both Riccardo and the doctor, inveterate enemies locked in their metaphysical struggle, unanimously (if for different reasons) reject Hegel's attempt to construe an intelligible sense to history: the doctor reads Hegel in Auschwitz (Hochhuth's bad guys always read too much) and mocks "the philosophers who squeeze / the horrors of world history / through countless convolutions of their brains, / until at last they look acceptable," and Riccardo, trying to counter his father's belief that there must be some higher meaning in human suffering, vehemently asks whether his father would have him "look down, supercilious and serene, / with the notorious glazed eyes / of the philosopher, / and dialectilize a meaning in this murdering"; in German he says *hineinhegeln*. A similar discussion in the other play: Churchill, who does not know Hegel, suggests that is was the cunning of reason or of history itself (in German, *der Weltgeist*) that prompted Hitler to drive all gifted physicists into exile, but Sikorski (sharing the playwright's views) does not want to accept these "barbaric accounts." There is no solace in a well-ordered but illusionary meaning, and Hochhuth's recurrent rejection of Hegel clearly reveals the question that obsesses him most deeply—whether or not all suffering, in Auschwitz, Dresden, and other man-made hells, is not totally devoid of meaning and whether, as Theodor Lessing suggested in his *Geschichte als Sinngebung des Sinnlosen*, 1919 / *History: The Meaningless Made Meaningful*, the act of constructing history is not a hopeless attempt to veil the unbearable chaos. Hochhuth's preliminary answer that man's fate in history is "absurd" yet "full of hope" strikes me as but another ruse to suppress the more awful insight darkly lurking in Hochhuth's mind.

But Hochhuth gives us his thoughts as a playwright, not as a philosopher, and it is hard to ignore the fundamental and sharp discrepancy between his piercing questions and his odd combination of theatrical means derived from the repertory of the classic and modern stage. While Peter Weiss in his recent partisan plays affects a strenuously simple style appealing to the tired tastes of the jaded intellectuals, Hochhuth prefers a more traditional and perhaps anachronistic *Volkstheater* which evokes memories of Schiller's great confrontation scenes between historical personages and their idealized antagonists, using a freely moving verse which "carries the speech more readily than prose" and yet aims to give order and shape to fleeting ideas; unfortunately, Hochhuth's language usually lacks vitality, intensity, and profile. He still wavers between writing morality plays and historical drama; his instinct for the "great scene" is sure and surprisingly theatrical, but he is far less certain of his stage economy and wastes much energy on naturalistic episodes, on silly remarks about the United States, and on women without a single spark of life; paradoxically, the playwright who almost alone among his contemporaries prizes the individual above all else has not created many individuals on stage. Half-numbed by the noisy discussion about the historical Pope and the British prime minister, literary critics have yet to admit that Hochhuth has learned a great deal, and that his second play is far better than *The Deputy.* He has wisely pruned the disturbing surfeit of naturalistic minor parts, abandoned his attempts to combine free verse and local dialects, and has created, in his Churchill, an ambivalent and rich theatrical character worthy of the late Charles Laughton's art. Hochhuth's awful and far-reaching questions about the ultimate meaning of history and his scenic prowess are far less incompatible today than they were a few years ago.

6. Friedrich Dürrenmatt

WHEN FRIEDRICH DÜRRENMATT first surveyed his earlier plays in his lecture on *Theaterprobleme* (delivered 1954) / *Problems of the Theater*, 1964, he complained about his "Protestant difficulties with the art of drama" and suggested, in rather involved syntax, that Catholic authors enjoyed theatrical possibilities not available to others. Dürrenmatt is the last theologian among the German playwrights (for the time being, anyway), but he has never hesitated to make the best of his particular predicaments. Intensely preoccupied with his own problems of belief and the theater, he haunts his audiences by ingenious use of grotesque stage techniques, confuses his critics with a homespun theory in which self-defensive commonplaces are curiously combined with epigrammatic insights, and hides rather than reveals his spiritual concerns.

Friedrich Dürrenmatt comes from an old Swiss family that has been rooted since the early seventeenth century in Bernese territory. He was born in 1921 in the village of Konolfingen, where his father was pastor, and moved to the city of Bern when he was thirteen years old. Dürrenmatt's fragmentary studies of literary history, philosophy, and science at the universities of Zurich and Bern seem to have been a rather haphazard affair; he always liked astronomy, read a good deal of Kierkegaard, Franz Kafka, and Ernst Jünger, but thought of himself as a painter in the expressionist tradition. In the mid-'forties he wrote his first prose sketches (later collected in *Die Stadt*, 1952 / *The City*) and, after moving to Basel and then Ligerz, tried to make a meager living as theater critic, free-lance contributor to the Zurich cabarets, and writer of potboilers, which in his hands turned into piercing examinations of guilt and punishment. For some years he also wrote radio plays for West German broadcasting stations.

Dürrenmatt's prose relates intimately to his plays: in *Der Richter und sein Henker*, 1952 / *The Judge and His Executioner* he anticipates fundamental situations in his later theatrical works; his near-novel *Grieche sucht Griechin*, 1955 / [Greek gentleman seeks Greek lady] *Once a Greek . . .* , 1965, mobilizes all the richness of his bizarre imagination; and in his first-rate narrative *Die Panne*, 1956 / [The Breakdown] *Traps* 1960, justice is meted out as if in a game, and Alfredo Traps, a contemporary Everyman selling textiles, is ennobled by an encounter with absolute fate and hangs himself at dawn.

Dürrenmatt's first three plays, *Es steht geschrieben,* [1947] / *It is Written; Der Blinde* [1948] / *The Blind One;* and *Romulus der Grosse* [1949] / *Romulus the Great,* 1964, made him a local competitor to Max Frisch, but the Munich premiere (March 26, 1952) of *Die Ehe des Herrn Mississippi* / *The Marriage of Mr. Mississippi,* 1964, later produced in New York as *Fools are Passing Through* [1959], opened up West German and European stages to him; and after the productions of *Der Besuch der alten Dame* [1956] / *The Visit* [of the Old Lady],* 1958, and *Die Physiker* [1962] / *The Physicists,* 1964, Dürrenmatt became the first German playwright after Brecht to be staged and discussed both in the Soviet Union and in the United States. Dürrenmatt is more bitterly critical of his Swiss fellow citizens than the melancholy Frisch, but he is far less restless than his Zurich compatriot. Living in Neuchâtel (rather than in Bern), Dürrenmatt often travels to collaborate with foreign producers of his plays, but he does not seek out distant landscapes and inspirations. He likes to refer to himself as a "village slowpoke," but we have to take his biographical suggestions with a grain of salt.

Es steht geschrieben [1947] / *It Is Written,* Dürrenmatt's first play, reveals many of his ideas about God and man and much of his stage technique, used later with greater discipline. In the German town of Münster, God's New Jerusalem has been established by the fiery Anabaptists who, in their own confused way, attempt to run their personal lives and the laws of the community in accordance with the strictest precepts of the Word Revealed; and while their longing for absolute purity quickly changes into terrorism directed against Catholics and Lutherans, an army is being formed to lay siege to the rebellious town. The Catholic bishop of Münster, a pensive humanist, is leaving, and in an atmosphere of anarchy, true belief and open treason emerge: Jan Matthison, the leader of the Anabaptists, is killed trying to defend the town alone against the enemy before the walls; Bernhard Knipperdollinck, the richest man of the community, freely gives away his gold to seek a genuine Christian life; and the greedy Johann Bockelsohn seizes power and crowns himself King of the New Zion. After a great feast he and poor Knipperdollinck both dance ecstatically on the roofs under a large pale moon, to express the fulfillment of their lives. The enemy enters through the crumbling walls and both are sentenced to death on the wheel. They die side by side, but Knipperdollinck has the strength to articulate, in his last agonies, the final truth: on the wheel, his tortured body changes into a "holy vessel, filled to the brim with grace."

Dürrenmatt creates a world rich in saints and fools, but he concentrates on Knipperdollinck and Bockelsohn, who rise and fall, fall and rise, in a counterpoint of fate: rich Knipperdollinck becomes poor Lazarus, and poor Bockelsohn (who was found in the gutter by two Münster street sweepers) rises to be a new King Solomon. We first see Knipperdollinck in his patrician home, together with his wife Katherina and his clear-eyed daughter Judith. Challenged by Bockelsohn, he divests himself of his golden chain, throws away his gold in the marketplace and, clad in rags, sets out, accompanied only by his daughter (his wife having meanwhile joined Bockelsohn), to quest after "poverty and peace." Bockelsohn entrusts the sword of justice to the wise man, but Knipperdollinck does not want to leave the dungeon, for there he is "free to commune with God and the rats." While Knipperdollinck literally falls to his fulfillment, Bockelsohn rises to his: he takes treasures and power, sings the praises of the flesh (surrounding him in the form of fifteen new wives), creates a new fantastic nobility of his loyal followers and, using an old map, begins to portion off the world. Calling himself "a son of the earth," he wants to rush through the dark night "like a meteor." Dürrenmatt does not intend to make a facile distinction between good and evil: the man of earthly pleasures and power and the radical Christian dance and die together under an inscrutable heaven, and the play does not suggest that grace is reserved for Knipperdollinck alone. Grace is infused from above, freely and unpredictably, and cannot be demanded, for whatever reasons or merits, from below; it is a mystery totally incomprehensible to man.

Dürrenmatt may be a late heir to the playwright Niklas Manuel (1484–1530), a fighter for Bernese Protestantism, but as a man of our age he feels "afflicted with the tumor of doubt"; and while suggesting the mystery of grace, he also makes his own clever arrangements to undercut high and intense emotions and to obscure his own inner conflicts by a show of tough technicality. In the scenic technique of his first play he relies on bathetic counterstatements of many kinds: he joins Max Frisch in using Thornton Wilder's anti-illusionary tactics, employs some of his characters as brash or wistful commentators, mobilizes the music against the elevated language of the actors, and juxtaposes scenes of intense feeling with scenes demonstrating the shabby realities of history. But faith prevails, perhaps against the theatrical intentions of the author: Thornton Wilder is left behind, and Knipperdollinck and Bockelsohn rise to their dance and their death, singing long lines of expressionist verse, and out of the self-reflective scenic arrangement, pure mystery emerges triumphant. I am inclined to believe that its power carries over into Dürrenmatt's second play, *Der Blinde* [1948] / *The Blind One*, in which (literally) blind faith triumphs over Satan, and an eyeless duke confesses that to be crushed by God means to reside in His grace. This dithyrambic Dürrenmatt strikes me as least troubled by his usual distrust of the world, the theater, and his faith.

Die Ehe des Herrn Mississippi [1952] / *The Marriage of Mr. Mississippi*, 1964, marks an important transition in Dürrenmatt's intents as a playwright. He returns to the essential metaphysical issues of his earlier work, but moves for the first time from the historical atmosphere of past centuries into our own age, or at least into a contemporary, if highly abstract, constellation of moral and political forces. His is a schematically ordered reality, and from the fashionable salon in which the complicated plot develops, or (as in Sartre's *No Exit*) comes full circle, one window opens on an apple orchard and a northern cathedral, and the other on a Mediterranean landscape of cypresses and an ancient temple. Anastasia, whose husband has just died of an alleged heart attack, is visited by the state prosecutor Florestan Mississippi, who mercilessly demonstrates to her that she, with the help of a devoted count, poisoned her husband (who had betrayed her with Florestan's wife Madelaine); and after she confesses her crime under the pressure of his arguments, the state prosecutor for his part confesses that he has poisoned his unfaithful wife Madelaine and that as penance he wishes to marry Anastasia on the spot. By contracting the new marriage bond he thinks to punish himself for his private rather than public execution of his wife; and Anastasia will, he believes, become a better woman by attending executions and paying daily visits to prisoners: as an "Angel of the Prisons" she may expiate her crime. The torments of his marriage inspire Mississippi to ever stricter pursuit of criminals, and when his three-hundred-and-fiftieth death sentence is carried out, he becomes a political liability to the government but attracts the attention of the reconsolidating Communist party (now the "Party for People, Faith, and Country"), eager to enlist a man evidently capable of effective action. Saint-Claude, the Communist organizer, delivers an ultimatum to Florestan: either the state prosecutor must serve the party, or he will be destroyed by having the secrets of his past made known to the nation—both he and Saint-Claude were once pimps, offering "white flesh to fat squares." Mississippi sternly rejects both the demands of the government and of the Communist party; Saint-Claude unleashes the revolution (nowhere are revolutions arranged more easily than in contemporary Swiss plays), and after it has failed and a new government has been installed, Mississippi, badly mauled by demonstrators, returns to his nearly demolished apartment and there finds Anastasia with Count von Übelohe-Zabernsee, who insists on telling the whole truth about his former involvement with Anastasia. The government tries to rush Florestan to an insane asylum, but he escapes home because he wants to know from Anastasia whether she has ever really loved the count; he poisons her coffee in order to extract the truth from the dying woman. But she has poisoned a cup of coffee, too, and in the end the stage is littered with dead and dying. Saint-Claude is shot by a Communist execution squad, and yet all unite in a *Chorus mysticus* in which utter failure becomes the mark of grace, and the drunken count, as the last Christian knight errant, appears in the mask of Don Quixote to continue on his eternal quest for the miracle of love.

In the organization of this metaphysical horror show (with some reminiscences of Frank Wedekind), a new economy, concentrating all events into one symbolically deteriorating salon around a small coffee table, happily counteracts Dürrenmatt's inexhaustible love of Marx Brothers' gags. Dürrenmatt still operates with Thornton Wilder's technique of broken illusions, but he has acquired a new grasp of the possibility of working poetically *with the stage* and makes the stage apparatus part of the game; portraits of the principal characters are quickly lowered and then raised out of sight, and the drunken count gracefully floats through space. As an ally of the nineteenth-century Viennese popular stage, of Alfred Jarry and of Eugene Ionesco, Dürrenmatt moves to the brink of a darkly poetic theater. But Dürrenmatt does not really wish to hide the strictly allegorical structure of his play: his three unusual men have all decided to change or save the world, each according to his absolute idea, and unfortunately they all encounter Anastasia, whose fatal and inert beauty incarnates the world, impervious to change. Florestan Mississippi fights for the awful justice of the Old Testament: when he was working for Saint-Claude's brothel he stumbled upon a Bible, was converted to the word of the prophets, and now devotes his life "to the gigantic effort to restore the law of Moses." He turns down his friends' suggestion that he abandon divine justice and burn God ("You cannot burn God, because He Himself is the fire," Florestan boldly retorts), and in his marriage with Anastasia he sees a unique opportunity to prove to the world that the strictest obedience to the Law may transform the murderess into "a higher and better" human being. Saint-Claude, who once found a copy of Marx's *Capital* in the pocket of a murdered pimp, went through his corresponding conversion, joined the Communist party, and dreams of a final battle in which—he anticipates the New Left by ten years—believing Marxists will fight the Soviet Union as a distortion of the pure idea. The playwright most closely sympathizes with the impoverished Count Bodo, whom he throws into the "melting pot of the comedy" to explore the nature of God's grace: Count Bodo, drunk and foolish, plagued by tropical diseases, accepts his degradation in the eyes of man, condemns Florestan's elevation of the Law over forgiveness, and loyally loves Anastasia (who promptly betrays him) not as a "just" but as an "unfortunate" woman. Dürrenmatt makes it clear that all three fail in their encounter with Anastasia: Florestan dies mistakenly believing that she is pure; Saint-Claude is destroyed by the power with which he has allied himself; and the count will have to continue on his quixotic search. Again, the play ends in expressionistic, if not mystical, verse, and the Christian count (like Knipperdollinck and the blind duke) praises the God who presses him to the beam of the cross and thus raises him on the mystical wood toward His inscrutable face. The count and his unusual friends have failed, but it is precisely their failure which intimates the closeness of grace.

The plays of the 'fifties reveal Dürrenmatt's increasing concern with man's fundamental encounter with the "other world," a concern expressed with a lean, almost classical, elegance of theatrical organization. Man confronts the absolute, be it cursed, holy, or both; and in his response to the challenge becomes fully aware of himself and realizes the best or worst of his potentialities. In the graceful comedy *Ein Engel kommt nach Babylon* [1953] / *An Angel Comes to Babylon*, 1964, God dispatches His love and light to earth in the form of a young girl. She is mistreated by King Nebuchadnezzar, who is offended that she was intended for a beggar and not for a lonely ruler, and later she cannot stay with him (whom she loves) because she is threatened with being betrayed by the court theologian, the scheming chancellor, and the king himself. Hand in hand with the beggar Akki (who closely resembles Brecht's Azdak), she continues her search for love in the desert and demonstrates in her fate that this earth, as in George Bernard Shaw's *Saint Joan*, is not ready to welcome its saints.

In *Der Besuch der alten Dame* [1956] / *The Visit* [of the Old Lady], 1958, which made Dürrenmatt well known outside Europe, it is not a charming young girl who brings love to the reluctant, but a stubborn and ageless woman who wants justice and retribution. The little town of Güllen (in dialect, "manure") has stagnated economically while other towns are booming; local industries are ruined, the town administration is bankrupt, most of the citizens are unemployed. Everybody expects help from Claire Zachanassian, once a local girl and now the richest woman on earth, who has expressed her intention of returning to her hometown after forty-five years' absence. Preparations are made for a festive welcome, and the shopkeeper Ill, once her lover, is nominated to be the next mayor of the town; he will be in a position to negotiate the details of her donations, loans, and investments. Claire, together with her butler, weird servants, a pair of eunuchs, husband number seven, a casket and a black panther, arrives, but hardly according to schedule. After all the clichés of greeting have been spoken, she coldly announces that she has returned to Güllen (which she has intentionally ruined) in order "to buy justice." In 1910, Ill had denied in court that he was the father of her child (who later died), and she is now ready to offer five hundred millions to the town and five hundred millions to be distributed among individual families if "somebody kills Ill." The mayor resolutely refuses the offer on behalf of the shocked community, but soon people, including the unemployed, begin spending freely; suddenly everyone is sporting strikingly new yellow shoes. In vain Ill seeks the protection of the authorities, but he finally resolves to stay and shoulder his responsibility. Güllen's citizens cannot long withstand temptation: in a community meeting they demand justice, and Ill, who submits to the verdict of the community, is strangled by the most muscular member of the local gymnastics club. The town physician declares that Ill died of a heart attack caused by joy at seeing his town rescued from ruin, and the mayor is handed Claire's check over Ill's corpse, before Claire has it embalmed in memory of better days. The moment for the happy end has come, and the Gülleners gather at their splendidly refurbished railroad station to recite Sophocles' chorus from *Antigone* in praise of man, their text as perverted as their mercurial lives.

Dürrenmatt presents his dramatic account of "absolute revenge" in a lean construction elegantly superior to all of his earlier plays and to many of the later ones; language, except for a few intentionally lyrical spots, and scenic inventions, including the cunning use of stage synchrony in the manner of the nineteenth-century Viennese popular playwrights, are of perfect functionality. But it is the sparse texture itself that raises questions of interpretation, because it is easy to ignore textual suggestions and, as has often been done, to declare *The Visit* either a social satire aimed at our contemporary consumer society (at a time when such satires are a dime a dozen) or a passion play rephrasing a timeless Biblical situation. We have to combine the possibilities of both readings; it is Claire Zachanassian who pits against each other the community, greedy for money, and her former lover, and then quietly sits back to see what will happen. Of vicious charm, stubborn, and removed from petty life by her riches, her artificial limbs of pure ivory, and her experience in a Hamburg bordello and elsewhere, she has been planning the script of Ill's retrial for many years. Claire knows that people are susceptible to temptation, and she is not mistaken: shortly after her arrival the buying spree begins, and the representatives of the political, religious, and intellectual establishments are not exempt from the general fever. On the contrary: the policeman has a new gold tooth, the mayor wants to build a new town hall, the pastor buys a new church bell which rings out in deceptive glory above the town, and the schoolteacher, an erudite humanist proud of his knowledge of Greek mythology and his apt allusions, takes to drink because he feels his humanism crumbling from moment to moment and knows that he, too, the avid reader of the ancients, is turning into a greedy killer. But while the people of the community are corrupted by their hunger for material goods, Ill rises to tragic insight and sudden nobility of soul: awkwardly intent at first to gloss over his blame for Claire's sufferings and the death of his child by referring vaguely to the difficulties of "life," he gradually comes to see where he went wrong. At the community meeting his tormented and lonely cry for God's mercy suggests that he has chosen to die in order to atone for his crime. His fate and that of his fellow citizens are bound together in a single knot of redemption and terror: driven by their bottomless greed, the modern consumers of Güllen commit murder; but what looks from the outside like murder is, when viewed from the inside, a meaningful death that has changed a shabby shopkeeper into a noble, tragic hero. Brutal destruction of human life for material reasons and voluntary expiation are one, and we should not close our sensibilities to Dürrenmatt's terrifying suggestion that in the realm of the hidden God, justice still goes its own paradoxical and troubling way.

The critic and philosopher Lucien Goldmann relates the ideas of the French Jansenists of the mid-seventeenth century to their overwhelming disgust with a political reality massively resisting change, and I suspect Dürrenmatt is closer to Pascal's world than the social interpreters of his plays would care to admit. He cannot escape the idea of withdrawal from a hostile world and the unforeseen consequences of such a withdrawal in an age of organized terror and constant war. In his earlier "unhistorical historical comedy" *Romulus der Grosse* [1949] / *Romulus the Great*, 1964, Dürrenmatt examined the phenomenon of a "Caesar of the chickens"; Romulus Augustus dislikes the empire built on bloodshed and slavery and decides to withdraw to his rustic chicken farm rather than to act the emperor when Germanic tribes threaten the country. The end of the hated empire will come sooner, he believes, but he is also aware that he will have to pay for his contemplative inactivity with his life if the Germanic warriors overrun his retreat. But Dürrenmatt early divests the protagonist's withdrawal of all heroic glory: when Odoaker, the enemy general, arrives at the farm and Romulus fully expects to be killed, it turns out that Odoaker, too, is a peace-loving chicken farmer at heart. He convinces Romulus that it would be in the best interest of all if Romulus would formally accept the submission of the tribes and then retire in honor with a comfortable salary. Continuing to do what he has done all his life, but now for pay, Romulus finds that his central concerns have become patently "absurd" in this unexpected reversal of his fate.

In *Die Physiker* [1962] / *The Physicists*, 1964, Dürrenmatt moves from the playfully suggested fifth century of *Romulus* to the age of Hiroshima. The horizon darkens, and to withdraw from the world now means to leave all power in the hands of those who degrade man to a slave. In an insane asylum (which Dürrenmatt locates in Neuchâtel, more to provoke his fellow townsfolk than out of any theatrical necessity) are interned three physicists who, one after the other, strangle their lovelorn nurses so as not to be distracted from their scientific thought by personal feelings. While the state prosecutor unsuspectingly plays into the hands of the asylum director, the three physicists confess to each other that they are not really mad, but have particular reasons for feigning madness: Johann Wilhelm Möbius, who has been longest in the asylum, has deliberately chosen to seem mad (claiming that King Solomon appears to him), for he has made theoretical discoveries which, if put into practice, would endanger the very existence of the world; and his two fellow patients are highly gifted physicists who, fascinated by his early publications, alarmed the secret services of their countries and were trained to track him down and to convince him to join the respective power groups whose offers, whether they imply laboratories near Moscow or in New Mexico, do not differ much. Möbius persuades his colleagues that the world would but distort their scientific discoveries, and since both Mr. Kilton (who claims to be Newton) and Comrade Eisler (who plays Einstein) are honest men, they agree that science would be best served if all remained in the asylum voluntarily, continuing to pretend madness; the murdered nurses, Möbius somewhat glibly suggests, were sacrifices to save mankind from vaster killings. But the three physicists have underrated Dr. Mathilde von Zahnd, the head physician, who is power-mad. Appearing in their midst, the hunchbacked virgin Mathilde declares that she has long monitored all their conversations, has drugged Möbius and copied his manuscripts before he destroyed them, and now intends to seize world power by means of the total technology derived from Möbius' inventions. Once again, the three physicists are to continue playing their roles, but this time it is for good, and what just a moment earlier was the semblance of free choice has now become inescapable necessity. Möbius has failed to act, and the mad Mathilde holds the unhappy world in a grip of terror.

Kilton and Eisler are perhaps excellent physicists, but politically they are as simple-minded as Dürrenmatt, who cannot resist the central-European urge to neatly equate the Soviet Union and America, an equation particularly popular among those who have never lived in either country. Kilton believes in pure research and distinguishes sharply between abstract and applied knowledge, but when he cannot locate Möbius he does not hesitate to join the secret service to be trained for the mission of discovering the whereabouts of the most talented physicist of all time; he demands absolute freedom for continued research, re-

gardless of its practical uses, and yet he has long been busy
reporting his findings via secret transmitter to his superiors (he
does not know that all his broadcasts have been monitored or
jammed by Mathilde). Eisler, who represents the union of Lenin-
ism and physics, calls Kilton a "deplorable aesthete" because
physicists do have to consider their social responsibility; and yet
when asked by Möbius how he himself handles his social responsibility, Eisler candidly admits that he has left all political business to the party and merely hopes that the party's actions will
be after his own heart. Neither he nor Kilton can offer Möbius
more than well-paid employment in a gilded cage provided by
their respective defense establishments, and Möbius rather easily
articulates their common belief that their only hope as good
physicists is to opt for total withdrawal, remaining "mad and
wise, interned but free, scientists but without guilt." It is reason
itself, he argues intensely, that urges such a choice, for scientific
research has advanced to a point at which it has become lethal
to humanity; scientists, if they wish to save humanity, cannot
but "take back" what they know.

But Möbius' idea of withdrawal is challenged by two voices
in the play, each revealing in its own way that the act of withdrawing or retracting has its fatal dangers: where one person in
this world does not act, another will. Möbius' nurse Monica,
deeply in love with the lonely man, has discovered the truth and
demands of Möbius that he leave the ward with her; he has been
given the gift of supreme knowledge and is therefore obliged
to commit himself in life, even if his commitment should bring
shame and cruel hardship upon him, and to fight in the outside
world for his discoveries. Monica dies at his hands for what she
has said, but she is right, and her beliefs are indirectly confirmed
by the other (evil) voice that reveals to Möbius that "taking back"
merely opens the way to the other force, now dominating the
world. Dr. Mathilde von Zahnd openly declares that she acted
where Möbius did not; and when he failed to commit himself
to the discoveries granted him by King Solomon, the king told
her to undo his disloyal follower and to act in his stead. What
has once been thought cannot be revoked, and Möbius will spend
the rest of his days dreaming (in a dark vision textually reminis-

cent of Romulus' vision of the crumbling empire) of man's fall from wisdom and of an earth contaminated, parched, and senselessly reeling through an inhuman universe. The technical perfection of Dürrenmatt's play does not contradict the terror of its final vision, for it is a perfection distinctly bordering on sterility: classicist arrangement has become purely algebraic, the usual techniques of reversal and repetition function almost automatically, and through the arid mechanism of the theatrical events one hears the playwright's cry of despair. Visions of emptiness and a barren stage together suggest that Dürrenmatt has come to an irreversible moment of crisis; if withdrawing or not withdrawing from the world both jeopardize man's fragile integrity, the most essential assumptions of Dürrenmatt's thought are at stake.

Dürrenmatt's theory of the theater, first sketched out some ten years after his first play, constitutes an occasionally obscure attempt to state why an author of today cannot write traditional tragedies and why he is still drawn to see the tragic, realized at the core of comedy, "as a terrible moment, as an opening abyss"; in practice, as Jacob Steiner has shown, Dürrenmatt echoes his theoretical uneasiness about genre when he subtitles his plays "fragmentary" or "tragic" comedies. Dürrenmatt's central argument against pure tragedy, toward which the best of his plays converge, combines the dubious and the legitimate: relying on a rather idealistic concept of the hero as a great historical doer (offset on the German stage by Georg Büchner's Woyzeck and Gerhart Hauptmann's proletarian protagonists), he asserts that Napoleon was possibly the last hero in a world of visibly concrete forms. In the age of Hitler and Stalin, history is made by "world butchers"; and since clear contours, irreplaceable individualities, and direct responsibility are rapidly disappearing, we cannot any more assign personal culpability, that first prerequisite of tragedy: we are guilty too, collectively. The old world and its literary mirrors thrived on the concrete, but in the new, anonymous, statistical universe (Dürrenmatt sometimes sounds like a German *Kulturpessimist* of the Right) it is the writer's task to create something visible. In comedy we are to look at the world as "mysterious misfortune," and therefore we cannot do without productive distance or perspective. In order to guarantee distance, comedy works with gags (*Einfälle*), invented materials, parody, and the grotesque. In his notes to the revised version of his first play (1969) Dürrenmatt discusses Brecht, Hochhuth, and Peter Weiss, and comes closer to defining his particular theatrical strategies. He sketches in a technical typology of the comic and opts for a play in which the comic does not reside in character alone or, as it did in the comedy of manners, in character and situation, but rather in predominantly tragic figures harnessed to comic situations. This third and encompassing type of comedy, he implies, becomes true "world theater" (*Welttheater*), reminiscent of the mystery plays of much older traditions.

Responding to the challenges of Brecht, Dürrenmatt sharply articulates his theoretical interests and, perhaps, some of his authorial frustrations. Mocking Brecht's long opposition to Schiller, Dürrenmatt dryly suggests that Brecht really went Schiller's way, only much farther: Brecht was the most extreme of the "sentimental" poets who cannot accept reality as it is. While Schiller rebelled against a world which he showed to be evil, Brecht progressed from being a rebel to being a revolutionary who wanted to demonstrate that the world was changeable and who advised his audiences exactly how to go about changing it. But Dürrenmatt does not share Brecht's basic assumptions; the world, he believes, has been transformed less by political action than by population explosions and mass technology, and the demand that the world be changed means little to the individual and is a mere slogan for the masses: to the individual, nothing is left but a feeling of impotence, coinciding with the awareness that a time is coming in which everybody should do his own job (*das Seine*) "resolutely and bravely." Dürrenmatt praises Brecht's technical boldness and precision and deals, in more recent comments (1969), with Brecht's stage technique in a curiously irascible way. He keenly defines the alienation effect as "an emergency brake that stops the plot so that people can think," but suggests that in his own plays the alienation effect resides in the material itself and not (merely) in the fashion in which the play is produced: his own plays, he adds, can therefore dispense with Brechtian productions. Dürrenmatt almost claims the real alienation effect for his own plays and aspires to compete with Brecht in terms of the *Schiffbauerdamm* rather than on his own level.

But Dürrenmatt's essence emerges from his plays rather than from his theories about them, and I am inclined to share the views of those who believe that his plays should be explicated against a horizon of religious issues, circumscribed by thoughts about the hidden God, unpredictable grace, the immutable world, and human beings troubled by the question of whether or not their earthly efforts are at all important to a terrible divine force. Moving through a wide spectrum between expressionist (not to say "mystical") passion and a cold vision as haughty as Jehovah's, Dürrenmatt's dramatic art has undergone considerable transformation. In the plays of the late 'forties, the reluctant believer wanted to counteract his terse metaphysical commitment, visible in historical images, by his mock-heroic techniques—including repetition, reversal, and the grotesque dehumanization of what is most alive. In the 'fifties he achieved control over his gags, freed himself from history (or its abstraction), and promptly found himself confronted by the question of whether contemporary man should strive only for God's grace or rather care for his fellow men; it was the time of his projected collaboration with Max Frisch and, later, his experiments with *Frank der Fünfte; Oper einer Privatbank* [1959] / *Frank V: The Opera of a Private Bank;* if it was to be an alternative to Brecht's *The Threepenny Opera,* it was surely an unsuccessful one. I find Dürrenmatt's plays of the 'sixties, or rather those following the slick but challenging *Physicists,* rather disappointing variations on earlier achievements: *Herkules und der Stall des Augias* [1963] / *Hercules and the Augean Stables,* an expanded radio play, bitterly complains about the stables of Swiss bureaucracy; and *Der Meteor* [1966] / *The Meteor* rehearses a few dexterous repetition scenes and then takes a curiously self-centered escape into discussions of fame, publishing, and vile literary critics. Dürrenmatt's recent revision of his first play about the Anabaptists [1947] clearly demonstrates the continuing if not paralyzing struggle in his mind: in the revised version, the question of the individual redeemed by grace is half pushed aside by the question of whether the world can be a humane place for all, and the transcendental and the social thrusts diverge. The playwright himself, caught between the conflicting demands of heaven and earth, has become a tormented figure closer to our troubles than any of the characters in his later plays.

INTERMEZZO 3: *Problems of Fiction*

THE NAZIS WANTED to see the novel regress to late nineteenth-century conventions, and their fascist realism reflected the violent opposition of the small-town petit bourgeois, afraid of the complicated industrial world, to the cosmopolitan writers who had thrived in the cities of the Weimar Republic. Putting their power brake on literary development, the Nazi organizations favored those novelists who still saw Germany as an agricultural country (as it had indeed been in the earlier nineteenth century) swarming with sturdy peasants, blonde maidens, and less than articulate heroes who resembled the vikings of old; analytical intellect was proscribed, and blood and soil were to form the essence of rustic (and totally unreal) Arcadias.

After May, 1945, writers had the difficult task of coming to terms with what had happened in Hitler's *Reich* and of reestablishing links with European and American fiction. Free at last to pose ultimate questions concerning death and German history, they embraced a great number of narrative strategies, ranging from a piercing factualism intended to reveal how people had really suffered and died, to the emblematic compression of the revived short story and the allegorical approach. Theodor Plivier (1892–1955) in his *Stalingrad*, 1945, the best of the German war novels, soberly dealt with the destruction of entire armies at the decisive turning point of the world conflict; the language was crude but compassionate, and the novel itself followed the dying soldiers, betrayed by their *Führer* and the High Command, deep into the cellars and foxholes along the banks of the Volga. In his *Die Stadt hinter dem Strom*, 1947 / *The City beyond the River* Hermann Kasack (1896–1966) explored, in a calm prose reminiscent of Kafka, the symbolic habitations of those who had recently died and were now sinking away into absolute nothingness, and he conveyed the sense of lethargy shared by many in the burnt-out cities. Thomas Mann published his monumental and yet meticulously organized *Doktor Faustus*, 1947/1948, but few readers were aware that his highly allusive story of the demonic German composer Adrian Leverkühn, as recorded by the humanist Serenus Zeitblom, was a resplendent "terminal book" (Erich Kahler) that concluded an entire epoch of European fiction. Contemporary critics (with the exception of Ernst Fischer, who with justice objected to Mann's aestheticizing discussion of fascism) stressed its political relevance, but later interpreters are more inclined to define *Doktor Faustus* as an important achievement because it unites in a final statement all the rich strands of Thomas Mann's steadily developing art.

In the 'fifties a small generation of younger writers stepped forward and proclaimed its own "age of distrust"—a few years later than in France perhaps, but no less radical, for in Germany the involvement of the fathers in the Nazi regime and the strategies of the older novel were subjected to simultaneous scrutiny. Following the early discussions of Group 47, German revulsion against inherited fiction came in waves of attack; and it is difficult to describe the patterns of conflict, since renewed exploration of narrative methods did not necessarily correspond to a bolder confrontation with society. For some years writers seemed to choose those narrative methods that antedated middle-class realism by at least a century or, more recently, those that had an essential share in its decomposition: Günter Grass took up the prerealist structure of the picaresque tale, while others, including Alfred Andersch and Heinrich Böll, worked increasingly with the internal monologue, which changed the epic world into a flexible constellation of personal perspectives, unencumbered by the cohesion once imposed by a consistent point of view. Yet in the first wave of distrust the methodological attempt to get beyond realism and the omniscient narrator did not always go hand in hand with courageous attention to social change: Uwe Johnson invented his *nouveau roman* as a means of returning to childhood landscapes; and Günter Grass and Heinrich Böll, in their intense loyalty to the bread-and-coffee paradise of the socially isolated lower middle class, completely overlooked the cool new world of businessmen and consumers that was vividly presented in the novels of Martin Walser. Developments were contradictory and compressed: only a year separated Grass's *Die Blechtrommel*, 1959 / *The Tin Drum*, 1962, from Walser's *Halbzeit*, 1960 / *Half-Time*, two completely different novels both intent upon unmasking the world from the limited perspective of a rather peculiar first-person narrator.

During these years Arno Schmidt (b. 1910) contributed decisively to the technical possibilities of fiction, and in his idiosyncratic way anticipated many of the experiments of the following decade. His narratives *Brands Haide*, 1951 (the title refers to the name of a forest), and *Das steinerne Herz*, 1956 / *The Stony Heart* suggest some of the virtues and limitations of his aggressive approach. Schmidt still has a story to tell (filled with lean girls and rare books), but he takes a radically subjective stance and, after giving a single organizing cue in a lone noun or phrase, tries to present the exact process of psychological associations as precisely as possible—often indulging in vulgar idioms, in extensive quotations in many languages, and in ax-grinding directed at the state, the military, religion of any sort, and people unfamiliar with the works of James Fenimore Cooper, Charles Dickens, and the eighteenth-century German writer Christoph Martin Wieland (1733–1813). His themes and his methods are strangely at odds: his genre scenes present a kind of Robinson Crusoe and his girl Friday in a North German village (before or after the next atomic war); but the protagonist releases, with the author's explicit consent, a stream of consciousness that documents an intellect more sturdy than refined attacking the material resistance of a narrow world. Provincialism and innovation could not possibly be mated in a more productive misalliance.

While writers of the 'fifties were instinctively disinclined to follow the lead of older authors, the young novelists of the 'sixties tend toward highly articulate polemics on theoretical issues, and relentless experimentation aimed at radically reducing the fictional element in fiction. Instead of epic detachment young writers want a striking immediacy that will carry its own evident reality; they resolutely reject the inclusive scheme of the realistic novel, which was characterized by the aspiration toward a total image of society, by immovable characters often summed up in recurring leitmotifs, and by linear plots artistically imposed on chaotic experience. But in rejecting the past, young German writers find themselves in a position different from that of Robbe-Grillet and his allies, for in Germany the past is closer to the present than in France: it is relatively easy to condemn Balzac (1799–1850) but more difficult to argue against Thomas Mann, who carried the nineteenth century far into our own and managed to embody a humanistic tradition that remains essential to German intellectual life. Reinhart Baumgart (b. 1929) respectfully defines the embarrassment his generation encounters with Thomas Mann: Mann appears to them as a "huge and distant figure," an "example behind glass" who has not been followed by any disciples (except perhaps by the novelist Baumgart himself). Baumgart feels uneasy about Mann's "ostentatious discipline" of narration; too much is rounded off, structured, organized; and in the desire to "establish order at any price," little allowance is made for "impenetrable experience." I suspect that Baumgart's objections to Mann's point of view also imply a critique of the inclusive novels of Robert Musil, Hermann Broch, and Heimito von Doderer; and while German and American professors are turning the interpretation of these authors into major scholarly industries, few practicing writers today share the reverence for these patriarchs of modern German fiction. The young writers slyly pretend that they do not have any fathers at all.

But any search for immediacy of narration inevitably creates great difficulties: if the narrator is compelled to abdicate, the author must search for his guarantee of "reality" either in the presence of exhaustive objective data or in the inner processes of his own all-absorbing consciousness. Alexander Kluge has chosen the predominance of the "outside" as the organizing principle of his prose experiments; his *Lebensläufe,* 1962 / [Biographies] *Attendance List for a Funeral,* 1966, and his *Schlachtbeschreibung,* 1964 / [Description of] *The Battle,* 1967, present a fundamental gesture of "showing." Like a movie director who focuses on the impersonal objects of the world, Kluge seizes upon language as constitutive of reality, and instead of creating particular characters or situations, he "demonstrates" idioms, reports, or protocols as modes of contemporary being. His description of the battle of Stalingrad (in some contrast to Theodor Plivier's compassionate account) consists of interviews, biographies, and documents, including the verbatim German army reports from

November, 1942, to February, 1943; the old-fashioned narrator has turned into a Pop artist who puts language on display but fails to explain why we should see value in flat duplications of totalitarian clichés and historical texts which, since they are purposefully arranged in structured sequences on the printed page, are as near to or as removed from reality as Little Dorritt's tears. In his *Felder*, 1964 / *Fields*, and *Ränder*, 1968 / *Margins*, Jürgen Becker (b. 1932) takes the other, perhaps more productive, option and concentrates on the continuous processes of his own subjective perception; his reality is constituted by his consciousness, incessantly absorbing the "outside" into whirlpools of memories, dreams, and hopes. But while they explore his many verbal resources, Becker's exercises of consciousness soon turn into stylistic exercises reminiscent of Raymond Queneau's (1947), and the art which he so distrusts returns by the back door in syntactic arrangements and textual sequences. In *Margins* Becker centers his recollected experience of Mediterranean and Rhenish landscapes around a middle zone of silence, suggested by a white page at the heart of the slender book, and the lively transcript of ever-changing perception suddenly submits to the organizing force of sophisticated form. We are watching something very like the rebirth of the Romantic Self.

1. Wolfgang Koeppen

WOLFGANG KOEPPEN (b. 1906) began writing in the early 'thirties, but his voice was drowned out (as one of his characters says) "by the shouts of the loudspeakers, the din of war, the cries of the murderers and their victims." In the last years of the Weimar Republic, Koeppen was on the staff of the distinguished *Berliner Börsen-Courier* (in which Brecht published some of his best early theoretical essays), he survived the dictatorship doing odd jobs in the film industry and, in the early 'fifties, literally burst upon the literary scene with a series of explosive novels in which, displaying a fully mature technique, he dealt mercilessly with contemporary society and politics. At a time when most of his contemporaries were looking back on the war in paralyzed terror or escaping to new idylls, Koeppen almost alone insisted on discussing the evident consequences of the Hitler years. Sadly, and with increasing rage, he faced the transitional years in which he saw an unthinking restoration of the old powers combined with the overwhelming and mindless temptations of the consumer society. In the late 'fifties and early 'sixties Koeppen set out on long journeys to the four corners of the world and published a series of travelogues which are vivid documents of his geographical explorations, as well as the bitter fruits of self-imposed exile from a country in which economic recovery offered a poor substitute for sorely needed spiritual transformation.

In his first postwar novel *Tauben im Gras*, 1951 / *Doves in the Grass* Koeppen, taking his cue from Dos Passos and his German disciple Alfred Döblin, constructed a compact but inclusive account of a single day in a Munich just recovering from the starvation years. American planes droning overhead suggest that a war is still going on somewhere; and beneath the cloud of noise and anxiety there are people who go on chasing after something that promises happiness: an aging film star, who, disgusted with his withering wife, pursues young women; a self-taught chemist who experiments with drugs in the cellar of a ruined house; two black U.S. soldiers; visiting schoolteachers from Massachusetts; and Philipp, a middle-aged writer, who encounters one of the traveling American girls and feels cold and lonely in the cheap room they take together. I suspect that Koeppen's colorful and desperate mosaic contains an oblique argument against inherited metaphysical views which surround modern man with false protective shells of belief. Among his set of major figures, he carefully introduces Mr. Edwin, a distinguished American poet and expatriate (a successful blend of T. S. Eliot and Thomas Mann's Gustav Aschenbach) who lectures in the local *Amerika Haus* to a polite audience on Homer, Vergil, Dante, Goethe, and Man but does not see that the teeming city outside radically negates what he is attempting to say; the microphone does not work anyway. Mr. Edwin argues in vain against the implied message of Koeppen's novel: some intellectuals, Mr. Edwin warns his audience, "show man independent of God . . . without values, free, endangered by snares, unprotected from the butchers [like doves in the grass] but proud of imagined freedom from God." But the novel suggests that the "intellectuals" are right and Mr. Edwin wrong: only two people, a black soldier and a youngish girl, embrace happily while the others all go on searching for meaning and human warmth; the distinguished lecturer himself ends his day in the company of homosexuals in the darkest alleys of Munich.

At first sight, Koeppen's *Das Treibhaus*, 1953 / *The Hothouse* resolutely confronts the power centers of the newly established Federal Republic and (almost unprecedentedly in German literature) dares to locate the narrative in parliamentary meetings, committee rooms, and the executive dining rooms frequented by high officials and foreign correspondents. Koeppen is not, of course, a realist in the established sense of the term, and his sure handling of the inner monologue and occasional Joycean Night-Town visions stretches almost to the breaking point the limit of political and social realities. Keetenheuve, the novel's central sensibility, both likes and intensely dislikes politics; a former exile who has returned to Germany to serve his country as a member of the Social Democratic parliamentary fraction, he feels more and more bored and disgusted with daily routine. He has just attended the funeral of his wife and is facing mounting political pressures: the ruling conservative party wants to send him to a new exile by offering him the ambassadorship to Guatemala, but conflicts are also growing within his own faction because the party chairman Knurrewahn (who strongly resembles Schumacher) dislikes the egghead and pacifist Keetenheuve, who opposes the party's intention of building a new, democratic army. Keetenheuve spends two restless days in conferences and luncheon meetings; once again he seeks warmth, in the embraces of a Salvation Army girl (who is closely watched by her lesbian companion), and finally, disenchanted by the furtive union, he runs to the river and throws himself off the bridge, while the neon lights of a nearby café ironically beam the magic word *Rheinlust* far into the night. Final lust, final fulfillment; death by drowning in the German Rhine.

In Koeppen's third postwar novel *Der Tod in Rom*, 1954 / *Death in Rome*, cold fury prevails over melancholy despair; and as the allusion to Thomas Mann's *Death in Venice* indicates, there is growing discomfort with the literature of the past, which did little to relate private woes to the brutal force of German history. Koeppen offers a melodramatic story of surprising chance encounters and the generation gap: Mayor Pfaffrath, once a high functionary of the Nazi regime, has come with his entire family to Rome to meet his brother-in-law, the former SS general Judejahn, in order to discuss Judejahn's return from one of the Arab states (where he has been serving as military adviser) to a newly conservative West Germany perhaps ready to forgive and forget. Yet the younger sons refuse to have a share in the deal: Siegfried Pfaffrath, a composer who writes difficult symphonies in the style of Adrian Leverkühn, dreams of regeneration in distant African places, and Adolf Judejahn, the general's son, has humbly entered a seminary to prepare for priesthood. It is Judejahn himself, however, who, with his physical force, angry aggressiveness, blind obedience to past commands, and sexual obsessions, dominates the configuration of individual fates and, finally, in a last outburst of rage and disappointment, shoots a Jewish woman in order to fulfill the *Führer*'s orders and suffers a fatal stroke in the fierce noonday heat. Alluding to Thomas Mann's concluding statement in *Death in Venice* that a "dutifully shocked world received the news" of the poet's death, Koeppen dryly remarks that the busy world was not at all interested to hear about Judejahn's death or that of his last victim.

Among the emerging authors of the 'fifties, Wolfgang Koeppen explored the question of organized power and individual sensibility in the context of the recent German past more energetically than anybody else and yet was unable to free himself entirely from the burdens of traditional German *Innerlichkeit*, which elevated subjective inwardness above the possibly shattering encounter with the exigencies of everyday political life; he experimented before Böll and Walser with the technical advances of the modern novel and yet remained a close ally of Goethe's Werther: behind the intricate epic juxtapositions and sophisticated narrative counterpoints lurks the familiar young man from the German "novel of development" who combines an abstract enthusiasm for humanity with a good deal of psychological solipsism and finds, in Koeppen's more modern articulation, the *monologue intérieur* and the *style indirect libre* an excellent technical way of separating his restlessly ruminating ego from the merciless harshness of surrounding reality. Philipp, Siegfried Pfaffrath, and Keetenheuve (who keeps his e. e. cummings volume close to his political documents) are finely organized artistic temperaments, constantly disappointed by relative, shabby, inadequate experience; and like their romantic relatives of the past, they cannot forgive the world for the agonizing, autonomous riches it harbors outside their creative minds.

The German critic Marcel Reich-Ranicki has pointed out that Koeppen's central figures are related to the heritage of German romanticism, but that is not the entire story; Koeppen transforms the romantic heritage in a strikingly modern way. In the symbolic fabric of his novels Koeppen connects the political issue of power with the more personal issue of sex; and from this interaction (reminiscent of Heimito von Doderer's more sophisticated theory of political and sexual perversion) emerge the contours of a threatening world in which the introspective intellectual time and again confronts a massive and fatal "force," of which the political power and rapacious sex are essential elements: political pressure constitutes "visible" evil while the overbearing force of sex is "invisible" evil, and where the visible and the invisible coalesce, almost archetypal Nazi ogres appear, their lethal combination of political and sexual aggression symbolizing to Koeppen's protagonists evil incarnate: Keetenheuve feels this way about Frau Wanowski, a former leader of the Nazi women's organization, who has now dragged his wife to perversion and death; Siegfried Pfaffrath meets evil in the SS general Judejahn, whose last ejaculation is one with his murder of the Jewess. The trouble is that there are few paths to salvation open in the modern world; when Siegfried seeks a more spiritual fulfillment in the arms of a handsome Roman youth, he (unlike Thomas Mann's Aschenbach) finds himself locked up in a rotten bathhouse with a meretricious boy. Retiring from losing battles against the "force" and escaping into disillusionment, Koeppen's intellectual has little hope of changing the world according to his impassioned vision of absolute justice. In transforming alienation into exile, geography may offer some relief, but it is an exile from reality that Koeppen really wants.

2. Gerd Gaiser

GERD GAISER's views of life and society are derived from the postromantic German *Jugendbewegung* of the early 'twenties, the adherents of which sought salvation from the pressures of industrial civilization in a German forest myth and, not unlike recent American youths, a close-knit collective life. Historically, the central ideas of the *Jugendbewegung* (recently described by Walter Laqueur) lent themselves all too readily to being used and perverted by the Nazis, who, concerned as they were primarily with power, did not develop a systematic ideology of their own but merely concocted one from the ragbag of German conservative thought. Looking steadfastly into the past, Gaiser deplores the fact that the ideals of the *Jugendbewegung*, sacred to many of his generation, had been first manipulated by the Nazis for their own ends and, after the war, totally ignored by the consumer society emerging from the ruins; and Gaiser's disappointment results in an elegiac attitude that determines the character of his supreme craftsmanship. He has the sure touch of one working in loneliness, against the grain of the age.

Like many distinguished German writers of the past, Gerd Gaiser (b. 1908) is the son of a Swabian Protestant minister and received a good deal of theological training before he decided that his true vocation was the fine arts. He studied in Stuttgart, Königsberg, Dresden, and Tübingen, traveled in many European countries, and completed his formal education with a dissertation (1934) on early baroque Spanish sculpture before starting on a teaching career. During the war Gaiser served with the air force in Rumania and Scandinavia, and finally surrendered to the British; after the war, he instinctively returned to his native section of Germany, tried unsuccessfully to make a living as lumberman and painter, and returned to teaching in 1949. He has received many distinguished awards, including the Fontane Prize (1951), but his novels and many collections of stories have found few readers outside Germany and are appreciated within the country by the older and middle generations rather than by the younger group with its insistence on social commitment.

Gaiser's *Die sterbende Jagd*, 1953 / [The Dying Hunt] *The Last Squadron*, 1956, skillfully secretes deeply personal views in a pastel-colored war novel free of carnage and gore. It is a requiem for the chivalry of the young German fighter pilots during the first years of the war. In a mechanical age the "knightly" way of engaging an individual enemy in sportsmanlike duels in the grand manner of "Blue Max" has little future; the well-prepared Operation Revolving Stage, arranged to provide cover for a convoy of heavy ships in the northern seas, seems a success at first, but the flying fortresses carry the day, and the fighter pilots "found to their surprise that this day, on which they thought they had fought well, had been the first day of their defeat." Rather than tell a fast-moving story Gaiser prefers to combine sixty vignettes of individual experiences into a composite image of a vanishing way of life; there are wing commanders, privates, sergeants, and lieutenants, but what holds the novel together is the dominant sense of forlorn hope and loss overwhelming the individuals as inexorably as the fog engulfs their planes. The mosaic technique contains the danger of fragmentation, but Gaiser links his individual "splinters" of experience by imposing a sustained time span consisting of the thirty-six hours that happen to coin-

cide with the final breakup of the old *Luftwaffe;* and the synchrony of incidents serves to reveal the beginning of the end as
perceived through many eyes and sensibilities: the many subtle
modifications of attitude among the characters point to inescapable and radical change. Gaiser's idiom inobtrusively and effectively fuses German tradition and the technical vocabulary of
the pilots; in his language, Gaiser may, at times, incline to a
finely spun impressionism, but when dealing with the rapidly
shifting patterns of air battles, his syntax has sharp-edged precision and will continue to provoke questions of major moral
and social import.

Gaiser's *Das Schiff im Berg: Aus den Papieren des Peter Hagmann,*
1955 / *The Ship in the Mountain: From the Papers of Peter Hagmann*
is not one of his best novels, but suggests much of the darker
side of his philosophy of history. The archeologist Hagmann and
his assistant Hedda have been called to explore newly discovered
caves in a Swabian mountain (close to Gaiser's native village),
and from the notes of the scientist the history of the mountains
emerges as a symbol of universal fatalities. A cosmic perspective
opens up, the four elements coming first; geological, biological,
and climatic changes later; and finally man, stubborn, "transitory." Many people defend their mountain until they are killed
or driven away by others, who in turn must soon defend their
spoils: stone-age men, Helvetians, Romans, early Christians,
unfree peasants, marauders of the Thirty Years' War, vagabonds,
early explorers and, more recently, an air force communications
center whose staff quickly disperses or dies when Germany
capitulates and the Allies begin combing the forests. Hagmann
has his fleeting moment of happiness when Hedda faintly responds to his feelings; however, within a week she is killed in
a car accident, and after the caves have been despoiled by vulgar
tourists, Hagmann returns to his mountain from which (like the
local peasants) he expected "the ship," that is, the fullness of
life, to come. He has learned that man's attempt to be more than
nature is in vain and that suffering at least signifies an honest
individual existence. Again, Gaiser does not construct a sustained
plot; Hagmann's notes provide the sparse framework for an
abundance of individual episodes from different historical ages,

anecdotes, tales, and novellas, all merging into a stream of natural, rather than human, history in which the exuberance of geological evolution and botanical growth blindly triumphs over human resolution, action, and will.

In *Schlussball*, 1958 / *The Final Ball*, 1960, Gaiser joins those writers of the middle and the younger generations who bitterly condemn the new consumer society; but unlike those who almost exhaust their creative energies in social criticism he sets up, in a concurrent volume of stories entitled *Am Pass Nascondo*, 1960 / *On Nascondo Pass*, a poetic utopia where the social ills of the age are resolved in absolute humanity. The West German town of Neu-Spuhl (where *The Final Ball* takes place) and the heroic landscape near Nascondo Pass belong together because they are the negative and positive "fields" of Gaiser's imagination. In *The Final Ball* structure and message are one: the voices of people seeking fulfillment of their selfish interests can be heard but do not communicate with each other; thus the fragmentary story develops in thirty snatches of internal monologues "spoken" by a local seamstress, wise and foolish girls, the widow Andernoth whose husband has not returned from the war, a melancholy teacher (who sounds very much like Gaiser), a Kafkaesque school-board member, and the dead, forgotten in the scramble for new cars, new villas, and refrigerators. These voices try to unravel, at a considerable distance in time, what happened the night of the promenade of the graduating class (a woman committed suicide and an erratic young man cracked his skull while trying to kill) and, wittingly and unwittingly, reveal Neu-Spuhl as a hellish city of emptiness and despair; gilded efficiency on the outside and, as only a few know, rotten to the inhuman core.

The artist Gaiser prefers to dwell in a purer country which he has created for himself; near Nascondo Pass (constantly suggesting a test of human endurance) he pensively roams the bare and stony plateau of a landscape strangely reminiscent of Rilke's Valais or, as Curt Hohoff has succinctly suggested, of a fusion of the Swiss Engadine, Rumania, and Swabia in which childhood memories and war experiences merge. Bound by the Susurra River and Nascondo Pass, this region of rocks, gardens, and vineyards is stark and simple; there are, as in divided Germany, recurrent tensions between the well-ordered territory of Vioms and the more rustic Calvagora, but the narrator has settled in Promischur, where he does not have to be subordinate to anybody and can enjoy the humble pleasures of bread, water, and wine. Transfigured in unexpected ways, many characters from Gaiser's earlier novels, including Peter Hagmann and some of his fellow officers of the air force, appear in strange encounters, and the lonely man of Promischur goes on longing for the girl Ness, also familiar in Gaiser's early work; unlike life in Neu-Spuhl, however, solitude, love, and suffering are central and noble experiences that take place under a clear sky in a country where people speak a poetic tongue both allied to the archetypal Romance language and yet differentiated from any idiom burdened with the dross of raw life. Of all the escape routes which contemporary German writers take from the ugly society, Gaiser's poetic mountain road leads most directly to pastoral Arcadia, close to the clouds.

Gaiser's symbolic isolation in serene Promischur cannot entirely hide the bitterness of a man who, a generation or more ago, belonged to those young German enthusiasts who wanted to transform the world in the image of their conservative visions but were outdone by more radical competitors who relied on ruthless power rather than on romantic dreams. Many of Gaiser's central figures (including Colonel Frenssen in *The Last Squadron* and Soldner in *The Final Ball*) have a *jugendbewegt* past and nostalgically recall the splendor of the blazing campfires, the fiery opposition to the bourgeois and their whores, "their thirst for bitterness and for the lust which kills"; they still hear the folk songs, the guitars, and the flutes melting through the night. They had pristine visions of a strong Germany rising from disgrace and inflation; but, little aware of the complexities of the power struggle in the Weimar Republic, they soon found themselves bewildered, fascinated, and often overwhelmed by the more efficient Nazis who appropriated their idea of youth groups, their cult of nature, nation, and *Reich*, and most of their vocabulary. In his only volume of youthful poetry, *Reiter am Himmel*, 1941 / *Riders against the Sky*, Gaiser himself, like so many of his generation, did not respect the fine line which separated conservative dreamers from the manipulators of power who pretended to be dreaming; he came perilously close to identifying his private visions with the triumphant National Socialism. Later he recognized that he had served a cause which was not his own and vowed never again to be the dupe: "Might I be tempted again," the lonely narrator in Promischur asks, "tempted to do things which I do not know, and of which I don't know whose ends they serve? Rather, I will not serve anybody."

Gaiser's dilemma was that of conservative German patriots who saw the *Reich* reestablished by vulgar but successful power technicians rather than by men of tradition and integrity; and while others of his persuasion, among them Dr. Carl Goerdeler and his noble friends, conspired to kill those who had perverted their ideals, Gaiser was condemned by his almost geological view of history to choose silent, inactive endurance. His representative officers (Hemingway-like heroes struggling in the thicket of German political metaphysics) find themselves fighting a war of which they fundamentally approve but in the service of false masters; van Truck, in *The Ship in the Mountain,* explains to his more skeptical friend that he always considered the Nazis mere pacemakers who would be followed by a conservative order (an idea disproved by political events as early as February, 1933); and Colonel Frenssen, in *The Last Squadron,* exhorts the young pilots to fight for their loved ones but admits to himself that he does not believe in the war any more, although he does not want to disassociate himself from it. Frenssen, who studied theology and was a youth leader (like Gaiser), knows that Hitler is a madman but believes that he was sent by God to chastise Germany and that it is useless to attempt individual revolt against a fate ordained by God: *contra Deum nemo nisi Deus ipse*—against God nobody but God himself can act. He lends a metaphysical, almost religious aura to a resistible political dictator and, a victim of his own speculative inclinations, has no other choice but to serve without belief and to die during the last days of the war.

Gaiser has softened but not relinquished his conservative and patriotic views, in which a marked sympathy for the simple and pure coincides with a good deal of fatalism and a deep dissatisfaction with a new society concerned with material things of the prefabricated kind, rather than with the immanent values of Rilkean *Dinge*, shaped by the soulful hands of the careful craftsman. He has been accused of lacking "epic stamina," but the ugly new world of individual egotisms is expressed better in narrative mosaics than in the inclusiveness of the old novel; and transforming the limitations of his talent into a strength, Gaiser forms his episodes and internal monologues into loose conglomerations which exactly reflect what he sees of the discordant world; Hermann Broch, another conservative, coped with similar problems. Gaiser's concern with geological change and biological growth as the prime elements of life permeates his rich, occasionally almost scientific vocabulary; in the human realm he admires half-articulated tales of unusual endurance, puritanical women with old-fashioned Germanic names (reminiscent of D. H. Lawrence but with ideological rather than sexual implications), and sensitive educators without the required certificates; he has little patience with intellectuals, functionaries of any establishment, dark-haired foreigners, "operators," and those who live and die for money—people whose souls consist of guaranteed genuine "synthetics," as he says. Gaiser's bitter condemnation of the renascent "bourgeois," dominant in West Germany, strikes me as oddly consonant with the antipathies of the intellectual left, whose restored "capitalist" has as little soul as has Gaiser's *Bürger*; and, in an oblique way, Gaiser, the pensive conservative, and an aggressive liberal like Wolfgang Koeppen are brothers in spirit; dissatisfaction with a purely materialistic society cuts through right and left. In Germany, idealism wears many masks and faces.

3. Alfred Andersch

IN HIS WRITINGS as well as in his life, Alfred Andersch (b. 1914) has explored more concretely than anyone of his generation the crucial tension between action and reflection, social commitment and self-centered sensibility. A few months after his conservative father died, the young man joined the Communist party, and when Hitler came to power he headed the Communist youth organization of Bavaria. He was briefly held at the Dachau concentration camp (1933); his release almost coincided with his decision to break with the Party because it had not fought to the bitter end, to withdraw instead to unobtrusive office jobs which gave him ample leisure to read Rilke, continue his lonely hikes, and indulge in private studies of art history. Yet he could not forget those of his friends in the youth organization who had been tortured and killed, and when, as a soldier of the German *Wehrmacht*, he was confronted with comrades of a different kind, his resolution to stage a private revolt grew almost subconsciously; on June 6, 1944, Private Andersch threw away his gun and, near Nettuno, crossed the lines. It was the first "act" of his renewed social commitment; after some time in American POW camps, Andersch returned to Germany and was, for more than twelve years, among the most active and impatient critics, editors, and moralists; coediting *Der Ruf* (*The Call*), the representative periodical of the younger generation, and establishing broadcasting services modeled after the British Third Programme, he contributed decisively to shaping ideas and forms of Germany's reviving intellectual life. Not until the late 'fifties did he resign from his public functions with the South German Broadcasting Corporation and move to the Swiss Ticino, where he concentrated on his novels, his literary essays, and (almost alone among older German writers, who do not go to the movies) on illuminating criticism of the cinema, which he with good reason considers one of the key arts of our age. In spite of a streak of German inwardness, which he continues to exorcise in his narratives, Andersch is an articulate intellectual in the European liberal tradition; and after wavering, in his own kind of German extremism, between Lenin and Rilke, he has long been attracted by Albert Camus and Elio Vittorini, who, although concerned with more than personal affairs, were yet unwilling to yield their right to personal choice.

Andersch's *Die Kirschen der Freiheit*, 1952 / *The Cherries of Freedom* suggests much of the intellectual and literary assumptions of his early development. It is a *récit*, not a leisurely autobiography; interpreting rather than unfolding his memories of the 'thirties and 'forties, Andersch is constantly wondering how renewed engagement results from disinvolvement. He does not want to make the past more poetic but rather to purify it by making it more distinct; remembering, with moving loyalty, his dead Communist friends, Andersch admits openly that he feels the Communist party failed because it was unwilling to admit spontaneity of thought and action; and when dealing with the frustration that induced him to turn to apolitical art in the mid-'thirties, he does not fail to relate his private escapism to that of many others who "responded to the totalitarian state by total inversion." But in interpreting the past Andersch also hopes to contribute to a new poetic: since life culminates in isolated and sudden "choices" or "acts of freedom," modern writers cannot use the traditional German symbolic calligraphy which revels in prettified continuities. What is needed is a new mode of "immediate narration," a way of writing which would be as "sharply cut" as Louis Armstrong's jazz or Ernest Hemingway's prose. This is the last time in postwar years that anyone challenges the German literary tradition in the name of American vitality and force; after Andersch, the young writers of the 'sixties share the anti-Americanism of the European New Left and opt for Ché or Mao rather than follow Andersch's inclusive American sympathies.

In *Sansibar oder der letzte Grund,* 1957 / [Zanzibar, or the Final Reason] *Flight to Afar,* 1958, Andersch projects his personal experiences into a model situation in prewar Nazi Germany; there is a dense web of cunning and close escape, but the existentialist pattern to be demonstrated triumphs all too easily over the loose ends of life. On a gray day in late October, 1937, in the small town of Rerik on the Baltic coast, five people confront decisions that are fundamentally to alter their lives. They are Judith Levin, a young Jewish girl who has come from Hamburg to find a steamer for her escape to Sweden; Gregor, a well-trained Communist functionary on his last trip in the service of the illegal party which he hates because it failed to resist Hitler; the fisherman Knudsen, an old Communist whose beliefs have long been crumbling; Pastor Helander, who wants to protect an avant-garde statue (reminiscent of Ernst Barlach's work) that the *Gestapo* has ordered to be taken from his church; and a young boy who reads

Mark Twain and dreams of leaving suffocating Rerik for exotic Zanzibar "beyond the open seas." Within twenty-four hours these people are intimately involved with each other, because they cannot carry out their choices without each other's help. The Jewish girl and the precious statue are brought to Sweden by Knudsen, who resolves to return to his sick wife and to whatever he will have to endure; the young boy enjoys an hour of supreme freedom in a Swedish forest but without a word returns home with Knudsen, who will be his new father; Gregor, in engineering Judith's flight and the rescue of the statue as a "private undertaking," breaks with his organized past and decides to resist on his own; and Pastor Helander takes his army revolver and shoots the *Gestapo* official who comes in the morning to arrest him. From the net of interrelationships, the statue of the *Young Monk Reading* emerges as a symbolic image of normative attitudes: disciplined and yet free, attentive to knowledge and yet ready at any moment to get up and act in accordance with his inner self.

Concentrating on the fleeting acts of choice, seen as supreme moments of being, Andersch inevitably develops a narrative structure of spare, fragmentary description combined with the "quoted thought" of his individual characters. The strength of the story thus resides in the pervasive characters, or rather in the differentiated autonomy of their consciousness; the trouble is that Andersch is not equally successful with all five of them. He tries to separate the innocent world of the boy (who does not even know the word "freedom" but burningly feels the meaning of it in his daydreams of Zanzibar) from the adults' universe, determined by conventions and ideologies; but Helander and Gregor, who are highly skilled in articulating theoretical issues, predominate over inarticulate Knudsen and the paper Jewess. Helander and Gregor, hating the church and the party that failed, seek to develop new attitudes, preserving something of their past and yet asserting their individual stances; Gregor falls back upon Andersch's personal experiences, and Helander, who still bears a festering wound from the Verdun trenches, has much of the dignity of suffering which Andersch suggests in the fate of his own dying father in *The Cherries of Freedom*: Helander, I suspect, is Andersch's father as the son wanted him to be. Andersch ironically hides the central meaning of *Zanzibar* in the party message which Gregor is to bring to the dwindling group of his Rerik comrades: as Nazi political pressure was increasing, the party had decided to rebuild the network of illegal combatants in small cells of five who would be unknown to other cells and thus have a better chance of surviving. Contrary to the expectations of the party, Gregor indeed helps to build a compact group, consisting of five people who have chosen freedom by making spontaneous choices. They are the exemplary "cell" of five on whom the future of mankind rests.

German critics, who for pedagogical reasons often like neat patterns of character and event, have high praise for the Rerik five; but I prefer the more mature novel *Die Rote*, 1960 / *The Redhead*, 1962, because I feel that in this novel Andersch deals with escape, change, transformation, and his cherished character of the defeated revolutionary within a more complex environment: basically, Rerik was another German inscape, but Venice, with its iridescent past and its modern fusion of *calamari* and high life, gives the working novelist a much better chance of avoiding abstract situations with didactic overtones. After a long weekend of sudden reversals of fate, the lives of Franziska, a highly qualified German interpreter (whose fair hair attracts both Italians and Germans), and Fabio Crepaz, a violin player who once commanded the partisans of the region, come together in almost pastoral bliss and serenity. Franziska faces the question of escape and change in intimate terms: married to Herbert, a German corporation man of aesthetic pretensions, and involved in an affair with his boss Joachim, she decides to break with her past and, on the spur of the moment, takes the train from Milan to Venice to embark there on a life of her own. Trying to improvise before settling on a job, she suddenly finds herself involved in the conflict between a former member of the British Counterintelligence Service and his onetime German enemy and, staggering from the fatal scene of their final encounter, almost instinctively seeks refuge in the embrace of Fabio, whom she barely remembers from a previous chance encounter. Andersch does not relish explicit happy endings, but there is one in a sort of proletarian guise: Fabio, who has long since left his revolu-

tionary fervor for a life of stoic meditation, brings Franziska to
the house of his mother, where she will go on living as a working
girl and give birth to her child, whose father, Herbert, she will
divorce. Franziska has always longed to penetrate the mysteries
of the Italian houses, withering with age and besmirched with
the dirt of true life, for she suspects that they are places of
happiness where people preserve their "poor, bitter, and luminous secrets," unlike her German compatriots who, in a country
of boredom, mistakenly seek sterile cleanliness (*Reinlichkeit*) instead of moral purity (*Reinheit*). Her transformation fulfills her
hidden dreams.

Andersch's narrative art has become mature and differentiated: he has refined his combination of description and "quoted
thought"; and, in alternating passages, ascribed with architectonic
precision to Franziska and Fabio, he closes each "day," or set of
monologues, with some of the discordant thoughts of Pietro,
Fabio's father and one of the last fishermen of Mestre. Pietro
utters fundamental magic words like "children," "fish," "sea,"
and "sun," and provides a pervasive counterpoint to the swift
spy plot and the *recherché* ritual of High Tea in the world of Venice
homosexuals. Despite what German critics say, *Die Rote* strikes
me as a rich, austere novel of considerable sophistication, and
if Andersch has erred by devoting too much energy to the spy-
and-Nazi game he can successfully claim to compete with
Graham Greene's best entertainments; outside Germany it is less
of a crime to produce novels that combine a certain amount of
depth with pervasive suspense.

Marcel Reich-Ranicki has made a convincing case for Andersch
as a "defeated revolutionary," but is is important to stress the
implications of such a curt image; Andersch is as much a defeated
revolutionary as, on the right, Gerd Gaiser; yet he differs essentially from his conservative counterpart in tone and narrative
technique. Both have gained as novelists what they have lost as
men of political action because (to quote Fabio Caprez) "vain but
not meaningless" involvement yielded the fruitful distance
necessary to epic art. Unlike Gaiser, who seeks escape in elegiac
moods, Alfred Andersch seems a lonely German Stendhalian who
combines bitter liberalism with a searching psychological interest

in how people's thinking ties in with irrevocable turns of fate; and, concerned as he is with the filtering mind rather than with impersonal realities, Andersch concentrates on unique moments of existential decision rather than on prolonged periods of slow psychological development. In his recent *Efraim*, 1967, Andersch confirms many of his views on art and experience and again demonstrates his deft handling of character and scene. George Efraim is a British journalist who is sent to Berlin (where he was born of a Jewish family in the early 'twenties) to report on the mood of the city during the Cuban missile crisis and to track down a young Jewish girl who disappeared from the house of her mother long before the persecutions began. He does not complete either assignment, but in a radical act of self-discovery (relating him to Franziska and the Rerik five) he realizes that the trip to Berlin constitutes a return to his own childhood and begins to write in German again after many years. Step by step he tries to find out whether his world really lacks all freedom of choice, as he has so often affirmed. For a brief moment it seems that lonely Efraim may find understanding in Anna Krystek, a young actress trained in Brecht's ensemble, but she does not want to leave Berlin, and he remains alone with the growing novel of his life. Andersch suggests his belief that writing should stay close to experience, "every sentence to imply a fact or at least a thing," and fully subscribes to Efraim's belief that novels reveal how people relate to others. Trollope is mentioned approvingly, and the recurrent figure of the old Communist (here a Berlin coal merchant who speaks in down-to-earth dialect) is done with an irony and compassion reminiscent of Thomas Mann, if not Theodor Fontane.

Alfred Andersch's artistic development clearly demonstrates that his postwar polemics against "arty" writing were of polemical rather than normative relevance. He was among the first to clamor against "style," against "beautifying" literature, and the literary artifact that contrasts so oddly with the vicious realities of our age, but it was precisely his stubborn interest in man's response to the new "border situations" of modern life that inevitably prompted him to develop a highly complicated method of his own; and although he successfully avoids the convoluted syntax of the German *Bildungsroman* from Adalbert Stifter to Thomas Mann, he has turned his own combinations of paratactical description, "quoted thought," and self-analysis into an instrument as sophisticated as the old "calligraphy" he dislikes. The artist cannot escape the exigencies of art.

I suspect there is a growing gap between the West German New Left, oriented toward problems of alienation, and Andersch's intellectual world with its elements of existentialism, liberal socialism, and considerable sympathy for the great American writers of "life," Mark Twain, Herman Melville, and William Faulkner. But the German left, old or new, cannot do without him. To the young writers of the 'sixties, the battles of the workingman have turned into abstract history, but Andersch still remembers the smell of the backrooms, the shabby leather jackets, and the handbills; he sympathizes with resolute involvement, yet, averse to ideological slogans of any kind, he keeps his word (as he says) "at the sharp tip of his pen"; he wants the work of art to articulate human truth (as does Pastor Helander's *Young Monk Reading*) and untiringly insists (as does hardly anybody else on the left) on the artist's sensibility. There are few German writers today equally qualified to tell how much of the revolutionary ecstasy of the age continues to burn with a fierce flame and how much has long since turned to bitter ashes.

4. Heinrich Böll

FEW CONTEMPORARY German authors are more widely known than Heinrich Böll (b. 1917), whose stories are regularly discussed in German schools, closely read in American colleges, and perceptively praised in the Soviet Union. In his own honest way Böll fulfills many varied expectations: his revolutionary anger at the establishments of state, church, and army springs from conservative inclination; his bitter distrust of the modern communication industries from a strong moral sense; and his implacable hatred of power from boundless compassion for the wounded and the defenseless. Catholics, Marxists, and belligerent intellectuals in Germany and elsewhere have legitimate reasons for admiring his moral force but often choose to overlook the more ambivalent challenges posed by his work.

Toward the end of the 'fifties Böll was nearly everybody's "good German," but more recently he has annoyed his ideological friends: his serious moral commitment remains the unshakable foundation of his work, but he now demonstrates a new freedom of artistic choice, a thoughtful finesse, and a searching concern with the potential ironies of message and form. As Adenauer's gadfly Böll contributed greatly to changing German literature, but his recent prose thrusts him in the direction of the bitter excellence of Georges Bernanos, Graham Greene, or Evelyn Waugh.

Heinrich Böll's ancestors were English ship carpenters of the Catholic faith, who during the Reformation clung to their inherited religion and emigrated first to Holland and later to Cologne. Böll began writing novels at seventeen; and after he had finished the *Gymnasium* he worked as an apprentice in a bookshop and studied German literature for a few weeks before the war began. Böll served for six years in the German army in France, Russia, and elsewhere, was wounded four times, taken prisoner on the Western Front, and finally released from an Allied POW camp in eastern France; and although he occasionally likes to talk about his childhood, the record of his traumatic war experiences must be deduced from the lives of his fictive figures; he rarely touches upon them beyond and outside a detached work of art.

Many of Böll's characters roam restlessly through cities and desolate railway stations, but their author does not share their desire for incessant travel. In the mid-'fifties he discovered Ireland as his Isle of Poetic Dreams (a country that is, contrasted to West Germany, modest, spiritual, and infinitely alive), but he has chosen the path of the hard worker, precise craftsman, and good father, and continues to live in a house on the edge of Cologne where, unaffected by distinctions and awards, he alternates work on his novels, short stories, radio plays, and essays with first-rate translations. Together with his wife Annemarie he has translated many Irish and American authors, including John Synge, Brendan Behan, and J. D. Salinger; and his review articles on Mary McCarthy, François Mauriac, and others indicate that his knowledge of European and American literature lacks neither depth, scope, nor critical judgment.

But despite his settled ways, Böll continues to develop as a writer. In his early prose Böll searched for green islands of human compassion, developing a technique of reported thought and a highly stylized *monologue intérieur*. He did not yet cope firmly with the drawbacks of the form: his search for the isolated individual implied a dispersion of narrative interests (resulting in excellent short stories and loosely organized novels made up of encounters and situations), and he identified himself too closely with his characters; if they became maudlin, he did, too. But in *Billard um halbzehn*, 1959 / *Billiards at Half Past Nine*, 1962, one of the most important recent German novels, both from a political and from an aesthetic point of view, Böll's art gains markedly in force: an ingenious compression of the time scheme links together disparate memories and varied chronological sequences; the narrator, who rarely speaks for himself, now exercises an unobtrusive check on the sentiments of the individual narrative voices; compassion and anger are in productive balance; and language has become brittle and imperturbably sober. In the narratives of the 'sixties, including *Ansichten eines Clowns*, 1963 / *The Clown*, 1965; *Entfernung von der Truppe*, 1964 / *Absent without Leave*, 1965; and *Ende einer Dienstfahrt*, 1966 / *End of a Mission*, 1968, the artist Böll comes fully into his own. Concerned with the individual's inevitable alienation from all the organizations and institutions that manipulate his life, Böll experiments with different sets of narrative premises; and closely checked rage, corrosive satire, and the willful free play of art miraculously combine. Stated simply, Böll tried in his early work to combat the false heroics of German life and literature by rediscovering the world of Dostoyevsky's wounded, poor, and offended, but in the 'sixties he is fighting the late heirs of the Nazis, moving closer to the strategies of Jonathan Swift, "the desperate Dean," whose grave he visited on his trip to Dublin.

Böll's first published narrative, *Der Zug war pünktlich*, 1949 / *The Train Was on Time*, 1956, displays many of the virtues and vices of his early work. It is the story of the young soldier

Andreas who returns from his leave at home knowing that he is going to be killed within a few days, finds a moment of happiness with a Polish girl, and dies, exactly at the anticipated hour and place, when Polish partisans blow up the car in which he is traveling (away from the war). In Andreas' encounter with the girl Olina all abstract loyalties are destroyed: it is a night of feeling, music, and mutual confessions, and the young people dream of escaping together to a lonely spot in the Carpathian mountains where they would be undisturbed by soldiers or partisans. Böll convinces (as Theodore Ziolkowski admirably demonstrates) by showing the inevitability of Andreas' fatal quest, but structural perfection suffers badly: the story is extraordinary in its first half for its atmospheric precision, meaningful use of leitmotifs, and skillful transition from reported thought to Andreas' *monologue intérieur*, but in the second part Böll utterly lacks control of the sentimental motifs of Olina, the prostitute with the Fragonard face, the Beethoven sonatas (in the bordello), and the "B" movie *Liebestod*. But in Andreas' and Olina's moment of happiness Böll early defines an essential element of his vision; from the senselessness and the inhumanity of the war Böll almost compulsively returns to encounters between unheroic men and women, encounters momentary and yet binding like a sacrament for all the future.

In his novel *Wo warst Du, Adam?*, 1951 / *Adam, Where Art Thou?*, 1955, Böll carefully prepares the martial backdrop for important confrontations: between Sergeant Schneider and the Hungarian peasant girl Szarka, whose hands smell of leather, earth, and onions; between the German soldier Feinhals, who is to die when he reaches his father's house in the spring of 1945, and the Jewish schoolteacher Ilona, who is transported to a concentration camp. Dealing with plagued lives in the destroyed German cities, Böll does not change his mind; the irrevocable encounter, increasingly and openly related to the sacrament of marriage, stands for spiritual salvation and provides, in a universe of hunger, cold, and emptiness, warmth and bliss. In the compact novel *Und sagte kein einziges Wort*, 1953 / [And Never Said a Mumbling Word] *Acquainted with the Night*, 1954, husband and wife tell the story of their endangered marriage in alternating lonely monologues: Fred, a somewhat shiftless man, has left his wife Kate and the children, because he could not stand living in their crumbling one-room apartment, constantly invaded by the noises of unfriendly neighbors. But after trying to replace his married life with contrived one-night encounters with his wife in cheap hotels, he suddenly sees her with the eyes of love again as she crosses the street, and in his moment of mystical realization decides to return home to their shabby but sacramental life together. Similarly decisive and irrevocable is the encounter between the young man and the girl in *Das Brot der frühen Jahre*, 1955 / *The Bread of Our Early Years*, 1957: a glance, a moment; and a decision for all eternity is made. Walter Fendrich, who grew up in the hungry years and never had enough of the bread of love, makes a "passable living" as a washing-machine expert and is to marry his boss's daughter; but when he meets Hedwig he feels immediately that he will not part from her side, "neither today nor any day to come," willfully destroys his established materialistic routine and, as if struck by the lighting of love or grace, enters a life of meaning and fulfillment.

Among Böll's earlier narratives, his *Haus ohne Hüter*, 1954 / [House without a Guardian] *Tomorrow and Yesterday*, 1957, occupies a particular place because it is his first full-fledged novel of considerable scope. He skillfully handles a complex group of three-dimensional characters and does not hesitate to introduce a massive element of fierce satire, something which has become more characteristic of his later work. Most of the narration is presented by five "voices" which exemplify what happens when fathers are senselessly killed in war and life has to proceed without them: two women who have lost their husbands (Nella Bach and Frau Brielach), two fatherless sons (Martin Bach and Heinrich Brielach), and a loyal man (Albrecht) who has lost his friend, try to carry on despite their irreparable losses. For both Nella, born of a well-to-do family, and the plebeian Frau Brielach, the great encounter is past, and both are tempted, each in her own way, to escape bygone days. Frau Brielach joins her life and that of her son to a series of "uncles," each of whom lives with her, pats or scolds the boy, and one day disappears to make way for the next "uncle"; Nella has a few affairs of small consequence, wavers between hectic party-going and shameless apathy, and seeks salvation in the "third reality" of possible memories, dreaming of a "life which has never been lived and could not be lived because the time allotted to it was past."

The novel *Billiards at Half Past Nine* marks an important turning point in Böll's development and his first literary contribution of more than German relevance. He works with themes and formal strategies which he has rehearsed before, but he exerts admirable control over his methods, has learned how to distance himself productively from his characters, and judiciously balances his feelings in a dirge inspired by implacable rage. In *Billiards at Half Past Nine* Böll treats a single day (September 6, 1958) in the life of the Fähmels, a prominent family of Cologne architects; it is a "great day" because on it everyone makes important discoveries about himself and others. A great day, and a long day: the Fähmels and some of their friends reach in their reminiscences far back into the past of their lives, of the clan, of the city, and of the country; and from their memories a record of German historical experience emerges in a complex of sharply outlined images. It is a surprisingly successful attempt to capture the history of a German family within a lucid moment of transformation.

Heinrich Fähmel came to Cologne as a poor young man from the countryside, but he had his future exactly planned from his very first day in the city (September 6, 1907); he purposefully developed a ritual of intriguing habits, including an order of paprika cheese for his daily breakfast, won the competition for designing the new monastery of St. Anthony in the Kissa Valley, married Johanna Kilb, thus becoming a member of a patrician clan, and found himself respected, rich, and popular at an early age. His son Robert Fähmel constantly returns in his memories to the decisive week of July 14 to 21, 1935, when he protected his friend Schrella on the ball field (as Günter Grass's Matern protects Eddie Amsel), joined a group of young people who were pledged not to partake of the "host of beasts," and subsequently has to escape to Holland. Later he was allowed to return to Germany, on the condition that he should enlist in the *Wehrmacht* as a demolition expert; he takes his revenge during the last days of the war when, heading an expert demolition crew, he blows up St. Anthony's, the work of his father. Robert's son Joseph has become an architect, too, and works for a firm that is rebuilding the monastery. Inspecting the foundations of the building, he discovers chalk signs in his father's hand indicating the spots where the explosive charges were to be placed; shocked by his discovery, he resolves to leave his job with the reconstruction firm and to think once more about his future. Joseph is not the only one who discovers Robert's part in the destruction of the building; when old Heinrich and Robert accompany the new abbot on an inspection tour of the reconstruction site, Heinrich instinctively realizes, from Robert's gestures, that it was his own son who destroyed his most famous architectural achievement. Yet he is not hurt: he has come to see that people are more important than bricks; and when, that evening, his eightieth birthday is celebrated and a huge cake (baked in the form of the monastery) is brought in, he cuts the top off the cake and serves it to Robert as a sign of their ironic final reconciliation.

Robert Fähmel develops his own mystical strategy for combating history, eluding time by daily withdrawing to the Hotel Prinz Heinrich, where he plays billiards with the bellboy Hugo and ruminates about his part, telling Hugo his own story and listening to what Hugo has to say. In the billiard game, which is as fascinating to him as is the pattern of flickering lights in the pinball machines to Fred Bogner in *Acquainted with the Night* and Albert in *Tomorrow and Yesterday*, he senses something that resembles a mathematically ordered work of art, unfolding within its own strict laws and occurring outside time; and while the balls click timelessly, his voice loses itself in the horizons of time ("in den Zeiten"). His daily game of billiards creates a "geometrical figure of green nothingness . . . paths of comets, white and green, red over green," and he experiences "music without melody, painting without pictures." His game protects Robert against the demands of time: "There, time was not a quantity which indicated anything . . . on this green blotting paper it was blotted out; in vain the clocks sounded, vainly their hands moved." But Robert's escape from time is ended when his friend Schrella returns from exile and suddenly embodies "the constant presence

of time"; confronting his oldest friend (whose sister was his wife),
Robert realizes that he cannot withdraw from time and finally
(like Heinrich, his father) accepts what is "here, today, now."

The author shares with both Heinrich and Robert Fähmel an
aversion to historical time in that he orders his world according
to an inflexible pattern highly resistant to modification by psychological or historical developments; people are either "lambs"
or have evilly "partaken of the host of the beasts"; either they
are powerless, or they ruthlessly exercise a power that continues
to be theirs through the years (May, 1945, meant little change
to them). Robert Fähmel, the self-appointed shepherd, time and
again thinks of the "lambs": Ferdi Progulske, the boy who threw
a primitive bomb at a Nazi bully (it merely singed his feet);
Robert's cousin Georg, who provided the black powder for the
homemade explosives; Edith Schrella, who was to be the mother
of Robert's children; her father, who hid Ferdi under the counter
among the beer pipes before the *Gestapo* came; Edith's brother,
who escaped to England where he read Hölderlin and taught
German; the unknown boy who passed on secret messages; the
waiter Groll, who sent money to Holland to keep Robert alive—
and there are the "little lamb" Marianne, Joseph Fähmel's fiancée
who, in May, 1945, was almost killed by her suicidal Nazi mother
but was rescued by humble folk, and Hugo, the orphan, on whose
face a gentle smile reflects the helplessness of all the "lambs."
Most of the "lambs" have been killed by those in power or, like
Edith, have died in the bombed city, but most of those who have
"partaken of the host of the beasts" (including those monks of
St. Anthony who joined in the Nazi rites) continue to live, thrive,
and exert their power without sadness or remorse: Otto Fähmel,
who spied on his brother and disdained his parents, died in
Russia, but his friend Nettlinger, who once whipped Schrella and
Robert with barbed wire, functions as a high official of the federal
government; Bernhard Wakiera, nicknamed "Wackes," Robert's
former gymnastics teacher, was the town's police chief under the
Nazi regime and in the Federal Republic continues to be an
important man in conservative politics. It is fascinating to observe
the developing tension between the natural order of the family
(fundamental to Böll's vision) and the moral division of the

world; in Böll's early narratives the beasts were outside the family, but in *Billiards at Half Past Nine* they have invaded the family sphere. In the final battle the moral order must triumph over natural law: Robert Fähmel adopts Hugo, his spiritual son; old Heinrich Fähmel considers Schrella, returning from exile, a new son of his own; and a spiritual community (in which family relationships continue to be important) is constituted by choice.

In his novels and narratives of the early 'sixties Heinrich Böll nearly abandons the often rehearsed techniques of his earlier work and, sure now of his craft, begins to experiment with a wider range of forms and epic strategies; his *Clown* may be close to his earlier technical interests in reported thought and internal monologue, but in *End of a Mission* and *Absent without Leave* he tries methods which he never used before. Böll's mood has certainly darkened; at a time when the powerful establishments of state, church, army, and "good" society again determine the life of the individual, meaningful encounters between people are lethally threatened by institutional pressures; those who want to retain their integrity as human beings must do their utmost to withdraw from the organizations that busily manipulate the crowds for their own interests.

In *The Clown* twenty-seven-year-old Hans Schnier tells of a lonely March evening in his deserted apartment and his decision to confront society as a guitar-strumming beggar on the steps of the Bonn railway station. Hans once left school out of love for Marie, the poor daughter of a Communist without a party, and instead of choosing an appropriate middle-class profession, he became a jester; for five years he was successful at his art of showing the absurdities of daily life in ingenious pantomines. But Marie, who shared his restless travels, lost two children prematurely and, longing for a more settled life, joined a discussion group of liberal Catholics. After Hans had refused to submit to a state-approved marriage ceremony and to sign a document guaranteeing the Catholic education of his future children, she left him in "metaphysical terror" and married Heribert Züpfner, one of the prominent Catholics of the West German establishment. Hans's fight for Marie is a hopeless affair: he tries to establish communications by a series of desperate telephone calls, only to discover that Marie has not opened his daily letters and has left with her husband for Rome. Hans Schnier's prominent and foolish father tries in vain to convince his son to accept his failure; and when his brother Leo (who is being trained for the priesthood in a nearby monastery) refuses to see Hans for reasons of mere school discipline, Hans paints his face white, takes his guitar, and walks over to the railway station, where he sits down on the steps, plays his little ditty about Pope John, and appeals to the compassion of the travelers. A first coin drops into his hat, but there is little hope that he will move Marie's heart when she returns on the Rome Express.

In spite of his small apartment high up on the fifth floor Hans Schnier is a West German underground man in radical alienation from society. He began to go his own way when his sister was killed in the last months of the war and he burned her possessions on a funeral pyre of his own making; unable to forget as easily as most of his compatriots, he is haunted by the "terror of the detail" and fears being "addressed by half-intoxicated Germans of a certain age, because they speak of the war and reveal themselves as murderers when they are really drunk." He thinks of his teacher Brühl, who was not a member of the Nazi party and yet preached the necessity of defending the holy German soil against the "Jewish Yankees" and asked for merciless punishment when Hans was to undergo a drumhead trial by the Nazi youth organization; and he also remembers the district party leader who defended Hans against the accusing functionary of the youth organization, and his own mother, who loyally supported the National Socialists until the very end but who recently chaired a committee for racial reconciliation and often lectures to ladies' clubs in the United States. Hans refuses to accept alternatives open to others: he recognizes only four genuine Catholics (Pope John, Alec Guinness, the girl Marie, and the Negro boxer Gregory), cannot stand his Catholic friends who sip expensive wines while they discuss problems of world poverty and who have mobilized Marie's longing for a legally approved home against his purer loyalties; and when he goes to Ulbricht's Germany he quickly discovers that the functionaries there are as concerned with proper tradition as are his friends in Bonn and are shocked when he suggests that he would like to perform a new act entitled "Election to the Central Committee" before GDR audiences. Marie was his only hope in an absurd world of offensive law and unfair order; and once she has left him he has nothing to show to the world but his suffering self.

In *End of a Mission* Böll skillfully surrounds his fierce determination with an effective camouflage of syntax and idiom; as R. W. Leonhardt has shown, matter and mode of presentation collide in explosive incompatibility. His narrator reports on a trial before the court of Birglar, a small town in the Rhineland; although the case is an unusual one, the authorities want to play it down, and appoint a man well known for his humanity (and soon scheduled to retire) as presiding judge. Two upright carpenters with some artistic leanings, fifty-year-old Johann Heinrich Georg Gruhl and his son Georg, are accused of a surprising transgression: on a hot day in July, 1945, they were seen in the fields near the main road burning a jeep of the German *Bundeswehr* and banging their pipes together in the rhythm of *Ora pro nobis;* when interrogated they confessed in their homely Rhenish dialect that they had wanted to arrange a little "happening." A professor from the Academy of Art does indeed testify that their burning of the jeep was a "quinquimusal" event, because the five muses of architecture, sculpture, dance, music, and literature were involved; and since the authorities do not press the case (but want to see the trial finished within a day and without publicity), the wise judge sentences the accused to damages and six weeks in prison, for he does not want to see their art degenerate into mechanical repetition; the army has to return the wreck of the jeep to the Gruhls because it constitutes the material of their art. The point is that the narrator himself takes the side of the authorities; he writes his report in the extremely traditional style characteristic of the German novella of the late nineteenth century but does not see that his style works against the import of his narrative. As an accomplice of the authorities, he creates a polished traditional syntactical texture, but beneath it beat the hearts of the two noble anarchists, and the jeep burns on as a fiery symbol of productive disorder.

Böll is not a Catholic writer in the dogmatic sense; his char-

acters move in a Catholic world, but they are little concerned
with transcendence. Böll's is an epic world of cathedrals and
churches, early and late masses, litanies and rosaries, nuns and
abbots, but rarely a universe of haunting mysteries; he may share
the anger of a poor parish priest who dislikes the mechanical way
in which traveling church dignitaries run through their daily
mass, but he is not obsessed by the issues of grace, eternity, and
redemption. His Catholicism, like his topography of Cologne,
amounts to a number of props used to indicate the way of life
which he knows best; only in a rare instance does Kate Bogner
feel, in church, "the infinite peace emanating from the presence
of God." It is Böll's open secret that he is concerned with the
immanent results rather than the transcendence of religion; he
observes what people (who happen to be Catholics) do to each
other and leaves theological niceties to professional theologians
and church dignitaries, whom he does not like much. To him,
religion implies an essential "anthropological" question, and
he inevitably favors in his later work an enlightened attitude long
proscribed by the institutions of all historical religions; Pastor
Kolbe in *End of a Mission*, to the astonishment of his superiors,
announces to his village congregation that people may be good
without being good Catholics, or even religious at all. Perhaps
the moralist Böll is less religious than the "immoralist" Grass,
whose highly artistic blasphemies in their own tense way main-
tain a running dialogue with the challenging mysteries of Christ,
salvation, and grace.

Böll's universe includes good and evil people cast in a Dickensian mold of instinctive Christianity: the good people have compassionate hearts and weep easily, and the evil ones possess
hearts of flint and eyes that remain dry. The good always share
and give, the evil retain for themselves or take away; and in the
political sphere the good become "lambs" who suffer at the hands
of power, while the evil become "beasts" who ruthlessly exert
their might. But Böll's attitude emerges distinctly as puritan and
petit bourgeois. Good "lambs" are introspective, close to a tightly
knit communal way of life (like early Christians before Constan-
tine or Communists before Stalin), and given to a kind of homemade spirituality rather than to material things; evil "beasts" are

robust and self-assured, indulging themselves in expensive luxuries such as fifty-cent cigars, tailored suits, and gin fizzes taken in the late afternoon on the terraces of their villas. Böll (like Uwe Johnson) does not like intellectuals who talk too much and hide in their endless speeches their secret collusion with the powers that be; and his sense of plebeian proprieties is offended by the snob (he does not see that snobbery may be a form of aesthetic protest against the gladly conforming "beasts"). Böll relates his moral dichotomies to a symbolic pattern of drinking and eating, and his system of culinary morality immediately reveals whether somebody belongs among the good or the bad. In contrast to Dickens and Gogol, who like their feasts rich and substantial, Böll prefers the simple, leaving the groaning board to the "beasts." Böll's good people drink water, *Schnaps*, beer, and interminable cups of coffee, while bad ones (including many intellectuals) sip French wines with complicated names; "lambs" are usually satisfied with *Butterbrot* and sausage, while the "beasts" do not disdain fashionable menus and have a deplorably delightful time choosing mock turtle soup and *entrecôte à deux*.

From Böll's narratives emerge two dominant characters who, in their symbolic essence, suggest where the center of the world lies: the good woman of Cologne who feeds the hungry, and the restless man who, saddened by terrifying memories of war and power, receives bread (or a cup of coffee) into his hands. Again and again motherly figures set aside food for the beggars or wanderers who come to the door, nuns distribute soup or pudding, and factory girls share their meager breakfast with hungry boys; in the story of Fred and Kate Bogner (*Acquainted with the Night*) Böll sharply contrasts the bleak house of the church authorities, a place of boredom and gossip, with a little food store in which a smiling and beautiful girl serves coffee and simple cake and would not dream of taking money from customers who are in need. In his autobiographical narrative *Als der Krieg zu Ende war*, 1962 / *When the War Ended*, 1964, Böll, describing his way home from prison camp, tells of a simple woman who, at a little railway station, suddenly emerged from behind the building and thrust a piece of bread into his hungry hand. It is an archetypal image that radiates throughout his world.

But in actuality Böll suggests a commitment that is far less political than he would have us believe. His good people tend to congregate in their own catacombs, because they fear contact with the evil world; and yet they feel prompted, at least sometimes, to fight back in their own improvised way. Böll praises their "nobility of helplessness" and yet approves of such incongruous raids against the threatening power as throwing a homemade bomb or burning a jeep; and with his utterly unhistorical view he seems little concerned about the question of whether the Third Reich can without further ado be identified with the Federal Republic. I think he finds himself a prisoner of his ambivalent premise of politically active inaction: he sets the pure apart in their own communion and thus reconfirms the pernicious German tradition of "spirit" vs. "power," all the while knowing that a spiritual *Innerlichkeit* without deed represents a threat of its own kind. He tries to escape the dilemma by staging an occasional happening (funny but without consequence) or introducing a trigger-happy grandmother who fires a misdirected shot at a parading Bonn functionary (a piece of antifascist *Kitsch* much admired by Georg Lukács): it is fascinating to see how quickly the absolute purity of the "lambs" is likely to change into absolute terrorism. The trouble is that Böll's good people are good German petits bourgeois who do not want to get involved with the daily business of politics; traditionally unable to think except in the most extreme terms, they continue to dream of an absolute idyll and are unwilling to soil their hands with something disturbingly relative.

Inside and outside his native country, Heinrich Böll was for a long time the most popular of the new writers, but I wonder whether his popularity did not rest on his early work rather than on the more virile sophistication of his later prose. He was among the first who, in a Germany devastated morally and materially, searched for a human and (as he said in his *Frankfurt Lectures*, 1966) "habitable" language; after the Nazis had triumphed, he had to start from scratch, far below the level of the socially committed literature of the German 'twenties. During the late 'forties and 'fifties, Böll protractedly developed his art (writing some excellent short stories), but it was only with *Billiards at Half*

Past Nine and the subsequent narratives of the 'sixties that he refined the rich virtues of his craftsmanship. It is another problem entirely that his moral commitment, of the absolute sort, actually masks a fundamental disgust with the inevitable politics of small, daily, pragmatic steps. It is all or nothing once again.

5. Martin Walser

MARTIN WALSER (b. 1927) likes to pose as the loyal son of an Alemannic tavern keeper from the idyllic shores of Lake Constance, yet in the 'fifties he was among the first young writers to boldly confront the emerging industrial society. After returning from the war, Walser studied history and German literature, worked for broadcasting and television stations and, once he had had his experiences with the mass media and had published his early stories and a first novel, returned in 1957 to the small town of Friedrichshafen, where he continues to live, not far from the place he was born. Many critics praise exclusively his bitter social criticism, but perhaps it is equally important to consider the virtues of his highly sophisticated and restless intelligence, constantly groping for adequate literary forms.

Martin Walser's beginnings go back to Kafka. As a student he wrote a first-rate dissertation on Kafka's narrative obsessions (1961), and his early prose labored under the burden of Kafka's terrors. His first collection of short stories, *Ein Flugzeug über dem Haus*, 1955 / *A Plane over the House* combines the kind of situation that recurs again and again in Kafka (an individual suddenly and inexplicably confronted with incomprehensible events) with other, perhaps more seminal, motifs and concerns: a plane thundering over the house indicates a darkly fateful turn of affairs, but Walser shows a more objective interest in the psychological complexities of modern marriage, in the traditional culture—to him a disintegrating collection of mere feathers—, and in social criticism, presented in lively parables with a sly grin. I would consider "Der Umzug" / "The Move" the most important story in Walser's transition from Kafka to social themes. A good-natured mechanic and his wife Gerda (who, like all the wives of Walser's lower-class heroes, comes from an upper middle-class family) live in a proletarian neighborhood, but when a windfall brings unexpected money, they move to a wealthier neighborhood. Yet in the new place, the neighbors seem to be afflicted with a curious disease: they sit motionless on their balconies or move slowly and cautiously. No birds sing in their sterile gardens, and their big black cars roll silently out of the garages. When the friendly mechanic notices that his wife is succumbing more and more to the disease, he escapes back to his old neighborhood, where people have gaunt faces but go about their daily work with quick, vital gestures. One is almost reminded of Rex Warner's and William Sansom's attempts in the late 'thirties and early 'forties to use their newfound knowledge of Kafka's parables to broaden the possibilities of the socially committed narrative.

In his compact first novel *Ehen in Philippsburg*, 1957 / *Marriage in Philippsburg*, 1961, little praised by American reviewers, Walser seems to be nervously filing away at his narrative technique. Eager to grasp the whole world of the new German upper middle class and yet intensely suspicious of the Olympian stance of the omniscient nineteenth-century narrator, Walser selects a few strands from the social tissue, concentrating on the experiences of four men who live in the city of Philippsburg in southwestern Germany (possibly Stuttgart) and participate in the rituals of the local cocktail circuit, the sexual interchanging of the "in" group, and the intense political scrambling. But in this sham, success-worshiping society, living means defeat, and those who want to protect their integrity and individuality must die. Hans Beumann, who (like Balzac's Eugène de Rastignac) comes with great expectations to the city, quickly sacrifices his youthful enthusiasm and accepts an editorial job financed by an industrialist whose daughter Anna is to be Beumann's wife; the lawyer Albin, who prides himself on his affairs with shopgirls, glances in the rearview mirror of his car "seeking contact" with Cecile, and in that moment runs into a cyclist and kills him; and Dr. Benrath's wife Birga commits suicide because she can no longer tolerate her husband's prolonged affair with Cecile; after Birga's death has been discovered, Dr. Benrath and Cecile face each other, "two people in a rotten apartment," and the man flees his mistress because she and his wife were inextricably bound together in the dialectics of his desire. Walser occasionally weakens the impact of his sober narrative by indulging in social melodrama—Anna's abortion, Albin's responsibility for the death of the cyclist, and Birga's suicide are indirectly commented upon by the new director of the Philippsburg radio station when he announces that his programs are designed to further harmonious family life—and by introducing, as an almost metaphysical protagonist, the writer Klaff, who goes on fighting for his integrity, loses his socially conforming wife and his job as doorkeeper at the theater, and finally kills himself to express his refusal to become involved in a social mechanism which utterly defiles the mind. Walser succeeds much better in dealing with the complicated case of Cecile's lover, Dr. Benrath, than with that of the maudlin underground man Klaff, who leaves his unpublished manuscripts, reminiscent of Kafka's diaries, to the mercenary Hans Beumann, who rises rapidly in the communications industry. Yet the dangers of social melodrama are reduced because of Walser's technical progress; clearly anticipating his major novels of the 'sixties, he articulates social relationships in a complex net of internal monologues, in which three figures (Beumann, Dr. Benrath, and Albin) express their situation in their own terms, while Klaff speaks through his manuscripts. The impersonal narrator who "translates" consciousness does not have to laboriously interpret political implications.

In his novels of the 'sixties, Walser controls his epic ambitions (now he is eager to embrace the totality of the social world) by using one restless, shifting central sensibility to mirror people and events. His novels *Halbzeit,* 1960 / *Half-Time* and *Das Einhorn,* 1966 / *The Unicorn* are, at least at first sight, the rambling confessions, revelations, and disordered thoughts of one Anselm Kristlein, who pursues a picaresque career as traveling salesman, as an advertising expert in the rapidly expanding West German mass media, and later as a more or less successful second-rate writer who appears at fashionable parties and public round-table discussions.

Half-Time and *The Unicorn* are different in tone and yet intimately related to each other by a recurrent pattern of events.

The earlier volume shows Kristlein (who, when a philosophy student, had married the daughter of a professor) trying to find a place in the sales and advertising jungle, drawing on the spiel of his business colleagues and his secondhand knowledge of Madison Avenue jargon; in the later volume, he has moved from Stuttgart to Munich, operates on the higher level of sales campaigns and publishers' advance contracts, and now offers his confessions in a more literary language, sustained by Joycean allusions and intricate pastiche. His language may have changed somewhat, but not his relentless longing for fullness and fulfillment: while the salesman may have instinctively felt its driving force, the writer Kristlein loquaciously describes his fateful quest and has little doubt that his life should properly be spent in a passionate search for love, childhood, death. There is a repetitive rhythm which tends to keep narrative exuberance in check: after many adventures and misadventures with actresses, secretaries, hairdressers' assistants, teachers, and village girls, Anselm unexpectedly encounters an "exotic" girl of overwhelming charms, but finally returns, a sick man, to his marital bed and to his wife, the *magna mater*. In *Half-Time* the girl is Susanne, who brings the memories of an exiled Jewish family back to the forgetful city; in *The Unicorn*, the magical girl Orli, born in distant Paramaribo of a Jewish mother and a Dutch father. At a camp site Orli utterly bewitches Kristlein, plagued by circulatory troubles, a mild sunstroke, and an acute case of priapism, and compels him to turn to a renewed search for geographical and psychological childhood. Yet after Orli has suddenly left him he returns as usual to his waiting family and, as his vital forces ebb, fuses in his feverish dreams the name of his wife Birga and that of the exotic girl into "Birli" and "Orga," fatal puns suggestive of his rovings between stillness and desire, his haven and the endless quest.

Unlike many of his contemporaries, Walser knows a good deal about the seismographic changes in West Germany after the dislocations produced by the war, the monetary reform, and the rapid emergence of the open industrial society. He cannot entirely hide his basic "populist" sympathies with tired waitresses and intelligent truck drivers, but he coolly explores the interdependence of advertising and everyday speech, the techniques of traveling salesmen, and vestiges of Nazism in the great corporations. In *Half-Time* there is an excellent scene showing a management meeting of the Frantzke Corporation, at which a former high official of Hitler's *Sicherheitsdienst* efficiently organizes a sales campaign by employing the militant language and techniques of his Nazi past; and a saddened observer (nonconformist because homosexual) remarks that former Nazis are always supremely efficient because it makes no difference to them whether they are organizing a roundup of Hungarian Jews, defaming monasteries, or plotting how to increase the sale of canned chicken.

In this world of organization men, a salesman carries (as if he were really a *Christ-lein* or "little Christ") the burden of all humanity on his frail shoulders; and Walser himself suggested that in the emblematic figure of the salesman the paradoxes of modern economics are combined with those of the writer's uncertain function. Anselm feels the despair of being superfluous (salesmen are interchangeable), and yet he dares to hope that the entire fabric of society depends on his selling largely unwanted goods which, in turn, stimulate industrial production. When Kristlein has advanced to being a writer, he continues to feel that it is his responsibility to sell his verbal products to consumers who may or may not want to buy, and still he secretly hopes that the writer's intellectual wares are somehow essential to the subterranean economy of the mind. Salesmen and writers, who both work with words, share daily despair and the furtive hope that they are of some ultimate use to mankind.

Yet these political and sociological issues are but part of Walser's more fundamental concern with reality and art, and of his consistent preoccupation with the function and value of literature. Neither *Half-Time* nor *The Unicorn* has plot or character in the conventional sense: there is only Kristlein's consciousness, an insatiable and relentless maelstrom sucking in and spewing out fragments of impressions, experiences, and feelings; Walser himself has offered the ingenious defense that he had no intention of writing a "novel"; rather, he wanted to present "an accumulation of everything which an author could articulate at a given time, whether a story, reflections, descriptions, or verbal scraps."

His problem is that, like a good nineteenth-century novelist, he yearns for the totality of the world and yet cannot bring himself to follow Balzac (although he does have recurring characters), because he distrusts authors who claim to know all there is to know about what Walser considers an impenetrable reality. The writer cannot trust anybody but himself, or a character who is as close to him as the salesman to the writer; he cannot pretend any more to be an epic lawgiver, interpreting with undisputed authority things he can view only from the outside. His task is to gather details, and nothing but details, hoping that his heap of splinters may hold some meaning; he himself will never interpret. Walser does not justify this narrative method of humble circumspection by offering abstract reasons, but rather by suggesting that it was recent German history that caused his radical skepticism; the Nazi years were enough to transform the character of any human being, even the simplest one, into a "real thicket." After those years we can no longer rely on "predictable" characters (which Thomas Mann would characterize by means of speaking names or leitmotifs), nor would it be possible, Walser suggests in *The Unicorn*, to recognize a man's temperament from the way in which his house is built or his garden tended. Today Gogol's Chichikov would have to know the wiring system of a house in order to know where to find his dead souls.

Walser depends exclusively on the expanding consciousness of the one character whom he knows as well as himself, and yet he insists that he avoids narrative solipsism. He does not present the traditional lonely hero "held together by a skin," but maintains that Anselm Kristlein has many existences and is right in considering himself a "parliament of personal pronouns" in which the first person represents the married, professional, eager salesman; the second fondly and slavishly submits to the unicorn's sexual desires; and the third meanwhile is checking on both and possibly on other selves emerging from Anselm's ego. Present experience and the word of the moment (in whose power Walser fervently believes) are closely related, but an immense abyss opens up between *past* life and *present* language; and it is Anselm's recurrent elegy on the "pastness" of things which reveals that all the exuberant richness of his language is but a desperate attempt to do the impossible and make the past a *now*. But the flesh does not have the power to remember, and the unfortunate Kristlein, who lives so much in the flesh, has reason to complain that the two systems, that of memory and that of language, are entirely different; and Walser, his friendly translator, shares his knowledge that recounting the search for Orli, the girl of ultimate enchantment, constitutes a final proof of the impotence of the word: "If only I could succeed with Orli in demonstrating that one could re-create the past through sultry, slippery words or words desert-dry or eremitical. . . . But one cannot have a real girl by simply speaking, singing, groaning." Yet this is exactly what he constantly does, in endless eruptions of prose, assuming that it would be in his power to bring the past back to life if he could only find the right word; and while Kristlein fails and tries and fails again, he rediscovers the richness of German and of many other languages. There may be a few pages that ramble and rattle, but others, including the monologue in Bernese dialect (a most puritanical idiom) carried on by a Swiss lady publisher while making love, or the final conjuration of Orli, in which Kristlein combines his ultimate passion with the archetypal force of love words from all ages, are, in their refined verbal intelligence, without equal in German writing today.

Martin Walser does not often speak about his work, but in his illuminating *Erfahrungen und Leseerfahrungen, 1965 / Experiences and Reading Experiences* there is an essay on Proust which contains all the clues for reading Walser's own prose. Ordinary people, Walser says, live a narrow, functional existence, but the great writer has a chance to grasp "everything," to show man in all his relationships, to "exhaust all the possibilities of consciousness," and to liberate human nature from functionality, habit, and narrow self-interest. Kristlein's search for the present past may be far from successful, but his wide-ranging failure contributes, because of his very obsession with detail, to freeing our consciousness from the bondage of the specific aim and the particularistic intent. Yet the monstrous accumulation of detail, amassed to break the curse imposed upon each of us by the modern division of labor, shows that Walser is working in closer proximity to Robert Musil than to Proust. A vulnerable intelligence of analytical inclinations goes beneath the surface of human behavior but finds itself increasingly in conflict with the aesthetic exigencies of organizing form. In his narratives as well as in his plays, Walser experiments *faute de mieux*.

6. Uwe Johnson

SLOW IN HIS deliberate gestures and precise in his sparse utterances, Uwe Johnson resembles a pipe-biting north German fisherman, rather than a successful young writer courageously challenging the age of the mass media; Robbe-Grillet's quick ability to articulate his theoretical insights in elegant Cartesian paragraphs and Uwe Johnson's careful double check on each of his sentences are worlds apart. Uwe Johnson (b. 1934) was early involved in German vicissitudes: he was educated for a time at a Nazi school in occupied Poland, moved with the trek of German refugees back to Mecklenburg, which was to become part of the Russian zone, studied German and English literature at the universities of Rostock and Leipzig, where Hans Mayer and Ernst Bloch taught in the early 'fifties, and decided, after a first manuscript had been turned down by the East German state publishing house, to go to the West; with cunning understatement he insists on calling his escape a mere transfer to West Berlin, where he hoped to settle with the permission of the city authorities. The publication of *Mutmassungen über Jakob*, 1959 / *Speculations about Jacob*, 1963, marked a turning point in German writing; it brilliantly illustrated the rise of a new, gifted generation and renewed energy for narrative experimentation; within a few years, Johnson received the Fontane Prize (1960) and the coveted Prix Formentor (1962), the latter of which made him internationally known. He is respected rather than loved by most of his readers, but he has not relented in his "difficult search for truth"; there are few writers in his generation who can compete with his Protestant dedication to his job (whether a novel or a textbook anthology to be compiled for an American publisher). The Allies may have destroyed Prussia, but what is most admirable in the Prussian heritage continues to inform his developing literary production, and once the current, somewhat superficial interest in the topicality of his East German "themes" subsides, his extraordinary contribution to the craft of writing will emerge with welcome clarity.

Uwe Johnson has often been called the writer of divided Germany by sentimental critics, but I fully agree with Marcel Reich-Ranicki that Johnson feels more at home in the territory between the Elbe and the Oder where he grew up than in the western provinces of Germany; a burning, wounded patriotism, territorial rather than political, makes him cling to "Eastern," not "Western," scenes. Again and again he protests, by powerful indirection, against the condescending skepticism of "Western" readers who do not believe firmly enough that a purer, though perhaps more human, way of life continues to assert itself behind the disfiguring slogans and economic regimentation engineered by "Eastern" functionaries. This most gifted writer of the German Democratic Republic just happens to work in West Berlin, and he draws intense strength from his visceral knowledge of life "over there." He cannot avoid interpreting all private woes (as did the great realists of the nineteenth century) in the most intimate alliance with political and public events; in each of his major novels, I suspect, an important political turning point in the development of the German Democratic Republic and the Soviet sphere of influence has a central function in shaping individual existence: the Hungarian Revolution and its post-Stalinist repercussions; the East German workers' uprising of June 17, 1953; and the building of the Berlin Wall. Johnson's famous first novel, *Speculations about Jacob*, investigates the death of a well-liked though taciturn East German railway dispatcher (Robbe-Grillet's *The Erasers*, 1953, shows similar preoccupations). Tortuously, and without final clarity, Johnson pieces together the character of Jacob Abs, the pensive dispatcher, from the memories and the conversations of his comrades, friends, and pursuers; and the many events preceding his death are interpreted from different points of view, including those of his sweetheart Gesine; of her friend Dr. Jonas Blach, a lecturer at Berlin University; and of a member of the secret police. Prompted by the Soviet intelligence agency, the East German state security service wants to enlist Gesine, who works in West German NATO head-

quarters, as an agent (Project Dove on the Roof); and Captain
Rohlfs of the East German agency attempts first to establish
contact with her through her mother, who promptly escapes to
the West, and then through Jacob himself. Jacob does not want
to help the secret police but, in contrast to many of his comrades,
loves his technical work so much that he does not hesitate to
ease the transfer of Russian troops to revolutionary Hungary by
clearing the East German tracks precisely according to order.
Only after he has done so does he suddenly join Gesine in West
Germany. But there he feels deeply disappointed at the crass
indifference of the consumer society, at the tolerance of unre-
generate Nazis, at West German condescension toward the man
from the "East," and at the Suez War, which convinces Gesine
that she should leave her NATO job. Jacob returns to his dis-
patching job, and a few hours after his return from the West
he is killed by a locomotive while crossing the symbolic rails
in the early morning mist. Was it accident, suicide, or a liquidation arranged by the state security service? We cannot know for
sure, but in our effort to find an answer we are confronted with
the overwhelming complexity of a modest life in a period of
violent change and revolution.

Uwe Johnson's *Das dritte Buch über Achim,* 1961 / *The Third Book
about Achim,* 1967, constitutes another attempt to overcome the
almost ontological difficulty of grasping human affairs "over
there." Speculations about a railway dispatcher are replaced by
conjectures about Achim, a famous cycling champion (and member of the People's Parliament) of the German Democratic Republic, but instead of collecting the reports of many friends and
witnesses, Johnson this time uses a relatively central sensibility
to pursue the search. He tells the story of Karsch, a West German
journalist who travels from Hamburg to the East to meet the
actress Karin, once his mistress. Through Karin, Karsch meets
Achim, who fascinates him because he seems to reap the benefits
of both spontaneous popular enthusiasm from below and political
consent from above. There have already been two books written
about Achim, but Karsch signs a contract with the state publishing house to write a third, more relevant, book which would

show Achim in his total involvement with society; and immediately Karsch finds himself confronted with increasing quandaries about knowledge, selection, politics, and art. One day Karsch receives an anonymous letter which contains a snapshot showing Achim marching with the revolting workers on June 17, 1953; and Karsch cannot but see that he has failed in his search for Achim's true image, for not even Karin was aware of Achim's involvement with the insurgents; and Achim himself does not want to admit the evidence of the photograph. In the end is a new beginning; Karsch returns to Hamburg, tells a close friend (who keeps posing searching questions) about his failure, and thus turns his provincial search for a true life story into an all-embracing metaphor for the impossibilities of literary narration in general.

Only in *Zwei Ansichten,* 1965 / *Two Views,* 1966, his third published novel, does Uwe Johnson begin to overcome his early thematic and methodological obsessions; there is considerable trust in the veracity of narrative statement, and the "Eastern" character has its counterpart in a "Western" figure, not employed as a mere analytic tool, but granted autonomous, if rather dubious, rights. We are told the story of two rather less than passionate lovers in the year of the Berlin Wall; Johnson does not even try to suggest that the West German photographer and the East German nurse cherish a particularly burning memory of the casual night they spent together when the young man visited Berlin and met the girl in the apartment of some West Berlin acquaintances. Yet the young man feels vaguely bound by promises which he made then and does not want to leave her without help when the wall goes up; and for her, the young man offers the only concrete chance to escape from a bleak life in which she feels herself to be gradually suffocating in a sullen, listless, and certainly unpolitical way. Her former lover travels repeatedly back and forth between Hamburg and Berlin to organize her escape; and finally a secret organization provides false papers, and the nurse makes her getaway disguised as an Austrian tourist traveling to Scandinavia. But there is no conventional happy end; the nurse decides rather to go on serving the sick than to chain herself to the irresolute, vacuous life of the West German photographer, who spends much of his time polishing his dashing sports car. "Eastern" loyalty to a job to be done and "Western" thirst for prestige do not mix well.

Critical attention has long centered on *Speculations about Jacob*, but it would be misleading to describe Johnson's swift development solely in terms of his first published novel; he has not ceased to stress that each of his stories had to be told in its appropriately different way. I do not believe that Uwe Johnson has been influenced by the *nouveau roman*; rather, he has invented his own "new novel" and fully shares some of the creative assumptions of his French colleagues, who in this "age of suspicion" want to develop narrative possibilities independent of an obsolete omniscient narrator and to grasp the latest transformations of reality. In his essay "Sur quelques notions périmées" (1957) Robbe-Grillet defines his objections to realism, socialist or not, and suggests some of the attitudes clearly implied in Johnson's practice: aversion to that "Manichaeism of good or bad" which does not bother to offer substantiation for preconceived norms of virtue or evil; the indictment of a narrative universe constructed from an *a priori* scheme; and absolute refusal to accept the most striking quality of the world, namely its "being there" (*le fait . . . qu'il est là*). Robbe-Grillet's theoretical questions are of almost existential import to Johnson, who well remembers East German recipes for Socialist Realism; and while Robbe-Grillet has experimented with viewpoint and structure, Johnson, at least in his beginnings, has pressed his search for the "existing" much farther than his French ally has, and has not spared his reader the most astonishing peculiarities of narrative structure, syntax, and vocabulary. *Speculations about Jacob* does not only deal with East and West but actually thrives on its own East-West tensions; some elements of Socialist Realism, including the "positive" party functionary and characters unfolding in their professional milieu stubbornly survive, and yet are constantly modified by experiment. Socialist Realism and *nouveau roman* clash within the novel itself.

Johnson does not do away with the traditional narrator, but he does relegate him to a spot of little importance; the narrator's views of Jacob Abs compete with those emerging from the surrounding dialogue that grows out of the internal monologues of Jacob's girl friend, the intellectual, and the captain of the intelligence agency; and in the absence of a final statement, there is only an "infinite discussion between narrator, witnesses, and reader" (Gotthard Wunberg) which energetically excludes any preconceived or ideological interpretation of Jacob's life and death. But Johnson's thirst for the "existing world" changes grammar and verbal detail: asyndetical parataxis (gathering fact upon fact) dominates the sentence structure; groups of adjectives, or entire series of compound adjectives, relate to a single noun, apparently intended to achieve precise individualization but often resulting in disturbing descriptive mannerisms.

Johnson's *The Third Book about Achim* turns against rash ideological conclusions formulated in either East or West, but the author seems less tense; he controls his mannerisms and occasionally makes his story truly gripping. As narrator he closely follows the journalist Karsch, who wants to write a book about a representative "hero" of the GDR; although the narrator does not claim omniscience, he keeps both Karsch and Achim at a half-ironical, half-compassionate distance and sometimes comments on Karsch's desperate fight to see his man as he really is (Gide has arranged a similar exercise in *The Counterfeiters*). Karsch first tries to write a traditional realistic biography by selecting the main railroad station as a milieu emblematic of historical changes—ironically enough he discovers only much later that Achim's mother and sister were killed there by the Allies' bombs—but his difficulties increase when Herr Fleiss and Frau Amann of the state publishing house try to impose upon his search the official prescription for Socialist Realism and then oppose his work completely; and the champion himself has long accepted his public image as a genuine self-portrait. But one should not forget that Johnson himself has recently tended to discipline his passion for the technical; in *Two Views* he employs a single adjective instead of entire chains of qualifiers, inclines to traditional grammar more than before, and contents himself with a reliable narrator who, in alternating chapters, conveys the viewpoints of the West German photographer and the East German nurse. There is still a longing for concrete evidence; and the narrator carefully suggests in the last few pages that he met both his characters personally; thus he explains his knowledge of their lives (as did Goncharov's narrator in the last pages of *Oblomov* approximately a hundred years before Johnson). More indicative even of Johnson's new faith in the capabilities of a narrator is the gradual disappearance of objects from his world; in his early novels, his half-ironic presentation of "things" (or technical operations) overshadowed, in its precise thoroughness, human relationships, which seemed to be much less amenable to sure delineation; in his later stories these "islands of restfulness" (Günther Zehm) are so changed as to raise the human element to undisputed predominance. The writer is finally capable of dealing with human affairs again and does not have to rely on objects as the exclusive guarantees of certainty.

Opposing a disfigured image of the world as imposed on us by competing mass media or a central ideology (or both), Johnson fights bravely to find what is really *there* in the world, but his total development reveals a personal myth of human affairs; this myth, for a number of reasons, occasionally corresponds to the "Eastern" ambience familiar to him in his youth, rather than to the consumer society of the West. Johnson has been quite skillful in avoiding the issue of his literary masters; he admitted to being influenced by William Faulkner (available in the middle 'fifties in the GDR), but he was not equally outspoken on the question of the conservative German nature novel, a tradition reaching from Hermann Löns (1866–1914) to Ernst Wiechert (1899–1950), whose peaceful visions of a simple life devoted to human closeness he secretly shares. Johnson's instinctive insistence on rustic and Germanic names seems closer to the heritage of the German peasant novel or to Gerd Gaiser than progressive critics care to admit; and in moments of slackening control, Johnson is not incapable of sentimental landscape sketches like those which used to be integral elements of peasant *Kitsch*. In his wishful universe of deep soul and sage silence, the narrative cards are stacked against quick thinkers and articulate intellectuals who do not work with their hands but merely with paper and words; and Johnson's explicit sympathies are with the inarticulate craftsman who putters around with old furniture (Cresspahl); the near-silent dispatcher who cherishes his systematic work (he is even forgiven the Eichmann-like precision with which he clears the rails for the Soviet troops coming to crush the Hungarian revolt); the sports champion almost mystically one with his perfectly functioning bicycle; and the blonde nurse of rather limited intelligence who unerringly serves humanity in the sick ward. "Work," dedication, and loyalty count, and the self-centered concepts of the intellectuals—among them the English professor Jonas Blach—are more than suspect. Rarely has the old game of earthy *Gemeinschaft* vs. abstract *Gesellschaft* been played in recent German writing with more paradoxical sophistication of intellect.

Inevitably, Johnson's famous attention to "things" and his explicit views of the political tension between the two Germanies are related to his peasant-and-worker's myth of a simple, warm community. However, his "things" (above all, those in *Speculations* and in *The Third Book*) are far from being analogies to the objects of the *nouveau roman*. Robbe-Grillet either isolates his things (like the tomato in *The Erasers*) in the stark nakedness of absolute being or, in other instances, involves them in frenzied subjective vision; they are either absolutely "cold" or unbearably "hot." Uwe Johnson's old pieces of furniture, decorative mugs, and venerable tin plates are close to Rilke's *Dinge*, hallowed by long human use; and even his telegraphs, telephones, bicycles, and typewriters have the virtue of being involved in daily human work which endows them with a permanent dignity; Johnson includes the manufactured and the technical in the blessed realm of the Rilkean *Dinge* only if they are part of a working process; he reserves his bitter antipathies for "things" that are either emblems of prestige (like the sports car of the young West German photographer) or objects of mere commercial, that is meretricious, exchange. Jean Baudrillard rightly indicates that Johnson, in his attention to things and "serving" things, comes close to *marxisme artisanal* or rather (as I would say) to a belief in a closed society in which workingmen and their "things" dwell happily (if unthinkingly) together. I believe that Johnson has long felt that the simple human society of his dream can be found buried in the "East" rather than in the "West"; his emotional option surely derives from his visionary image of a territory charged with childhood memories and lacking in industrialization rather than from the brutal facts which he professes to seek. The "East" is now beginning to computerize its (profit-guided) industries as efficiently as the "West," and Johnson may soon find himself out of a dream country in which to shelter his secret and productive myth.

7. Günter Grass

GÜNTER GRASS burst upon the literary scene like a sudden thunderstorm and, with his natural exuberance and a language that was incredibly rich, made a mockery of the worn-out slogans about the death of the novel or the fatal sterility of the German idiom. In the later 'fifties and early 'sixties young people were quick to sense that Grass articulated the restive feelings of a generation totally unwilling to accept traditions that had failed and ideologies that were inhuman; and while many critics tried to ignore his merciless prodding by assigning his historical antecedents reaching from the baroque novel to Alfred Döblin (1878–1957), his younger readers enthusiastically lived along with his heroes, seriously analyzed their virtues and deficiencies, and, it has been suggested, brought German literature *to market again* in Berlin, Paris, and New York; it is another question entirely whether the antipathies between Grass and the New Left are not entirely mutual. Bold, cunning, and vital like a Kashubian horse thief, richly talented in many arts and crafts (from cool jazz to impeccable fish cookery), more directly involved in German politics than Heinrich Böll, Grass has come to be an extraordinary public figure, whose literary achievements are discussed even by those who have not read a book for thirty years.

Günter Grass was born in 1927 of Polish and German parentage in Danzig-Langfuhr, which he made the shabby heart of his narrative universe. As a boy he went through the prescribed schools and organizations, joined the *Jungvolk*, the Hitler youth group and, when war broke out, the air force auxiliary corps and the *Panzer* infantry. In April, 1944, he was wounded in battle, transferred to a Marienbad hospital, and taken prisoner by the American forces marching into Bohemia; after his release he worked as a farmhand and, for some time, in a mine near Hildesheim. (Gorki once said that he had learned his Marxism in the bakeries of Kazan, and Grass acquired his own pragmatic concern with social questions in the course of endless discussions with old Nazis, embittered Communists, and resilient Social Democrats at the bottom of the pit.) In the later 'forties Grass turned to cultivating his artistic gifts, worked as a stonemason, attended the Düsseldorf Academy of Arts, and continued his training under the supervision of Professor Hartung in Berlin. In 1956 Grass and his wife moved to Paris, where he worked in many media: his first volume of poetry was a moderate success; his plays and playlets, including *Hochwasser* [1957] / *Flood*, 1967; *Noch zehn Minuten bis Buffalo* [1959] / *Only Ten Minutes to Buffalo*, 1967; and *Die bösen Köche* [1961] / *The Wicked Cooks*, 1967 (a sprightly and sad vision of two lovers who refuse to betray a secret to competing groups of culinary maniacs), were far less successful than he had hoped; and at times Grass considered himself a disappointed playwright. But in 1959 *Die Blechtrommel* / *The Tin Drum*, 1963, was published and immediately combined the rewards of public scandal (the Bremen city government refused to grant a literary prize to Grass) with legitimate literary success international in scope; and the novella *Katz und Maus*, 1961 / *Cat and Mouse*, 1963, as well as *Hundejahre*, 1963 / *Dog Years*, 1965, another massive novel, amply confirmed Grass's highly personal combination of narrative exuberance, piercing insight, and skill with language. In the 'sixties Grass returned to Berlin, where he now resides with his family, increasingly participating, as artist and as citizen, in the political life of the city and the Federal Republic. In his play *Die Plebejer proben den Aufstand* [1966] / *The Plebeians Rehearse the Uprising* he discussed Brecht's politics and the East German workers' revolt, and later he traveled through West Germany to persuade his fellow citizens to give their vote to the Social Democrats, who promptly disappointed him by choosing to enter into the Grand Coalition rather than rule by themselves. Grass did not fail, however, actively to support the Social Democrats in the fall elections of 1969 and to speak up for his friend Willy Brandt, who was to be the first Socialist Chancellor of the Federal Republic.

In Grass's first novel, *The Tin Drum*, a hunchback named Oskar, approaching his thirtieth birthday and haunted by memories and anxieties, tells of his picaresque life, his particular vantage point being the cozy white bed of a West German mental institution to which he was transferred after being tried for the murder of a nurse. His precise memory roams with ease through past experience, and whenever memory does not suffice, his intense imagination, aided by his little child's drum, produces streams of images, smells, and colors: brown potato fields near the mouth of the Vistula River; the Danzig suburb of Langfuhr with its shops, churches, barracks, schools, and trolley cars; eels, sea gulls, and herrings; coco matting near bathhouses; and, after the war, the industrial landscape of the Rhine, the city of Düsseldorf, and yellow rye fields between the coal mines. He did not want to be an adult or a grocer like the others, Oskar asserts; therefore he decided to remain a permanent three-year-old who, though maturing in mind, sensitivity, and virile reserves, continues to haunt the adult world with his piercing and far-reaching voice; only after the death of the grocer Matzerath, his archenemy (who also happens to be his father) does Oskar decide to grow again, but he does not entirely succeed: he remains deformed, but proudly cherishes his fine hair, expressive eyes, and sensitive hands. The story of his life, as Oskar tells it, centers around the women to whom he has been stubbornly and sometimes perversely loyal: his sensuous mother Agnes, who did not exactly know whether she loved her sentimental Polish cousin Jan Bronski or the gay Rhinelander Matzerath whom she married; during the war years, Maria, who liked fizz powder, smelled of vanilla and mushrooms, and finally decided to marry Matzerath, senior; and, in the Rhineland, the nurse Dorothea, whom Oskar pursued with cunning, with endless curiosity and (as a ribald episode demonstrates) with impotent fury. Yet Oskar's experiences are not merely private ones; unlike the *picaro* of the old Spanish novel he cannot live outside history and constantly finds himself confronted with political events of growing importance. In search of his drums, he witnesses the burning of the Danzig synagogue after the "Crystal Night" of November 9, 1938, and finds his Jewish friend Markus (who had always provided drums at reduced prices) dead in his shop, which has been destroyed by Nazi storm troopers; on September 1, 1939, he happens to be among the hapless defenders of the Danzig Polish post office, and lives, in his own way, through the historical beginning of World War II; later, traveling with a troupe of acrobats to perform before German *Wehrmacht* audiences in the Normandy region, he has to pack his little bags rather quickly on June 6, 1944, when the Canadians arrive on the beaches and the invasion begins. He is a man—or rather a dwarf—of his age and cannot speak about himself without implying something about the rise and fall of Hitler's *Reich*, and the ensuing days of the merely economic "miracle."

The trouble with Oskar is that we have to accept whatever he says; and although a few parts of his confessions, true or false, are provided by his friendly male nurse Bruno (Book II, Chapter 17) and his friend Vittlar (Book III, Chapter 11), theirs are not "objective" voices, for they are manipulated by Oskar and only say what he wants them to say. Being the most unreliable of narrators, he is also the most challenging, erratic, and ambivalent character in recent German fiction, a moral monster with aesthetic talents and metaphysical anxieties who calmly observes a morbid world. When he had entered the world, Oskar asserts, he observed a dark butterfly resentfully drumming with its wings against the merciless light of naked glass bulbs; and like the butterfly Oskar does not cease to fight against the necessity of being. But his attempts to return to the womb are of uneven success, and he resolves to fight ruthlessly for himself. He protects himself against adults by withdrawing into a fake childhood, yet his path is strewn with people offended, wounded, and dead; he is responsible for the death of Jan Bronski because he drags him, against his will, to the Polish post office and, after the Nazi victors take away the Poles to shoot them, pretends to be a helpless little boy who has been kidnaped by the Poles; he tries twice to abort Maria's child when she is pregnant by Matzerath, senior (until he decides that he himself was responsible); he refuses to help his lilliputian mistress Roswitha Raguna and forces her to go out into an open yard where she is killed by a grenade; he leads his "Duster" gang with a swagger but promptly betrays the young people when they are tried by the authorities; and although Matzerath, senior, stubbornly refuses to sign a document turning Oskar over to the health authorities (who want to do away with him in accordance with their theories of racial "health"), Oskar does not hesitate to cause Matzerath's ugly death when the first Russian soldiers arrive. He has never killed with his own hands, but he is a vicious killer nevertheless.

Yet Oskar also embodies, as Henry Hatfield has suggested, the gifts of the artist in a dull society of grocers, functionaries, and squares. He has gathered a "little learning of wide scope," usually relies on Goethe and Rasputin or, as any good post-Nietzschean intellectual would, on Apollo and Dionysus. Only the admirable example of the wing-beating butterfly and his mother's promise that a toy drum was forthcoming persuaded him (as he says) to go on living after he was born; and his drum turns into his instrument of revolt, dream, and metamorphosis. For good reasons he constantly reminds us of the red-and-white colored fringe of the toy: the colors suggest the Polish flag (associated, in turn, with abstract heroism); his grandfather Joseph Koljaiczek's life of arson, close escapes, and revolt; an aura of fire, fierce feeling, and strange innocence. In the suggestive rhythm of his drumming, things past, implacable revolt, and a powerful transformation of feelings are one; and behind the hunchbacked cousin of Theodor Fontane's and Thomas Mann's talented outsiders, an archetypal troll full of ambivalent magic powers appears. It is his infinite self-assertion and his concern for his art that define the limits of his stance in the epoch of rising Nazi power. He does not revolt against the Brown Shirts but against the adult world; he joins the Poles at the post office because he wants to have his drum repaired by Pan Kobyella; he clearly separates his own gang from the more politically oriented sabotage groups of the Communist-led apprentices at the Schichau docks, and disrupts well-organized Nazi manifestations by drumming a waltz or "Jimmy the Tiger"—because he cannot stand their competing fanfares or, for that matter, those played by the musical corps of other political groups, including the Socialists or the Nationalist Young Poles. In the particular constellation of his native Danzig he comes close to being a virtual ally of the Nazis and yet occasionally functions as an antifascist, if only for wholly inappropriate reasons.

Yet Oskar's deepest secrets may well be religious or ontological; negating all philosophy except that of his ego, he cannot free himself of anxieties of the most existential nature. Throughout his Danzig youth he feels strongly attracted to the Church of the Sacred Heart and considers the figure of the Christ Child his most radical challenge. Jesus is the "most perfect Oskar"; unbelieving and nevertheless expecting a miracle (and little Jesus does drum when Oskar puts the toy in his wooden hands), Oskar constantly returns to the church, mobilizes his gang, has the Christ Child sawn off Mary's lap, and installs himself there to be adored by his friends, all well-trained Catholics perfectly able to say (Black) Mass with the correct Latin texts. He is one of the atheists who cannot live without intensely hating God, and even the most satanically clever curses he hurls at Christ confirm a bond without escape. The vicious little artist Oskar essentially longs for salvation from being—against, not with, time. His early decision to remain a three-year-old constitutes only part of his strategy of regression to the protective womb; others include his constant desire to hide under his grandmother's five skirts (he playfully imagines how pleasant life would be *inside* her body), his urge to hide under tables, behind closed doors or, at some crucial moments, in a wardrobe, in order to spy on his enemies or to indulge in drumming and sexual self-gratification (so closely related) in a sphere of warmth and protection. Obsessed by white-clad nurses *d'ogni forma* because they remind him of his mother, who was a nurse before she married Matzerath, Oskar turns into a compulsive repeater who, in his urge to stop time, constantly relives and rearranges past experiences in protest against present and future. But as time goes on he is forced closer against his inveterate enemy Death, or the "Black Witch," who is waiting to ambush him; in growing agony, he desperately tries to avoid the final, often anticipated encounter. Like Pirandello's Henry IV who would rather be mad than face time, Oskar, for his own reasons, sits in his white bed, reminiscent of the neat womb of motherly nurses, drums up his protective past on his white-and-red toy, and senses in fear and trembling the coming of the inescapable "Black Witch."

In his novella *Cat and Mouse* Grass masterfully checks his epic force and creates an intense and rich work of art that competes successfully with some of the most perfect stories of the nineteenth century; there is some significance in his remark that Heinrich von Kleist is one of his favorite authors. A striking chip off the Danzig block, *Cat and Mouse* unfolds the story of "Great Mahlke," a boy of curious obsessions and notable achievements, as told, many years after the events, by his reluctant admirer Pilenz, who is trying to clarify for himself what happened on a half-sunken Polish minesweeper in the Gulf of Danzig, near Neufahrwasser, back in 1944 or so. The boy Mahlke has to take great care to cover his large Adam's apple, which resembles a nervous mouse. He collects all sorts of things, including a screwdriver, religious medals, a can opener, and fashionable tassels, as "counterweights" to be worn around his neck in order to hide his abnormal mark. But when a famous submarine commander, the "Knights' Cross of the Iron Cross" around his neck, addresses the boys in school, Mahlke realizes that this is what he has to have; he steals the cross and wears it under his tie, but he does not enjoy it for long because the theft is investigated and Mahlke is transferred to a lesser school. Yet Mahlke cannot forget the "thing thing thing"; and when he joins the army he feels personally inspired by the Virgin Mary, who enables him to destroy many Russian tanks, for which he is finally awarded the "thing thing thing" himself. On leave, he hastens back to his old school, hoping to give a lecture like the submarine commander's to the students, but school director Klohse, reminding him of his theft, refuses permission, and Klohse's obedient colleagues agree. Deprived of his triumph, Mahlke does not want to return to the front, deliberately misses his train, rows out to the old minesweeper where he had built himself a hideout in the watertight radio cabin, and dives down, never to come up again.

Mahlke's friend Pilenz may be a more reliable narrator than the hunchback Oskar but, like Oskar, he is driven by feelings of involvement, responsibility, and guilt that emerge more clearly as the story advances; his confession does not come out easily, because he was raised a believing Catholic and formulates his story in a constant dialogue with Father Alban who, suspecting the therapeutic value of the text, urges Pilenz to cultivate his god-given artistic gifts. As a boy, Pilenz was among those who admired Mahlke boundlessly, aped his gestures, and eagerly reported stories of his courage; yet infinite admiration and loyalty turn into an awful burden, and Pilenz inadvertently admits (if often by mere implication) that he longed to free himself from Mahlke. He does confess that he was responsible for making a cat jump at Mahlke's "mouse" (that is, his Adam's apple), but he is far less outspoken about those last moments, when his friend, the cross and two cans of food strung around his neck, went down into the deep; he does not say why he did not return to the boat at night as he had promised. But only Pilenz's ambivalent view can penetrate into Mahlke's deepest secret: Pilenz knows that Mahlke was driven by the urge to be like his father who, while working for the Polish railroads, died a hero's death averting a dangerous accident. Pilenz is able to see Mahlke's grotesque will to go his own way and pays hesitant homage to a man who demonstrated unusual resilience in the cat-and-mouse game that fate plays with everybody.

Günter Grass's second full-length novel *Dog Years* is an extraordinary ragbag of wild yarns, clever parodies, tragic insights, piercing satire, and Rabelaisian gags; the structure may be loose, but the historical and political scope has widened, a world of convincingly "round" characters emerges, and language, fired by disgust and fascination, has become incomparably resourceful. Grass refuses to commit himself as a narrator and leaves the job to three other men who, being from Danzig and the nearby villages of Schiewenhorst and Nickelswalde, are all supremely qualified to compete with him in knowledge of local detail; they all know that Trolley Number Five goes to Niederstadt and continue to discuss, with piety and pedantry, the differences between Danzig-Langfuhr's two movie theaters a generation ago. But one of them, Herr Brauchsel, or Brauxel (*alias* Goldmäulchen *alias* Haseloff *alias* Eddi Amsel), seems particularly interested in editing the substantial manuscript; as an introspective man of considerable means (he owns a kind of scarecrow factory in an old mine near Hildesheim), he retains the literary services of his collaborators Harry Liebenau and Walter Matern, discusses their writings, suggests modifications, and combines his own contributions, entitled *Early Morning Shifts,* with Harry Liebenau's more epistolary part and the one hundred and three irregularly numbered *Materniads* of his rather picaresque third contributor, who happens to be his lifelong friend and enemy. He also makes sure that the garrulous collaborators stick to the chronological sequence: he himself concentrates on the late 'twenties and early 'thirties, Harry writes about the late 'thirties and the war years, and Walter about the postwar period; describing grotesque grandmothers, the narratives cover the exact time span of Oskar Matzerath's story; and inevitably, Oskar occasionally reappears, marching and drumming on the Danzig shore. Herr Brauchsel, relying partly on an old diary, writes of his own childhood, of "sunsets, blood, earth, and ashes"; dreaming of the rolling waters of the Vistula and the wide marshes, he remembers the days when he was fat and freckled Eduard Amsel, built his first scarecrows, and fought with his friend Walter Matern, who threw away the penknife which the boys had used in the rite of blood brotherhood. Windmills, peasants, birds, and later, the smell of chalk and classrooms in a landscape of boys: Eddi, beaten by others because he was helpless, sensitive, and half-Jewish, Walter, his protector who handled his early business affairs (selling his scarecrows to eager peasants), always wearing Eddi's new clothes, gnashing his teeth, and abusing his friend in famous fits of theatrical rage. In Harry Liebenau's contribution, consisting of love letters to his cousin Tulla Pokriefke and a concluding fairy tale (*Endmärchen*), the circle widens, and Eddi and Walter appear among a crowd of students, teachers, petits bourgeois, Nazi storm troopers, and local artists; the real dog years have begun, the National Socialists dominate Danzig and most of Europe, and those who resist are tortured and killed. In luminous detail Danzig-Langfuhr once more comes alive, but the shadows quickly lengthen: the sensitive girl Jenny is humiliated by Tulla; Eddi is nearly killed by a gang of storm troopers led by none other than Walter Matern, whereupon he changes his name to

Haseloff, quickly escapes to Berlin, and there continues to organize ballets and scarecrows; and Harry Liebenau himself, after wavering between Jenny and Tulla, joins (as did Grass) the air force auxiliary corps and the *Panzer* infantry and during the last months of the war learns his lesson about life and death. In the concluding *Materniads*, Walter, in his own disorderly way, reports on the first years after the war; released as antifascist from a POW camp, he sets out on a picaresque tour of revenge to punish those functionaries, officers, military policemen, and judges who have made his life miserable and, while enjoying their hospitality, sleeps with their wives and daughters, kills their chickens and canaries, and infects everybody with his gonorrhea (curing himself in a fashion not recorded in medical literature). When he is in danger of becoming a bourgeois, he fortunately meets Harry Liebenau, who arranges a round-table radio discussion about German guilt (the star speaker: Matern). Then in Berlin he encounters Eddi Amsel, who again begins to cling to him, and who takes him, in a descent worthy of a true epic, to his mine to show him his scarecrows; they are together, and alone, again.

Grass anticipated the ambivalent relationship of Eddi and Walter in Pilenz's terse loyalty to Great Mahlke in *Cat and Mouse*, but in *Dog Years* the ambivalence of feelings combines almost lethally with the political situation. Matern protects his friend Eddi against belligerent boys and cruel fellow students, but loyalty has its own burdens, and after Matern has caught Eddi donning a Nazi uniform and constructing his mechanical men in his villa, he personally leads a group of Nazi bullies to the house and almost kills his friend, who loses all his teeth in the struggle, collapses in the snow, and suffers for the rest of his life from the consequences of the freezing cold. But as soon as Eddi has left Danzig, the lonely Matern begins to drink, steals SA funds for his *Schnaps*, tries to make a living as an actor, gets into trouble with the political authorities again, saves his skin by voluntarily joining the army in 1939, and is finally transferred to a punitive battalion, because he has abused the highest functionaries of the regime. He lies constantly about his responsibility for hurting Eddi (his daughter Walli senses the truth); yet when they meet again and Eddi half-ironically confesses that he continues to be fascinated by Germany, the land of forgetfulness and primeval scarecrows, and offers Matern the old penknife of blood brotherhood, miraculously dragged from the sands of the Vistula River, Grass comes close to suggesting the idea of an almost mystical, recurrent communion between Germans and sons of Jewish fathers, destined to hate and love each other eternally.

Dog Years may be among the most baggy monsters of recent German fiction, but Grass expertly relates his concern with Amsel and Matern to parallel vicissitudes of other characters and to a number of subsidiary motifs; he is particularly successful in his story of Jenny and Tulla, but his chronicle of the dogs Senta, Harras, and Prince (Hitler's pet) does not add much. Young Tulla Pokriefke, who first appeared in *Cat and Mouse* (and was, as Henri Plard has suggested, clearly anticipated in the informer Luzie Rennwand, who destroyed Oskar's "Duster" gang), belongs among the truly unforgettable figures of the Danzig world: lean, bony, smelling of carpenter's glue, she embodies an almost mythic force of malevolence, and inevitably fascinates the crude as well as the sophisticated. In her relationship to chubby Jenny, who wants to become a ballerina, reappears something of Matern's attitude toward Amsel: attracted by and hating Jenny for many years, she pursues the young girl, who is not Jewish but of gypsy origin, with the attentions of a spiteful slave; and one cold January day she forces her to dance in the snow and, with Harry's help, builds her into a big snowman and leaves her in the cold. But it is precisely the moment of greatest personal humiliation which relates the fate of Jenny, the gifted gypsy pursued by Tulla, to that of Eddi, the talented half-Jew pursued by Matern; while Jenny dances in the snow, Matern leads his brutal Nazi buddies to Eddi's house. For both Jenny and Eddi humiliation means metamorphosis: Eddi changes his name and begins his new life in Berlin; and chubby Jenny, having suddenly acquired fragile grace, surprises the Danzig audiences, when she first appears in a ballet appropriately entitled *The Ice Queen* (Walter Matern plays the speaking reindeer), with a superior performance.

Among the literary tactics of *Dog Years*, parody and satire are of essential importance, sharpening the polemical intent and, often in unexpected ways, refining the poetic vocabulary. The few pastiches of Benn's poetry are cunningly integrated (recited by Matern in moments of despair); the satires on the booming round-table business, on the conservative publisher Axel Springer, and on leading German periodicals, including *Der Spiegel* and *Die Zeit*, are rather tedious expansions of overburdened gags. The Heidegger passages are another matter of varying success: Grass admirably characterizes the intellectual confusion of the generation of the 'forties, which indulged in the high obscurity of Heideggerian philosophy rather than see the base and ugly as it was; Matern, Liebenau, and others speak of "the being of being" and try to ignore the rat-ridden realities of the barracks and the heap of bones and skulls of Stutthof concentration camp victims right in front of their military training ground. As long as Grass works with the technique of reported thought, the Heideggerian idiom has its legitimate function, but as soon as he talks over the shoulders of his narrators and theorizes about the disparity between "high" philosophy and brutal experience, he is working against his own interests; it is not, as Hans Egon Holthusen suggested, a question of confusing the "formed" with the merely "thought," but rather the problem of narrative discipline and the integrity of fictive characters. But Holthusen has rightly pointed out a curious "backfiring" of the Heideggerian idiom; Grass may intend to use existentialist terminology against existentialism, but there are some moments when, in the reported thought of the narrators, Heideggerian terminology and precise experience fuse in a new idiom of extraordinary richness. Thinking of the "ontic voices of the ships," Harry Liebenau indeed combines Grass and Heidegger in the most poetic way.

Günter Grass develops realism in a mannerist fashion; like Eddi Amsel's ballets, Grass's stories are a "precise chaos danced on tiptoe." Much of his art involves "the world as it is," as Hegel would say; and with the insatiable hunger of the true epic writer he tries to encircle, grasp, and hold the world in order proudly to name, to show, and to enumerate. He, the belated Homer of the German lower middle classes, is a lover of objects, which at times assume independent and emblematic significance; surprisingly enough, Grass himself confesses that it was Herman Melville who revealed to him some of the "thingness" *(Dinglichkeit)* of the world. At times Grass clings to nineteenth-century tradition and builds his *intérieurs* (for instance, the living room at the Matzeraths' or Grandmother Matern's chamber) in Balzac's fashion; increasingly, however, he develops a personal technique of endless asyndetic enumerations (often of the associative variety) that link one thing to the next. There are only a few enumerations in *The Tin Drum,* but they abound in *Dog Years:* the chaos of disparate substances carried by the floods of the Vistula River; the wares sold by Amsel, senior; the gifts offered by various ladies to Walter Matern to keep his favor; the wealth of shabby materials that Amsel uses to build his scarecrows. There is epic ecstasy in such detail.

But Grass's realism (he likes the term himself) explodes in twisted shapes; articulating through the organization of his narratives his distrust of harmony, coherence, translucence, and his generation's fierce opposition to a graceful classicism that clearly failed, Grass mobilizes his counterstrategies of disproportion, ugly incompatibility, and willed obscurity; Eddi Amsel's principle of constructing "eccentric" scarecrows contains much of Grass's own poetics. Grass's huge bag of tricks and methods include both the old and new: in the earlier parts of *The Tin Drum* he often relies on the metaphoric disparities of an extended conceit (Mrs. Greff's huge and impassive body related to a theater of war), but in *Dog Years* the conceit disappears, and incompatibilities and distortions are handled more efficiently in Dickensian characters and grotesque situations (the deeply humane Professor Brunies, fatally addicted to candy, cooks his own caramels over a fire in the forest); the trouble with Grass is that he is sometimes content to stop at playful jokes, which he tries to burden with symbolic meaning. Beyond a certain limit, disparity destroys itself.

Perhaps the most productive incompatibilities reside in Grass's ingenious method of epic impersonality. He does not impose his own views upon a recalcitrant world, but delegates the job of seeing and saying to narrators who are deeply involved in the world of guilt, blood, and shame; and while opposing the vices of the German past, Grass willingly grants narrative autonomy to the voices of people like Oskar, Pilenz, Liebenau, or Matern who, plagued by the age, know from their guts what they are talking about. They are superbly qualified to explore the German past; they are guilt-ridden or immoral narrators, manipulated by an author with strong moral leanings. Grass plays his own cat-and-mouse game with his narrators, a game which has not yet been explored for all its aesthetic and political implications.

Yet deprived of his narrators and confronted with more recent political events, the artist Grass is far less fortunate, for he lacks the aesthetically productive detachment afforded by temporal and structural distance; even within his two novels, the anemic third sections (Oskar in postwar Düsseldorf and Matern's West German pilgrimage), closer in space and time to the "now" of the narrating voices, do not have the full substance of the earlier sections relating events in faraway Danzig, thirty or more years ago. In his play *The Plebeians Rehearse the Uprising*, Grass confronts a famous playwright, who strongly resembles Brecht, with the workers' rebellion of June 17, 1953; but the play illustrates history more than it illuminates it. In his earlier Academy lecture (1964) sketching his plans for the play, Grass strongly attacked "culinary" Brecht as an "unspoiled man of the theater" who ignored the challenge of the new revolution; in the play itself, Grass is more willing to see the ambivalences of Brecht's character. The "boss" is just rehearsing a scene from Shakespeare's *Coriolanus* in his theater, subsidized by the Ulbricht establishment, when a delegation of workers, representing the revolutionaries just then beginning to march through the streets of East Berlin, appears on his stage and asks him to help formulate a document explaining the workers' demands. Showing a considerable grasp of revolutionary politics, the skeptical boss does not refuse outright, but first wants to know more about what is happening outside; and while they relate what is going on, he uses them as aesthetic material to solve some of his theatrical problems with the Shakespearean plebeians. After prolonged hesitation he wants to join the workers, but it is too late; the Russian tanks are driving through the streets, the revolution is suppressed, and of his cunning declaration (criticizing, in two paragraphs, the government's premature action against the workers and confirming, in a third, his loyalty to the ruling party), only the final part will be made known by the triumphant government. Grass does not make the "boss" a theatrical figure in his own right (his Brecht explains his reasons for indecision by quoting a pastiche from the real Brecht's poetry) but fully convinces in his deep concern for the workers' revolt, crushed by the Stalinists and robbed of its social relevance by the official speeches of the West German conservatives.

The political playwright Grass is a man of definite ideas about art and revolution (consonant with those of the politically committed citizen who leans toward a self-critical social democracy), but the novelist does not display a tightly-knit system of ideas. In his revolt against the novels of the immediate past, suspect of expressing a particular doctrine in a closely organized form, Grass concentrates on things, details, individuals, episodes, and loosely connected yarns; the obsessions of the narrators are more effective than the author's few ideas. Grass analyzes the vices of the German past at closest range: his petits bourgeois and perspiring Nazis are closer to experience than the SS Frankensteins emerging from the books of others, and in handling his ugly, guilt-ridden, and perspiring creatures he does not ignore daily betrayals, maudlin indifference, or the young German who is punished for mistreating kittens and promoted for persecuting Jews. Yet Grass's world is not organized along primarily political lines separating the beastly Nazis from the noble Jews; at the risk of provoking the more political-minded admirers of Grass, including George Steiner, I submit that his people are either insensitive, dull, crude "squares," or humane, sensitive, and aesthetically gifted "cats." His "squares," of course, do comprise the Nazi functionaries, while the "cats" include gypsies, Poles, Jews, and those artists who (like Grass) work in new media, whether drumming, scarecrows, sculptures made of knots, or complicated sound machines. Among the younger writers who emerged after the war, Grass is the most gifted, but the confusing richness and conflicting variety of his many talents have their own dangers; I find myself less shocked by Grass's portraits of urinating storm troopers than by his occasional self-indulgence in undisciplined verbiage, cheap puns, and funny but entirely inconsequential gags. Trying to penetrate a strained and distorted world, his loyalty to the sustained grayness of daily life is as essential to his art as his strategy of disproportion and incompatibility; there may be some meaning in relating his narratives to the baroque novel, but I would think it more appropriate to stress his close affinity to Nikolai Gogol's shabby and hellish grotesque.

8. Heimito von Doderer

ALONE IN HIS massive and occasionally eccentric independence, the Austrian writer Heimito von Doderer (1896–1966) emerged from the later postwar years as the legitimate heir to Thomas Mann. Doderer developed late and, as if corresponding in his own development to the late maturity of many of his fictive characters, he created in his declining years two or three novels which constitute his indubitable contribution to world literature. A man of varied experience, he was free of the bitter anger which fired, and sometimes poisoned, the imagination of many of his younger contemporaries: skillfully fusing past and present, Doderer did not hesitate to continue and to oppose nineteenth-century narrative traditions, and elements of realist technique that had become to others a burden or even a curse, he cunningly transformed into new strategies for capturing epic material. He was unabashedly in love with life, and his love made his narrative universe strong, human, and often radiant with joy. He was among the few writers of his time who, although intensely aware of all the dark abysses, insisted on creating simple people capable of laughing happily.

Doderer was born in Weidlingau near Vienna into a family of architects and engineers; he always felt strangely alienated from the traditions of his family because of his artistic and scholarly inclinations. Anticipating a career in the civil service of the monarchy, he briefly studied administrative law but later (1915) joined a cavalry regiment, fought on the eastern front (1915–1916), was taken prisoner by the Russians, and returned to Vienna (1920) on foot, crossing the steppes. Like René von Stangeler, his fictive *alter ego,* Doderer studied history, received his doctorate for a dissertation on middle-class historiography in fifteenth-century Vienna (1925), and for years made an uneasy living as a free-lance writer with scholarly interests. Doderer admitted himself that he (like many other members of the Austrian intelligentsia) joined the illegal National Socialist Party in 1933, but he disengaged himself when the National Socialists came to power in Austria (1938); and it is not impossible to conceive of a psychological link between his decisive break with his immediate past and his increasing concern with human obsessions, political and otherwise. In World War II Doderer served with the German air force in Russia and southern France (where he read Paul Valéry); in April, 1945, he was interned by the tolerant Norwegians and returned with other Austrian officers and soldiers to devastated Vienna. Doderer's notes and war diaries (1940–1950), collected in *Tangenten,* 1964 / *Tangents,* clearly demonstrate that the final stages of his intellectual and artistic development were extremely painful; only late in life did Doderer have the distinct feeling that he was coming into his own as a creative writer. His later novels he wrote with the fastidious precision and the dedication of his engineering forefathers; honors and distinctions, including the Austrian State Prize for Literature (1958), were lavished upon him in the late 'fifties and 'sixties, but he preferred to stay out of the limelight and to spend much of his spare time with close friends, discussing aspects of the narrative art in a back room of the hospitable little Havelka café, in the center of Vienna.

Young Doderer began to write when on leave from the eastern front (1916), continued writing during his years in the Russian prison camps (1916–1920), and published his first slim volume of verse (1923) and his first novel (1924) while an overage history student at the University of Vienna. In the late 'twenties he felt immensely strengthened by the example and achievements of his friend, the painter and writer Albert Paris Gütersloh (b. 1887), but only in the late 'thirties did themes and modes emerge that were to shape his mature work. The years 1938–1940 probably constitute the major turning point in his career as a writer:

breaking away from an ideological commitment, Doderer increasingly concerned himself with the question of self-fulfillment (*Menschwerdung*) and with the dangers an abstract order holds for the natural spontaneity of the individual and of social life; the narrative world of his later years began to coalesce. In 1938 and 1939 he worked on *Die erleuchteten Fenster oder die Menschwerdung des Amtsrates Julius Zihal*, 1951 / *The Illuminated Windows, or The Humanization of Councillor Julius Zihal*; from notebooks kept during the war years *Die Strudlhofstiege*, 1951 / *The Strudlhof Staircase*, developed as a substantial novel; and, returning to his earlier fragment, Doderer completed *Die Dämonen*, 1956 / *The Demons*, 1961, his most important book, filling it out with grotesque stories, *outré* narrative variations, and theoretical commentaries. Shortly before he died, the short novel *Die Wasserfälle von Slunj*, 1963 / *The Waterfalls of Slunj*, 1966, was published as Part I of a projected tetralogy; a moving story of son against father, it is also a true *livre sur rien*: pure, impeccable, translucent form, and yet intensely humane. Heimito von Doderer occasionally suggested that he had searched Beethoven's compositions for structural analogies to his own work, but it is with the fragile lightness of his compatriot Haydn that his final pages resound.

Doderer's long story *The Illuminated Windows, or The Humanization of Councillor Julius Zihal*, in many important ways anticipates the concerns of his later work. In contrast to some of his early narratives, in which distinct traces of expressionist syntax can be discerned, character and events are firmly "localized" in Vienna by utterance and topography, and the central theme of *Menschwerdung* and obsession combine in a single central figure. Councillor Julius Zihal, a little man who has spent much of his life in the almost Kafkaesque atmosphere of the old Austrian civil service, has retired, and after experiencing the rude shock of suddenly waking to a life without purpose, rapidly subjects his daily routine to a new concept of order which he creates during sleepless nights in his darkened apartment. His obsession is that of the voyeur, and restlessly exploring the illuminated windows facing those of his own apartment, Zihal, using first opera glasses and later a telescope, develops a strict and rigid system of observation which splits his life into almost meaningless days and hectic nights; by day, he reads the dry paragraphs of the civil service code, and by night he enters his detailed observations of half-naked women and young girls bathing into his "Observation Book," in which human beings are ruthlessly transformed into the mathematical formulas of his obsessive system ("Window I, 10:00; adjustment 27/100"). An almost deadly "perception of order" imposes itself on his life and increasingly separates the aging Zihal as if by a wall from the richness of potential experience. But the chronicler of his aberrations does not deny him the possibility of again becoming human: in another shock of true, not abstract, experience, Zihal encounters the corporally concrete charms of Rosa Opletal, an attractive lady *d'un certain âge;* his obsessions are immediately destroyed by the touch of her ample flesh, and, a true human being at last, Zihal joins Rosa for a performance of Mozart's *Zauberflöte* and later in marriage. The story is deceptively funny, and the Gogolian element of the grotesque (in its Austrian variations) sharply reveals the obsessive perversions that have infected and corrupted old Austria's soul as embodied in the civil servant Zihal. The chronicle of Julius Zihal's vicissitudes can surely be read as Doderer's first, parabolic answer to the aberrations of the Third Reich.

In his substantial novel *The Strudlhof Staircase* Doderer fully demonstrates the conflicting forces of his art: his epic hunger for "total" reality and his Flaubertian desire to convert the heavy mass of experience into light, brittle form; almost inevitably, a delightful masterpiece of architectural *art nouveau* (the Strudlhof Stairs connecting two Vienna districts) constitutes the symbolic heart of his narrative. Desire for "total" reality cannot be satiated by the story of a single life, and Doderer, as if following Balzac or, better still, George Eliot, unfolds an expansive Viennese horizon of lives and "plots," each of which complements, completes, and influences the other; true "being" does not tolerate isolation, and to be truly human means to communicate, to share, to be involved with others. To expansion in space corresponds depth in time; in a complicated combination of lived and remembered time levels, past and present merge, and the mind of the narrator (as well as that of his figures) moves freely from the summer of 1911 to the late summer and early fall of 1925: people do not disdain memory, essential to their individualities, and nothing of the past is lost. Dates of particular days are of essential importance, and after Doderer has put his most important characters on the stage in Part I, he makes sure that specific days form the core of Part II (August 23, 1911), Part III (August 29, 1925), and Part IV (September 21, 1925); the many events of the "final" day are (as in the later novel) told minute by minute and in constant awareness of flowing time. We are not to ignore the synchronism, the correspondence, the spatial coordination of groups, circles, and individual lives that together constitute the exuberance of being.

Yet there are major threads which dominate in the texture of the novel and, in analogy and conflict, once more confirm Doderer's incessant search for what can transform a mere "character" (determined by biology and environment) into a true "person," or human being, which with the help of patience, spontaneity, and endurance actually realizes the absolute core of its immanent potentialities. If there is a coherent story which binds together many other elements, it is that of the slow "humanization" of Melzer, another civil servant, who, lost in the continuous contemplation of his past, withdraws dangerously from potential contact with new experience. The narrator characterizes the hesitant, self-involved, and shy Melzer as a crayfish walking backward; and while in Melzer's meditations a recurrent "red of seriousness" suggests a future moment of blood and terror, he encounters his moment of truth when, in the late afternoon of September 21, 1925, on the Vienna Althahn (now Julius-Tandler) Square, he kneels on the pavement to help a woman who has been badly injured by a passing streetcar. Her blood streams over his hands and over those of graceful Thea Rokitzer, who happens to kneel beside him, but it is precisely in this moment of "red" terror that he breaks out of his shell, opens up to human experience and love. Shaken and yet unperturbed, he proposes to Thea (whom he has long secretly admired) almost on the spot.

Melzer's humanization connects intimately with the conflicting fates of Mary K. (whose leg was severed above the knee by the streetcar) and Etelka, the sister of his friend René von Stangeler. Noble and sensitive Mary K. (whom Melzer almost married in 1910) has had a contented if perhaps monotonous life that has not yet forced her to discover the "person" within her "character," but the brutal accident compels her to mobilize all her latent forces; she survives, and emerges (in *The Demons*) as the archetypal radiant woman whose Jewish ancestry links her spiritual triumph over her weakened body to the most ancient sources of resilience; the terrible moment on the pavement has actually initiated her into human existence. Mary K. is destined for later triumph but Etelka Stangeler-Grauermann for imminent failure: Etelka cannot discipline herself; she moves deliriously from affair to affair, from lover to lover, and finally takes an overdose of sleeping pills to end a life of chaotic emotions and restless discontent. But Doderer does not create his narrative world solely in order to demonstrate a theoretical concept of *Menschwerdung*. In reflecting on the fruitful confusions of rich experience, demonstrated in a complexity of "plots," he does not ignore the element of entertaining intrigue: as if to mock the professional reader of traditional novels, he assiduously develops the story of the lovable twin sisters Edith and Mimi Pastré. When Edith wants to help her German lover Wedderkorp, they conceive of a complicated project to smuggle good Austrian tobacco into Germany, which involves braving some intimate encounters *au lit*, in which one sister "plays" the other—but Mimi has an appendectomy scar which Edith does not have, and the sisters may deceive René or Melzer but never the well-instructed reader. Yet the motif of the intrigue is a "blind" one; abstract planning never succeeds in Doderer's world; the spontaneous force of life itself interferes with the tobacco intrigue and dooms it to inconsequential failure.

Behind all these events, adventures, and vicissitudes, the lovely Strudlhof Staircase (built in 1910 by Johann Theodor Jaeger) embodies the secret form of essential meaning: it is the "central actor" of the novel (as Doderer said), and a constant reminder of the unforgettable presence of the past. People cannot avoid the stairs, and its elaborate ramps, terraces, corners, lamps, and sculptures echo with scandals, conflicts, kisses, and memories; constituting the "focus" of the city, these stairs unveil the *genius loci* (also incarnated in sweet Paula Schachl), the "deepest depth" of Vienna and yet its complete "freedom of depth." With their complicated terraces and levels the stairs correspond strangely to the structure of the rising Semmering landscape and the waterfalls of Slunj (landscapes implying life and death in the later narrative): all structured forms revealing deeper secrets of art and life. René von Stangeler (who often voices Doderer's ideas) praises the Strudlhof Stairs as a "poem," and "ode in four stanzas"—"as incomprehensible as something alive, even though of stone." The architectural symbol indicates much of Doderer's idea of how human experience should be: these stairs make people walk slowly, and in constant awareness of something exquisitely shaped, colorful, and rich. Life should not be determined by quick purpose and short cuts (*[ein] zweckvoller Kurzfall*) but, like a walk on these stairs, illuminated by delicate joy at every turn of the way (*[die] Köstlichkeit all' ihrer Wegstücke*). The architecture of the Strudlhof Staircase expresses a Goethean plea for life dwelling freely on protracted delight and not disfigured by rushed, dehumanizing functionality.

Doderer's massive novel *The Demons* constitutes his undisputed contribution to the literature of our age. Refining earlier formal achievements and convincingly probing private and political issues, Doderer widens the scope of his observations, strengthens the relevance of his questions and, deriving ideas from the Viennese psychologist Otto Weininger rather than from Schopenhauer or Nietzsche, he resolutely competes with Thomas Mann's perhaps more metaphysically and aesthetically oriented analyses of fascism in *Doktor Faustus* (1947). Doderer's Zeitblom is Dr. Georg von Geyrenhoff, a meditative civil servant, who has just retired and wants to write a diary, or chronicle, of an entire group of people who fleetingly come together in the winter and spring of 1925–1926; following the example of Dostoyevsky's narrator in *The Possessed* (who abbreviates his name "G-ff"), Geyrenhoff tries hard to fulfill the historian's task for which, at least at first, he seems to be well qualified by his financial independence, maturity of outlook, and relative detachment from nearly everybody. His difficulties are those of the limited narrative perspective: as a chronicler he cannot be present everywhere and know everything and thus finds himself forced to employ, in order to be truly inclusive, the literary help of his friend, the writer Kajetan von Schlaggenberg (who contributes, among other things, a chapter on the everyday affairs of a lady of some *embonpoint*) and of the scholarly René von Stangeler; others, like Mrs. Selma Steuermann and Grete Siebenschein contribute by gently spying on their friends. But the final narrative, constituting the novel, actually consists of three textual levels: the first, fragmentary chronicle written by Geyrenhoff almost within view of the events of winter and spring of 1925–1926 but left unfinished because he feels, on May 15, 1927, that he has become disqualified for further chronicle-writing owing to his deeper emotional involvement with Friederike Ruthmayr, combined with the fact that he does not know much anyway; the later "edition" (1955) of his fragment which he uses as raw material while pondering his past in a lonely room high above his city; and, finally, the narrative efforts of the interceding author who, increasingly impatient with Geyrenhoff's labors and limitations, takes the "edition" (1955) of the fragment (1927) out of Geyrenhoff's hands and employs it for his own "novel according to the chronicle of Geyrenhoff." Thus, narrative perspective widens beyond Geyrenhoff's partial vision (as happens in Dostoyevsky's *Possessed* and Melville's *Moby Dick*); and the chronicler, who has sacrificed his distance to more intimate involvement, himself appears as an agitated character, ironically viewed from the outside.

Yet the correcting authorial voice cannot entirely silence Geyrenhoff, who has firmly implanted his observations of multiple events into the Viennese landscape and has employed the infinitely varied resources of Viennese German to indicate something of his own skepticism and keen wit. Geyrenhoff does not hesitate to interpret Viennese geography in sociological terms; he locates the city exactly on the border separating two traditional modes of living: the "West," shaped by the detailed contours of distinct individuality (inherited from Rome and Greece), small gardens, detached houses, and the self-assertion of the human being; and the "East," with flat and almost infinite horizons, lack of hard lines, souls "like smoke" merging into each other, and people, gathered in a communion sustained by helpless acceptance of fate. Unlike Thomas Mann's Zeitblom, who does not deviate from the decorous prose of the well-trained humanist, Geyrenhoff relies on many shades of written and spoken Viennese; he ordinarily uses the circumstantial language of the civil servant, but whenever abstract ideas threaten to prevail or to overshadow actual experience, he quickly adds—in comments, parentheses, or asides—a corresponding term from the popular speech, and thus explodes high seriousness by bathetic idiom; if he speaks about "agglomeration" he will not forget to add a sarcastic *"Knödelbildung"* ("molding of dumplings"). He falls back on an ingenious collage of idiomatic levels which Johann Nestroy perfected in the mid-nineteenth century; and opposing heroic abstraction of ideas, Geyrenhoff successfully prevents his chronicle from becoming like the traditional German *Bildungs-roman*, in which vivid character disappears behind elaborate discussions of educational issues.

Aiming at a "total" novel in the tradition of inclusive realism, Doderer again works with a multiplicity of plots, which are to create "the carpet of life." There are, again, stories of "human-izations" and obsessions, some muted, some fierce. Geyrenhoff himself "falls from his hobbyhorse" and discovers that he is deeply in love with Friederike Ruthmayr, who, in turn, has to break through the "wall of glass" that shelters her from direct contact with life; Mary K. finds absolute fulfillment with Leon-hard Kakabsa, a kind of proletarian Wilhelm Meister, who, working hard at his private studies of cultured German, Latin grammar, and Renaissance philosophy, achieves a humanization of his own; René von Stangeler quarrels endlessly with Grete Siebenschein before he comes to accept her right to independence of thought. There is, again, the blind motif of intrigue (the high-class operator Levielle tries to cheat Quapp von Schlaggenberg out of an inheritance), and there are hosts of card players, petty thieves, ladies eating mountains of whipped cream, Hungarian fascists, Prater prostitutes, learned policemen, friendly Jewish lawyers, playboys, unemployed historians, and ugly *concierges* (the only people whom Doderer really hates) to add intricate color, tension, and fullness. Again as in the earlier novel, certain days are "told" almost from hour to hour (above all, January 10, 1927,

and May 15, 1927), but the complex strands all converge on the
long hot day of July 15, 1927, when private lives are overshadowed by fateful public events that bode ill for the future.
The Viennese Palace of Justice is burned down by demonstrating
workers; police and demonstrators slaughter each other; the
Lumpenproletariat loots some districts; and amidst the fire and the
lawlessness emerge the demons who within twenty years will
cause far more brutal conflagrations. The fire and the smoke over
the city of Vienna foreshadow the death clouds over Bergen-
Belsen and Auschwitz.

Doderer always insisted that he was concerned with modern
demonology, or rather with the ideologies responsible for the
imminent dehumanization of humanity; but he sees political
issues as an element of a phenomenology of the mind. He defines
his problem in a psychological (and ahistorical) way and implies
that the demons may emerge in any realm of life, but particularly
in the central spheres of sex and politics: underlining the meaning
of his early Zihal story, he suggests that sexual aberrations anticipate or correspond to the practices of the totalitarian state.
Among Geyrenhoff's circle of acquaintances, the writer Kajetan
von Schlaggenberg and the youngish industrialist Jan Herzka are
victims of demons in sexual shape: Schlaggenberg untiringly
searches the most shabby cafés for rotund women, who alone
satisfy his tastes; and Herzka, who once saw in an old book on
witch trials the picture of a middle-aged woman being tortured,
desperately tries to rearrange his sexual experiences so as to
reproduce that unforgettable scene. Both Schlaggenberg and
Herzka are cursed with a sexual ideology, for they want to impose
an abstract system of "order" upon spontaneity; both are in
danger of transforming other human beings into the depersonal-
ized "objects" of their dubious transactions.

But Doderer does not merely describe the possessed. He also
presents internal evidence in the form of three manuscripts (each
a literary *tour de force*) inserted into the novel. Schlaggenberg
presents Geyrenhoff with a statistical and theoretical treatise on
his search for fat women, and Geyrenhoff rightly remarks that
Schlaggenberg's pseudoscientific terminology aptly illustrates the
emergence of an ahuman system of classification and a "second-

ary" language—later readers will be inclined to compare Schlaggenberg's terminology of selection and exclusion with the
memoranda of the SS offices, which were to organize the mass
liquidation of persons not conforming to an ideal type of their
own. Jan Herzka, in search of middle-aged ladies to be tortured,
finds himself confronted with a telling image of his own obsession when he and René Stangeler read through a late medieval
manuscript in which the horrified chronicler describes the curious
aberrations of his master, Achaz von Neudegg, a Styrian baron
who brings two ladies to his castle, subjects them to a fake witch
trial, and orders two young boys to "torture" them with velvet
whips, because he is obsessed with the idea of breaking their
dignity; and when the women have slept with the boys (to escape
further humiliation, as they think), he immediately releases them,
because his purpose has been achieved.

Dwelling in the depths of the soul and in the abysses of the
world, the demons may strike a Styrian baron in 1464 as well
as a modern writer; these demons coexist with humanity and are
merely waiting to come forth when the great fires begin to flare.
The third inserted manuscript (Mrs. Kapsreiter's *Nightbook*) suggests, by recording the nightly visions of a simple woman resid-
ing in the "Blue Unicorn" house (not far from the Strudlhof
Stairs), that horrible shapes and forms are teeming in cellars,
caverns, caves, and sewers which, in turn, are linked with the
fluid element of the rivers and the great oceans; at times these
slimy, muscular monsters assume an almost human form, as does
the Hitler-like Austro-Bavarian killer Meisgeier, and try, as does
Meisgeier on July 15, 1927, to rise up through the gratings in
the streets. Preconceived "concepts" of experience and absolute,
narrowing programs of life within the minds of obsessed men
correspond to the outside correlatives—the incubus (or, as simple
Mrs. Kapsreiter says, the *Kubitschek*), slimy sea monsters, and
polyplike, malevolent humanoids.

Doderer believes that there is normally a relative congruity
(*Deckung*) between inside (ego) and outside (world): man gladly
opens up to the glorious rush of experience, likes to "perceive,"
and, as if incarnating the female principle, to submit in a mystical
marriage to the force of the tangible world that penetrates into

the welcoming soul. Dehumanization begins when man withdraws into himself, narrows both his contact with experience and his field of vision, and fatally refuses to perceive that which comes from the outside (*Apperzeptionsverweigerung*); inevitably, the ego turns into a central imperious spot (*ein herrschsüchtiger Mittelpunkt*) and tries to impose its conceptual structures on the outside world. A "normative concept" (*Soll-Vorstellung*) assumes dominance over living spontaneity. Thus, an abstract, spectral "second reality" (*zweite Wirklichkeit*) triumphs over the primary tangible one and, by disrupting "given" relationships, turns the world into a hell of ideology triumphant. Refusal to perceive may occur in many degrees of intensity and many different forms: Melzer and Geyrenhoff are surely endangered by being too self-involved and by granting their past too much dominance over their present: Imre von Gyurkicz (in *The Demons*) chooses a second reality on purpose when he tries to build himself a new biography, complete with studied stances and objective emblems; Zihal, Schlaggenberg, and Herzka demonstrate in their private lives a total lack of congruity between ego and world. In the political sphere, the anti-Semites Dr. Kröger and Eulenfeld, and the Hungarian fascist Sevzcik (in *The Demons*) become, by implication, guilty of obstructing life by creating a neat system of preconceived political notions. Party organizations, on the right as well as on the left, are dominated by "second realities," but in analyzing the late 'twenties the conservative Doderer tends to find fault more with his friends on the right than with those on the left. He does condemn the collectivist doctrines of the Socialists, but the individual members of the paramilitary Socialist *Republikanischer Schutzbund* who, on July 15, 1927, help the wounded and carry the dead, look suspiciously like radiant angels in human guise.

Arguing against fatal "second realities," Doderer confronts the issues of revolution squarely and with some insight. Revolutionaries, he believes, are people who, wanting to escape the responsibility for their individual humanizations, close their eyes to the spontaneity and fullness of the universe, refuse apperception, and violently impose their total vision upon a recalcitrant world. Doderer wisely concentrates on a critique of the totalitarian aspects of revolutionary demands, but he welcomes a transformation of the world if it is based on changing "individual aspects under the conditions of nature"—the difficulty being that all his illuminating examples of such useful changes come from an idyllic pastoral and agricultural sphere and hardly relate to the issues of highly industrialized societies. I am tempted to say that Doderer's conservative attitude does not prevent him from articulating some of his essential ideas within Austrian anti-Hegelian traditions and from giving instinctive support to the social views of his compatriot Sir Karl Popper who, in more philosophical terms, has convincingly argued the case for sober changes, as opposed to the inhuman atrocities inevitably involved in instant and total transformations.

Doderer's most intimate secret is his axiomatic belief in the force and glory of life; he praises the "entirety of being" (*Gesamtleben*) and comes close to developing an ideological concept of his own to organize his view of the world: fortunately enough, it is precisely the virtue of the *Gesamtleben* that it amounts to a rich coexistence of many diverse, unique, individual, tangible, and definite elements. But a strong streak of Bergsonian vitalism informs most of his novels, and he will never hesitate to depreciate principles of abstraction, rearrangement, selection, and classification in favor of something that is infinitely alive, powerful in its very presence, and stubbornly concrete. Other "vitalists" have turned their idea of life against the creative intellect, but Doderer made it the instrument of an art that strives to protect the rich rotundity of the world from programmed rape by crude ideologists.

Useful Further Readings

(Superscripts [e.g. 1965^2] indicate new editions = 2nd edition, published in 1965.)

Switzerland

Social and Political Developments

Chopard, Théo. *Switzerland: Present and Future.* Bern, 1963.

Dürrenmatt, Peter. *Schweizer Geschichte.* Zurich, 1963.

Hauser, Albert. *Schweizerische Wirtschafts- und Sozialgeschichte.* Erlenbach/ Zurich, 1961.

Literary Trends

Böschenstein, Hermann. "Contemporary German-Swiss Fiction." *German Life and Letters* 12 (1958):24–33.

Calgari, Guido. *The Four Literatures of Switzerland.* London, 1963.

Schmid, Karl. *Unbehagen im Kleinstaat.* Zurich, 1963.

Weber, Werner. *Tagebuch eines Lesers,* pp. 267–290. Olten, 1965.

Wildi, Max. "Contemporary German-Swiss Literature: The Lyric and the Novel." *German Life and Letters* 12 (1958):1–11.

Wiskemann, Elizabeth. "Contemporary Writing in Switzerland." *Times Literary Supplement,* July 4, 1958.

Austria

Social and Political Developments

Bader, William B. *Austria between East and West.* Stanford, 1966.

Nenning, Günther. *Anschluss an die Zukunft.* Vienna, 1963.

Schulmeister, Otto. *Die Zukunft Österreichs.* Vienna, 1967.

Vodopivec, Alexander. *Die Balkanisierung Österreichs.* Vienna, 1966.

Literary Trends

Fleischmann, Wolfgang Bernard. "Introducing Austrian Literature." *Wisconsin Studies in German Literature* 8 (1967):475–483.

Langer, Norbert. *Dichter aus Österreich.* 4 vols. Vienna, 1956.

Magris, Claudio. *Il mito absburgico nella letteratura austriaca moderna.* Turin, 1963.

Musulin, Janko von. "Österreichische Literatur nach 1945." *Hochland* 59 (1967):437–444.

The German Democratic Republic

Social and Political Developments

Doernberg, Stefan. *Kurze Geschichte der DDR*. East Berlin, 1968.
  The official point of view.
Dornberg, John. *The Other Germany*. Garden City, N.Y., 1968.
Ludz, Peter Christian. *Parteielite im Wandel*. Cologne-Opladen, 1968.
Richert, Ernst. *Das zweite Deutschland*. Frankfurt/M., 1966.
Stolper, Wolfgang F. *The Structure of the East German Economy*. Cam-
  bridge, Mass., 1960.

Literary Trends

Demetz, Peter. "Literature in Ulbricht's Germany." *Problems of Commu-
  nism* 77 (1962):15–21.
Mayer, Hans. *Zur deutschen Literatur der Zeit*, pp. 374–394. Reinbek/
  Hamburg, 1967.
Raddatz, Fritz. "Tradition und Traditionsbruch in der Literatur der
  DDR." *Merkur* 19 (1965):666–681.
Reich-Ranicki, Marcel. *Deutsche Literatur in Ost und West*. Munich, 1963.
Winter, Helmut. "East German Literature." In *Essays on Contemporary
  German Literature*, edited by Brian Keith-Smith, pp. 261–280. German
  Men of Letters 4. London, 1966.

The Federal Republic of Germany

Social and Political Developments

Balfour, Michael. *West Germany*. London, 1968.
Dahrendorf, Ralf. *Society and Democracy in Germany*. Garden City, N.Y.,
  1967.
Grosser, Alfred. *The Federal Republic of Germany: A Concise History*. New
  York, 1964.
Richter, Hans Werner. *Bestandsaufnahme: Eine deutsche Bilanz*. Munich,
  1962.
Wallich, H. C. *Mainsprings of the German Revival*. New Haven, 1955.

Literary Trends

Grosser, J. F. D. *Die grosse Kontroverse*. Hamburg, 1963.
  Thomas Mann and the "inner emigration."

Holthusen, Hans Egon. *Der unbehauste Mensch.* Munich, 1951.
The beginnings of postwar literary criticism.

Jens, Walter. *Deutsche Literatur der Gegenwart.* Munich, 1962.

Lettau, Reinhard. *Die Gruppe 47: Bericht, Kritik, Polemik.* Neuwied/Berlin, 1967.

Reich-Ranicki, Marcel. *Literarisches Leben in Deutschland.* Munich, 1965.
A chronicle of developments, 1961–1965.

———. *Literatur der kleinen Schritte.* Munich, 1967.
Developments, 1963–1967.

Stern, Guy. "Prolegomena zu einer Geschichte der deutschen Nachkriegsprosa." *Colloquia Germanica* 3 (1967):233–252.

Widmer, Urs. *1945 oder die "Neue Sprache."* Düsseldorf, 1966.

Problems of Poetry (Intermezzo 1)

Hamburger, Michael, and Middleton, Christopher, ed. *Modern German Poetry.* New York, 1962.
An anthology including verse from Else Lasker-Schüler to Christoph Meckel.

Schwebell, Gertrude Clorius, ed. *Contemporary German Poetry.* New York, 1962.
Includes verse from Hans Arp to Rudolf Alexander Schröder.

* * * *

Allemann, Beda. "Non-representational Modern German Poetry." In *Reality and Creative Vision in Modern German Lyrical Poetry: Proceedings of the 15th Symposium of the Colston Research Society Held in the University of Bristol, April, 1963,* edited by A. Closs, pp. 71–79. London, 1963.

Enzensberger, Hans Magnus. "In Search of the Lost Language," *Encounter* 21 (1963):44–51.

Exner, Richard. "Tradition and Innovation in the Occidental Lyric of the Last Decade—German Poetry, 1950–1960: An Estimate." *Books Abroad* 36 (1962):245–254.

Flores, John. "Adjustments and Visions: Poetry in the German Democratic Republic, 1945–1969." Ph.D. dissertation. Yale, 1969.

Krolow, Karl. *Aspekte zeitgenössischer deutscher Lyrik.* Gütersloh, West Germany, 1961.

Lange, Victor. Introduction to *Contemporary German Poetry,* translated by G. C. Schwebell, pp. xiii–xxxix. New York, 1962.

Trends in the Theater (Intermezzo 2)

Benedikt, Michael, and Wellwarth, George E., ed. *Postwar German Theatre*. New York, 1967.
Includes plays from Borchert to Peter Weiss.

* * * *

Esslin, Martin. *The Theater of the Absurd*, pp. 191–195. Garden City, N.Y., 1961.

Garten, Hugh F. *Modern German Drama*. London, 1959.

"The German Theater in the 1960's." *Times Literary Supplement*, April 3, 1969.

Klarmann, Adolf D. "German Documentary Drama." *Yale German Review* 2 (1966):13–19.

Rischbieter, Henning. *Deutsche Dramatik in West und Ost*. Velber/Hanover, 1965.

Shaw, Leroy R., ed. *The German Theater Today*. Austin, Texas, 1963.

Tynan, Kenneth. "The Theater Abroad: Germany." *The New Yorker*, September 12, 1959, pp. 88–113.

Zipes, Jack D. "Documentary Drama in Germany: Mending the Circuit." *Germanic Review* 42 (1967):49–62.

Problems of Fiction (Intermezzo 3)

Baumgart, Reinhard. *Aussichten des Romans oder Hat Literatur Zukunft?* Neuwied/Berlin, 1968.

Hatfield, Henry. *Crisis and Continuity in Modern German Fiction*. Ithaca, 1969.

Heitner, Robert R., ed. *The Contemporary Novel in Germany: A Symposium*. Austin, Texas, 1967.

Thomas, R. Hinton, and Will, Wilfried van der. *The German Novel and the Affluent Society*. Toronto, 1968.

Vormweg, Heinrich. *Die Wörter und die Welt: Über neue Literatur*. Neuwied/Berlin, 1968.

Waidson, H. M. *The Modern German Novel*. London, 1960.

Alfred Andersch

Bance, A. F. "*Der Tod in Rom* and *Die Rote:* Two Italian Episodes." *Forum for Modern Language Studies* 3 (1967):126–134.

Burgauner, Christoph. "Zur Romankunst Alfred Anderschs." In *Alfred Andersch: Bericht, Roman, Erzählungen*, pp. 419–445. Olten, 1965.

Geissler, Rolf. "Alfred Andersch: *Sansibar oder der letzte Grund*." In *Möglichkeiten des modernen deutschen Romans*, pp. 215–231. Frankfurt/M., 1965.

Migner, Karl. "Die Flucht in die Freiheit: Untersuchungen zu einem zentralen Motiv in den Werken von Alfred Andersch." *Welt und Wort* 18 (1963):329–332.

Ingeborg Bachmann

Holthusen, Hans Egon. "Kämpfender Sprachgeist: Die Lyrik Ingeborg Bachmanns." In *Das Schöne und das Wahre*, pp. 7–13. Munich, 1958.

Lyon, James K. "The Poetry of Ingeborg Bachmann: A Primeval Impulse in the Modern Wasteland." *German Life and Letters* 17 (1964):206–215.

Schoolfield, George C. "Ingeborg Bachmann." In *Essays on Contemporary Literature*, edited by Brian Keith-Smith, pp. 187–212. German Men of Letters 4. London, 1966.

Triesch, Manfred. "Truth, Love and Death of Language in Ingeborg Bachmann's Stories." *Books Abroad* 39 (1965):389–393.

Johannes Bobrowski

Bridgewater, Patrick. "The Poetry of Johannes Bobrowski." *Forum for Modern Language Studies* 2 (1965):320–334.

Glenn, Jerry H. "An Introduction to the Poetry of Johannes Bobrowski." *Germanic Review* 41 (1966):48–56.

Johannes Bobrowski: Selbstzeugnisse und Beiträge über sein Werk. East Berlin, 1967.

Documents and essays.

Heinrich Böll

Bronsen, David. "Böll's Women: Patterns in Male-Female Relationships." *Monatshefte* 57 (1965):291–300.

Haase, Horst. "Charakter und Funktion der zentralen Symbolik in Heinrich Bölls Roman *Billard um halbzehn*." *Weimarer Beiträge* 10 (1964):219–226.

Plant, Richard. "The World of Heinrich Böll." *German Quarterly* 33 (1960):125–131.

Poser, Therese. "Heinrich Böll: *Billard um halbzehn*." In *Möglichkeiten des modernen deutschen Romans*, edited by Rolf Geissler, pp. 232–255. Frankfurt/M., 1965^2.

Reich-Ranicki, Marcel, ed. *In Sachen Böll: Ansichten und Aussichten.* Cologne, 1968.
Essays by various critics.

Schwartz, Wilhelm J. *Der Erzähler Heinrich Böll: Seine Werke und Gestalten.* Bern, 1967.

Sokel, Walter. "Perspective and Dualism in the Works of Heinrich Böll." In *The Contemporary Novel in Germany: A Symposium,* edited by Robert R. Heitner, pp. 111–138. Austin, Texas, 1967.

Ziolkowski, Theodore. "Albert Camus and Heinrich Böll." *Modern Language Notes* 77 (1962):282–291.

———. "Heinrich Böll: Conscience and Craft." *Books Abroad* 34 (1960): 213–222.

Paul Celan

Allemann, Beda. "Paul Celan." In *Schriftsteller der Gegenwart,* edited by Klaus Nonnemann, pp. 70–75. Olten, 1963.

Duroche, Leonard L. "Paul Celan's 'Todesfuge': A New Interpretation." *Modern Language Notes* 82 (1967):472–477.

Kelletat, Alfred. "Accessus zu Celans 'Sprachgitter.'" *Der Deutschunterricht* 18 (1966):94–110.

Lyon, James K. "The Poetry of Paul Celan: An Approach." *Germanic Review* 39 (1964):50–67.

Prawer, Siegbert. "Paul Celan." In *Essays on Contemporary German Literature,* edited by Brian Keith-Smith, pp. 161–184. German Men of Letters 4. London, 1966.

Weinrich, Harald. "Paul Celan." In *Deutsche Literatur seit 1945,* edited by Dietrich Weber, pp. 62–76. Stuttgart, 1968.

Heimito von Doderer

Hamburger, Michael. "A Great Austrian Novelist." *Encounter* 8 (1957): 77–81.

Hatfield, Henry. "Vitality and Tradition: Doderer's *Die Strudlhofstiege.*" *Monatshefte* 47 (1955):19–25.

Ivask, Ivar, ed. "An International Symposium in Memory of Heimito von Doderer." *Books Abroad* 42 (1968):343–384.

Jones, David L. "Proust and Doderer: Themes and Techniques." *Books Abroad* 37 (1963):12–15.

Politzer, Heinz. "Heimito von Doderer's *Demons* and the Modern Kakanian Novel." In *The Contemporary Novel in Germany: A Symposium,* edited by Robert R. Heitner, pp. 37–62. Austin, Texas, 1967.

Spiel, Hilde. "Der Kampf gegen das Chaos: Zu Heimito von Doderers *Die Dämonen.*" *Der Monat* 9 (1957):65–68.

Weber, Dietrich. *Heimito von Doderer: Studien zu seinem Romanwerk.* Munich, 1963.

Friedrich Dürrenmatt

Allemann, Beda. "Friedrich Dürrenmatt: *Es steht geschrieben.*" In *Das deutsche Drama* 2, edited by Benno von Wiese, pp. 415–532. Düsseldorf, 1968.

Bänziger, Hans. *Frisch und Dürrenmatt.* Bern and Munich, 1966[5].

Esslin, Martin. "Friedrich Dürrenmatt and the Neurosis of Neutrality." In *Essays in the Modern Drama,* edited by Morris Freedman, pp. 225–227. Boston, 1964.

Heilman, Robert B. "The Lure of the Demonic: James and Dürrenmatt." *Comparative Literature* 13 (1961):346–357.

Jäggi, Walter, ed. *Der unbequeme Dürrenmatt.* Basel, 1962.
   Essays by Reinhold Grimm, Gottfried Benn, Hans Mayer, and others.

Klarmann, Adolf D. "Friedrich Dürrenmatt and the Tragic Sense of Comedy." *Tulane Drama Review* 4 (1960):77–104.

Loram, Ian C. "*Der Besuch der alten Dame* and *The Visit.*" *Monatshefte* 53 (1961):15–21.

Mayer, Hans. *Dürrenmatt und Frisch.* Pfullingen, 1963.

Steiner, Jacob. "Die Komödie Dürrenmatts." *Der Deutschunterricht* 15 (1963):81–98.

Wellwarth, George E. "Friedrich Dürrenmatt and Max Frisch: Two Views of the Drama." *Tulane Drama Review* 6 (1962):14–42.

Hans Magnus Enzensberger

Bridgewater, Patrick. "The Making of a Poet: Hans Magnus Enzensberger." *German Life and Letters* 21 (1967):27–44.

Grimm, Reinhold. "Montierte Lyrik." *Germanisch-romanische Monatsschrift* N. F. 39 (1958):178–192.

Holthusen, Hans Egon. "Die Zornigen, die Gesellschaft und das Glück: Lyrik von Hans Magnus Enzensberger." In *Kritisches Verstehen,* pp. 138–172. Munich, 1961.

Noack, Paul. "Fremdbrötler von Beruf." *Der Monat* 15 (1963):61–70.

Schlenstedt, Dieter. "Aufschrei und Unbehagen: Notizen zur Problematik eines westdeutschen Dichters." *Neue Deutsche Literatur* 9 (1961): 110–127.

Max Frisch

Bänziger, Hans. *Frisch und Dürrenmatt.* Bern and Munich, 1966[5].

Bradley, Brigitte L. "Max Frisch's *Homo Faber:* Theme and Structural Devices." *Germanic Review* 41 (1966):279–290.

Brustein, Robert. "German Guilt and Swiss Indictments." *New Republic,* March 9, 1963, pp. 28–30.

Jacobi, Walter. "Max Frisch: *Die chinesische Mauer*—Die Beziehung zwischen Sinngehalt und Form." *Der Deutschunterricht* 13 (1961): 93–108.

Karasek, Hellmuth. *Max Frisch.* Velber/Hanover, 1966.

Schürer, Ernst. "Zur Interpretation von Max Frischs *Homo Faber.*" *Monatshefte* 59 (1967):330–343.

Staiger, Emil. *"Stiller."* *Neue Zürcher Zeitung,* November 17, 1954.

Wellwarth, George. "The German-Speaking Drama: Max Frisch: The Drama of Despair." In *The Theater of Protest and Paradox,* pp. 161–183. New York, 1964.

Gerd Gaiser

Bronsen, David. "Unterdrückung des Pathos in Gerd Gaisers *Die sterbende Jagd."* *German Quarterly* 38 (1965):310–317.

Hilton, Ian. "Gerd Gaiser." In *Essays on Contemporary German Literature,* edited by Brian Keith-Smith, pp. 111–138. German Men of Letters 4. London, 1966.

Hohoff, Curt. *Gerd Gaiser: Werk und Gestalt.* Munich, 1963.

Hülse, Erich. "Gerd Gaiser: *Schlussball."* In *Möglichkeiten des modernen deutschen Romans,* edited by Rolf Geissler, pp. 161–190. Frankfurt/M., 1965.

Günter Grass

Bruce, James C. "The Equivocating Narrator in Günter Grass's *Katz und Maus."* In *Monatshefte* 58 (1966):139–149.

Cunliffe, W. G. "Aspects of the Absurd in Günter Grass." *Wisconsin Studies in Contemporary Literature* 7 (1966):311–327.

Gelley, Alexander. "Art and Reality in *Die Blechtrommel."* *Forum for Modern Language Studies* 3 (1967):115–125.

Holthusen, Hans Egon. "Günter Grass als politischer Autor." *Der Monat* 18 (1966):66–81.

Loschütz, Gert, ed. *Von Buch zu Buch: Günter Grass in der Kritik: eine Dokumentation.* Neuwied/Berlin, 1968.

Parry, Idris. "Aspects of Günter Grass's Narrative Technique." *Forum for Modern Language Studies* 3 (1967):100–114.

Plard, Henri. "Verteidigung der Blechtrommeln: Über Günter Grass." *Text und Kritik* 1 (1963):1–8.

Steiner, George. "The Nerve of Günter Grass." *Commentary* 37 (1964): 77–80.

Willson, A. Leslie. "The Grotesque Everyman in Günter Grass's *Die Blechtrommel.*" *Monatshefte* 58 (1966):131–138.

Peter Hacks

Chiarini, Paolo. "Appunti su Peter Hacks." In *La letteratura tedesca del Novecento,* pp. 76–80. Rome, 1961.

Kesting, Marianne. *Panorama des zeitgenössischen Theaters,* pp. 239–242. Munich, 1962.

Helmut Heissenbüttel

Dohl, Reinhard. "Helmut Heissenbüttel: ein Versuch." *Wort in der Zeit* 12 (1966):50–64.

Hartung, Harald. "Antigrammatische Poetik und Poesie: Zu neuen Büchern von Helmut Heissenbüttel und Franz Mon." *Neue Rundschau* 79 (1968):480–494.

Hoeck, Wilhelm. " 'Vorüberlied und Dennochlied': Deutsche Lyrik zwischen Heissenbüttel und Benn." *Hochland* 56 (1963):119–136.

Schöfer, Erasmus. "Poesie als Sprachforschung." *Wirkendes Wort* 15 (1965):275–278.

Rolf Hochhuth

Bentley, Eric, ed. *The Storm over the Deputy.* New York, 1964.
Contains articles by Hannah Arendt, Robert Brustein, Alfred Kazin, and others.

Kaufmann, Walter. *Tragedy and Philosophy,* pp. 323–337. New York, 1968.

Marx, Patricia. "An Interview with Rolf Hochhuth." *Partisan Review* 31 (1964):363–376.

Raddatz, Fritz, ed. *Summa iniuria; oder, Durfte der Papst schweigen? Hochhuth's "Stellvertreter" in der öffentlichen Kritik.* Reinbek/Hamburg, 1963.

Contains articles by Hans Egon Holthusen, Albert Wucher, Rolf Hochhuth, and others.

Sammons, Jeffrey L. "The Deputy: A Minority View." *Yale German Review* 2 (1966):1–6.

Schwarz, Egon. "Rolf Hochhuth's *The Representative.*" *Germanic Review* 39 (1963):807–820.

Winston, Clara. "The Matter of the *Deputy.*" *Massachusetts Review* 5 (1964):423–436.

Zipes, J. D. "Guilt-Ridden Hochhuth: *The Soldiers.*" *Mosaic* 1 (1967): 118–131.

Fritz Hochwälder

Loram, Ian C. "Fritz Hochwälder." *Monatshefte* 57 (1965):8–16.

Thieberger, Richard. "Macht und Recht in den Dramen Fritz Hochwälders." *Deutsche Rundschau* 83 (1957):1147–1152.

Wellwarth, George E. "Fritz Hochwälder: The Drama within the Self." *Quarterly Journal of Speech* 49 (1963):274–281.

Uwe Johnson

Baudrillard, Jean. "Uwe Johnson: La frontière." *Les temps modernes* 18 (1962):1094–1107.

Detweiler, Robert. "Speculations about Jacob: The Truth of Ambiguity." *Monatshefte* 58 (1966):25–32.

Diller, Edward. "Uwe Johnson's Karsch: Language as a Reflection of the Two Germanies." *Monatshefte* 60 (1968):34–39.

Kolb, Herbert. "Rückfall in die Parataxe: Anlässlich einiger Satzbauformen in Uwe Johnsons erstveröffentlichtem Roman." *Neue deutsche Hefte* 10 (1963):42–74.

Migner, Karl. *Uwe Johnson: "Das dritte Buch über Achim": Interpretation.* Munich, 1966.

Popp, Hansjürgen. *Einführung in Uwe Johnsons Roman "Mutmassungen über Jakob."* Stuttgart, 1961.

Wunberg, Gotthart. "Struktur und Symbol in Uwe Johnsons Roman *Mutmassungen über Jakob.*" *Neue Sammlung* 2 (1962):440–449.

Zehm, Günther. "Ausruhen bei den Dingen: Notiz über Uwe Johnsons Methode." *Der Monat* 14 (1961/62):69–73.

Wolfgang Koeppen

Heissenbüttel, Helmut. "Wolfgang Koeppen—Kommentar." *Merkur* 22 (1968):244–252.

Jens, Walter. "Verleihung des Georg-Büchner-Preises an Wolfgang Koeppen: Rede auf den Preisträger." In *Jahrbuch der Deutschen Akademie für Sprache und Dichtung*, pp. 91–110. Darmstadt, 1962.

Günter Kunert

Horst, Eberhard. "Günter Kunert: *Verkündigung des Wetters: Im Namen der Hüte.*" *Neue Rundschau* 78 (1967):678–684.

Wilhelm Lehmann

Härtling, Peter. "Die Welt zurechtsingen." *Der Monat* 15 (1962):76–80.

Hohoff, Curt. "Poeta Magus—Wilhelm Lehmann." In *Geist und Ursprung*, pp. 162–164. Munich, 1954.

Prawer, Siegbert. "The Poetry of Wilhelm Lehmann." *German Life and Letters* 15 (1961/62):247–258.

Scrase, David A. "Wilhelm Lehmann." In *Essays on Contemporary German Literature*, edited by Brian Keith-Smith, pp. 19–35. German Men of Letters 4. London, 1966.

Siebert, Werner, ed. *Gegenwart des Lyrischen: Essays zum Werk Wilhelm Lehmanns*. Gütersloh, West Germany, 1967.

Weber, Werner. "Suite zur Gegenwart." In *Zeit ohne Zeit*, pp. 172–228. Zurich, 1959.

Nelly Sachs

Blomster, W. V. "A Theosophy of the Creative World: The *Zohar*-Cycle of Nelly Sachs." *Germanic Review* 44 (1969):211–227.

Enzensberger, Hans Magnus. "Die Steine der Freiheit." *Merkur* 15 (1959):770–775.

Geissner, Hellmut. "Nelly Sachs." In *Deutsche Literatur seit 1945*, edited by Dietrich Weber, pp. 15–37. Stuttgart, 1968.

Nelly Sachs zu Ehren: Gedichte, Beiträge, Bibliographie. Frankfurt/M., 1966. Contributions by Käte Hamburger, Horst Bienek, Hilde Domin, Walter A. Berendsohn, and others.

Martin Walser

Ahl, Herbert. "Klima einer Gesellschaft: Martin Walser." In *Literarische Portraits*, pp. 15-27. Munich, 1962.

Enzensberger, Hans Magnus. "Martin Walser: ein sanfter Wüterich." In *Einzelheiten*, pp. 240-245. Frankfurt/M., 1962.

Kreuzer, Ingrid. "Martin Walser." In *Deutsche Literatur seit 1945*, edited by Dietrich Weber, pp. 435-454. Stuttgart, 1968.

Peter Weiss

Carmichael, Joel. "German Reaction to a New Play about Auschwitz." *American-German Review* 32 (1966):30-31.

Fleissner, E. M. "Revolution as Theater: *Danton's Death* and *Marat/Sade*." *Massachusetts Review* 7 (1966):543-556.

Marcuse, Ludwig. "Was ermittelte Peter Weiss?" *Kürbiskern* (1966): 84-89.

Milfull, John. "From Kafka to Brecht: Peter Weiss's Development toward Marxism." *German Life and Letters* 20 (1966):61-71.

Moeller, Hans-Bernard. "Weiss's Reasoning in the Madhouse." *Symposium* 20 (1966):163-173.

Rischbieter, Henning. *Peter Weiss*. Velber/Hanover, 1967.

Roloff, Michael. "An Interview with Peter Weiss." *Partisan Review* 32 (1965):220-232.

Sontag, Susan. "Marat/Sade/Artaud." *Partisan Review* 32 (1965):210-219.

Wendt, Ernst. "Peter Weiss zwischen den Ideologien." *Akzente* 12 (1965):415-525.

White, John J. "History and Cruelty in Peter Weiss' *Marat/Sade*." *Modern Language Review* 63 (1968):437-448.

Index